Gordon Gammack:

COLUMNS FROM THREE WARS

Gordon Gammack:

COLUMNS FROM THREE WARS

EDITED BY Andrea Clardy

THE IOWA STATE UNIVERSITY PRESS / AMES

FRONTISPIECE: MARCH 1970, Vietnam. Gordon Gammack ready for a helicopter spy mission. *(Register and Tribune)*

Composed and printed by
The Iowa State University Press
Ames, Iowa 50010

First edition, 1979

Library of Congress Cataloging in Publication Data

Gammack, Gordon.
Gordon Gammack, columns from three wars.

1. World War, 1939-1945—Sources. 2. Korean War, 1950-1953—Sources. 3. Vietnamese Conflict, 1961-1975—Sources. I. Clardy, Andrea, 1943- II. Title.
D735.G25 950'.42 78-13973
ISBN 0-8138-0130-3

Contents

AUGUST 1, 1944. American war correspondents strolling about the grounds of a press camp in Normandy. From left, Hal Boyle, Associated Press; Ernie Pyle, Scripps-Howard columnist; Gordon Gammack; and Don Whitehead, Associated Press. *(AP)*

Preface

BY Andrea Clardy, EDITOR

LIKE THOUSANDS of other Iowans, I knew and trusted Gordon Gammack as a friend without ever having met him. We moved to Iowa in time to enjoy a few years of Gammack's amiable coverage of local people and places before he demonstrated in Vietnam that his fascination with the details of people's experiences could be an instrument for insight into international crisis as well as local color.

This book resulted from my close friendship with Julie Ellen Gammack, Gordon's younger daughter. The conception of a book that would present selected columns as a memorial tribute and as a model of excellence in reporting was hers and she has been the moving force behind its development. Her idea was warmly supported by Drake Mabry, Gordon Gammack's last editor at the Des Moines *Tribune* and his trusted friend, and by Merritt Bailey, Director of Book Publishing at Iowa State University Press. Their encouragement and assistance have been invaluable.

Lasting historical interest and elucidation of the American fighting man's experience were the criteria for selection of columns to be included in this book. The application of such criteria is clearly a matter of personal judgment. The cooperation of the Des Moines *Register* and *Tribune* management in releasing materials is very much appreciated. I would also like to thank Michael Kjome for his permission to include the full account of his experiences as a prisoner of war in Vietnam as it was recorded by Gordon Gammack.

With minor exceptions, the columns are presented as written. Deletions have been made within articles in the interest of conciseness. Some columns are out of chronological order so that the reader may see a story or thought carried through to completion. The style of using all capitals in random sentences has not been retained except where emphasis is important.

The text linking the articles was derived from columns not selected for inclusion and from Gordon Gammack's correspondence with Drake Mabry during the Vietnam trips. I am indebted to Elizabeth McClurkin for her services as manuscript editor.

Wes Gallagher, Keyes Beech, Peter Arnett, Drake Mabry, and Donald Kaul each responded enthusiastically to my request for contributions. They have provided essential perspectives on the experiences they shared with Gordon Gammack—the reporter they respected and the man they loved.

Foreword

BY Drake Mabry, MANAGING EDITOR, THE DES MOINES **TRIBUNE**

GORDON GAMMACK was excited about going to war. He was excited about a little old lady in Tiffin, Iowa, who raised six kids and sent them all to college by scrubbing floors. He was excited about a one-liner he heard on the golf course. He was excited about gossip that came to him over the newsroom transom.

Gordon Gammack was excited by people. All this made him an editor's dream: He would—and could—do nearly anything, anytime. With gusto.

This collection of his war coverage and the accompanying tributes from his more famous peers is especially fitting. It shows how he kept his reportorial head "screwed on tight" despite hardship and the sometimes overwhelming realization that he was involved in the making of history. The latter feeling sometimes leads to an outpouring of pompousness and drivel from one's typewriter.

I have read (or reread to be more precise) his pieces here. I find them hauntingly delightful. They rekindle a lot of memories—from boyhood, when I first started reading him, to a few years ago, when I became his boss. (Actually, Gammack didn't need a boss. You just turned him loose to follow his instincts. He made editors look good.)

He would have been pleased, and probably a bit embarrassed, by this book. I know he would have insisted that some of his nonwar stories be included. He loved those down-home vignettes of Iowans that regularly appeared in his column on Page One of the *Tribune* as much as the more glamorous battlefield pieces.

As his friends Wes Gallagher, and Keyes Beech and Peter Arnett—both Pulitzer prize winners—point out, it was natural that Gammack worried more about a soldier's fear and feelings than a general's bravado.

He grew with the job. His personal feelings about war changed during the three he covered in a span of 30 years.

His dispatches from World War II are tinged not only with the pathos of men in mud being shot at, but also with a bit of patriotism. Sacrifice for the good of the country and the world. He believed it, and he reflected the mood of nearly everybody in the free world.

In Korea, his pieces were more politically neutral, but as always he praised the troops on the front. It was in

Korea that he got into a roaring battle with the military brass—the first of a series—because he knew the names of American prisoners to be released by the Communists before anybody else. The brass lost. Typical Gammack. They were mad as hell because of what he did, but they couldn't remain mad at him personally. Gammack could be a very disarming reporter.

Early in Vietnam, he wrestled with doubts about his country's business of fighting the war. He spent a good deal of time trying to figure out whether we were right or wrong. His stories, I think, were more dispassionate and thoughtful. But he had more to write about: heavy drug use, revolt in the ranks, political overtones that filtered down to the front, wherever it was.

Vietnam sparked his second monumental clash with military brass. Again, he won. In Manila to cover the return of American prisoners held by the Communists, he devised a system of penetrating the news blackout to write about the health and the mood of the returning POWs.

It was a world exclusive. And he shared it with his reporter bunkmates only after the *Register* and *Tribune* had first published it for Iowa readers. Typical Gammack.

Introductions, I'm told, should tell you something about the man. Well, Gammack was first of all a reporter. I don't pretend he was a Hemingway from the Corn Belt. His syntax was not perfect, and he had this thing about semicolons. But seldom was a name misspelled. Seldom was he challenged on the accuracy of a quote. He habitually double-checked his facts.

Once, in Vietnam, he was in anguish because he lost his notebook in the mud up front. So when he got back to the relative comfort of Danang, he sat down and reconstructed the whole thing.

He was a family man. On both trips to Vietnam, he was gone on his wedding anniversary. Then he'd cable the office and ask somebody to have a Des Moines florist send his wife flowers. He was a marvelous host. He shunned strong drink in later years, but somehow managed to keep yours constantly refreshed while grilling the chicken.

He was not impressive looking. Somebody once described his wardrobe as discards from a garage sale. He is the only man I know who could buy a new pair of pants and within hours have them baggy from the hips down.

He was frugal with the company's money. He loved fresh strawberries, which were usually in season when he went to Vietnam, but he worried about paying $3.50 for them for breakfast. So when he ran out of money and we had to wire him a bundle, he promised to lay off the strawberries.

He had an ear for the telling quote. Bunking on the ground with two pilots at Khe Sanh, he heard one say to the other, "God, I hope we can get breakfast in the morning. I don't want to die on an empty stomach."

He was in his sixties when I asked him to go to Vietnam. It was a request, not an order. The hardships can be overwhelming at that age. The decision was his. It took him about 30 seconds to determine that I was serious, then he reached for the telephone to start the travel and accreditation arrangements.

He covered the war the only way he knew how: Get out in the boonies and talk to the troops.

The hardships were indeed great. Once, he left the Laotian border and I cabled him to go back and stick with the action a couple more days. He did, but later confessed he was so beat that instead of sleeping at night, he vomited.

After the POW exchange in Manila, where he lined up the complete story of Michael Kjome's years as a prisoner, he came home to write it. For days, he sat in his office cubicle in the northwest corner of the newsroom, pounding away at his typewriter. He wrote more than 100,000 words. It wasn't until later we found out that all the while he was fighting an agonizing pain in his gut.

He didn't know it then; it was cancer.

His POW series, that last great effort, won the National Headliner award, one of the nation's top journalistic recognitions.

But he couldn't beat cancer. Even when he knew, he set to thinking about ways for others to beat it. "Do you suppose," he calmly mused, "that if we spent as much on cancer as we have on wars that we could win one?"

PART 1

World War II

(OCTOBER 1943 - NOVEMBER 1945)

FEBRUARY 17, 1944. After war passed through Anzio, Italy. At right, an American half-track protects the road from German air attacks. *(U.S. Navy)*

Introduction

BY Wes Gallagher, GENERAL MANAGER, THE ASSOCIATED PRESS

IN A WAR there are several levels of activity: the politicians painting broad pictures of victory; the commanding generals concerned with broad strategies; the lesser generals and colonels leading troops into battles; the captains and sergeants; and finally, way down the line, the foot soldiers — fighting and dying in the mud, in the forests, in the sands of the deserts.

Death can come anywhere and anytime for the G.I.

Each level of war is covered by correspondents, particularly large wars such as World War II. The correspondents, unlike the politicians and generals, sometimes switch levels, moving from one to another, seeking that first casualty of war — the truth.

But there are some, a handful, who cast their lot with the G.I., who concern themselves with his trials and tribulations, who bark at the generals when he is treated badly, who see to it that the lowly G.I.'s name gets into the hometown paper so his parents or friends know he is alive or, sometimes, how he died.

In World War II, it was Ernie Pyle or Hal Boyle or cartoonist Bill Mauldin who painted the little picture of the war: the G.I.'s view.

Such a correspondent was Gordon Gammack. He roamed the western front looking for G.I.s from Iowa so he could bring their word back home. He pursued them from the division headquarter books to regimental headquarters, to the battalion, to the platoon, and then to the foxhole.

"I am Gordon Gammack of the Des Moines *Register* and *Tribune*. Anyone from Iowa here?" he would ask. When he found someone, he plunked down in the mud or snow and spent the day. The chances of getting killed in this pursuit were pretty good. But no matter how far forward the Iowan might be, Gordon would be there.

Hundreds of names flowed through his notebooks, and his stories and columns must have brought a measure of reassurance to hundreds of homes.

No war correspondent could ask for anything more, and none did his job better than Gordon.

JUNE 9, 1944. American assault troops on the beachhead—Normandy—on D-Day. *(AP)*

WHEN Gordon Gammack went off to report the news of World War II, his assignment was to cover the personal experiences of the men he joined. His introduction as a war correspondent to the readers of the Des Moines Register *and* Tribune *read as follows:*

"A top-flight reporter for the Register *and* Tribune, *Gammack has been assigned to North Africa where he will be attached to the 34th Division as War Correspondent. His instructions are to live with the many Iowans in that division and report what they are thinking and doing. He will narrate the big and little details of how American men live and die fighting in a strange land for the folks back home. He will bring to Iowans the personal news which fills the hunger of mothers and fathers and wives and brothers as nothing else can do. He will write what amounts to a letter home from the soldiers abroad for Iowa readers. Gammack has been with The* Register *and* Tribune *ten years and has covered everything from state legislature to football."*

Divisions such as the 34th were formulated on a regional basis. Coverage of such a unit involved a double focus: on the major political and military news of the war seen from a very immediate perspective and on the local boys through human interest stories.

The experience of getting to the front was, with minor variations, common to most of the American soldiers on the war torn side of the Atlantic. Gammack's commentary on his passage across to Europe and on some of his feelings about the role he was to play documented that experience in detail.

REGISTER, OCTOBER 10, 1943.

PORT OF EMBARKATION, ATLANTIC COAST—For a guy in the process of becoming a war correspondent, life is just a bowl of "ifs" and "whens" all tangled up in red tape.

From the moment the boss dumps your thoughts into a dizzy whirlpool of excitement and suspense with the news of your assignment, you wait like a jitterbug for every development.

You wait to learn whether the necessary arrangements can be made. For days you wait for word that the war department has finished investigating you and has accredited you as a war correspondent.

Then you wait—and this is the worst wait of all—for orders from Washington, D.C., to be on your way; that transportation across the Atlantic has been arranged.

Not Much Warning.

You've heard enough from others to know that the army doesn't give you much warning. You don't dare make plans more than a day ahead. You almost jump every time the telephone rings, every time the boss comes out of his office and starts casting his eyes around for someone who might be you.

Then it comes when you least expect it. You wander into the office late in the afternoon believing another day has passed without any word and you find that everyone's been trying to find out where you've been.

Your guess about little warning was more than right. It's Tuesday at 5 p.m. The orders are:

"Report at the port of embarkation at 3 p.m. Thursday."

You've got to wind up your affairs at home, travel more than 1,000 miles to Washington, buy all your uniforms and equipment, obtain your credentials and then travel some more—ALL IN 48 HOURS. You wonder how you can do it and after you do, you wonder how.

And now, in this way-station army camp, one more big "when" dominates the thinking of the hundreds of us who are waiting:

"When do we sail?"

The army doesn't want us to know the answer—and we don't. It might be tomorrow. It might be in a month. You didn't make the trip here from Des Moines in 48 hours because the boat was waiting for you.

The embryonic war correspondent does most of the wondering about the "ifs" and "whens" during the first six weeks (as in my case) from the time you first hear of the assignment until the present, but others do some.

Your friends and acquaintances who've heard about your plans ask questions.

"When do you go?" they ask and time after time you have to explain that you don't know, that you wished you did and that there isn't anything much more indefinite than the time the army will send for you.

"Lucky Stiff."

It's interesting to note the reactions of various persons to your assignment. Most think as you do and they say: "You lucky stiff. I'd give my right arm to have that chance. That's a swell break."

But occasionally you get a reaction like this:

"Do you have to do it? If that's what you want, O.K., but I wouldn't want any part of it."

Almost everyone asks you what your wife thinks about it all and it's nice to answer that she's been darn swell about it.

The red tape keeps you pretty busy while you're waiting to go. You take periodic jaunts to the Fort Des Moines army post for "shots" against typhoid fever, smallpox and tetanus with the understanding there'll be more of the needle-jabs later on.

Your application for war correspondent status has to be filled out seven times and you have to tell everything from your mother's middle name to the names of the clubs you belong to.

You write for your birth certificate and get a release from your draft board and a statement from your employer plus $10 to apply for a passport. You get photographed and fingerprinted. You go out to Camp Dodge to get some "dog tags" to hang around your neck.

And during all this time, as your boss unhappily discovers, it becomes increasingly difficult to keep properly interested in your day-to-day work.

Six and a half hours after I received instructions to go, I was on my way out of Des Moines. It was a mad scramble. A bag to pack . . . the immunization certificate to get from the army post—travelers checks and other financial papers from the bank to get and Carl Mesner of the Bankers Trust Co. is good enough to come downtown and oblige . . . telephone calls to Washington to insure a priority for air travel.

Doubts about the flying weather so a last minute decision to grab the night train to Chicago and fly from there.

Your spirits hit bottom for a while. It's no fun to leave your family for a long time and put thousands of miles between you. When the train pulls out it's lousy. Your thoughts race with the clickety-clack of the train all night and you don't sleep much. Hardly any.

In Washington you start scurrying around again. First to the mammoth Pentagon building. You receive a small green folder with your picture attached which certifies you as a war correspondent and an office girl affixes your fingerprints.

War correspondents overseas wear the clothing of army officers, without insignia of rank, so getting all that stuff is the next job and your hat is off to the men in the army clothing store downstairs in the Pentagon building who do the whole job for you, including alterations, in less than two hours.

Loaded down, you struggle along until you find a taxicab. There are six in a cab already but they shove you in anyway.

The driver grabs the big bag with all your new clothes and shoves it between the fender and the hood. Then he tosses the bag of another passenger in the window and on your lap and says "Hold this."

"Damned outrage!" snorts a colonel jammed in the back seat.

Well, that's Washington for you.

In the morning you hustle to the crowded Union station in Washington for another train and this time you're all duded out in your new uniform—and you soon wish you could get back to civilian clothes in a hurry.

The station is filled with soldiers and they start giving you the eye, some of them even walking around you while they stare and they give you that who-the-hell-are-you look and you almost feel like yelling to all of them that you're a war correspondent and that's why you've got a uniform but no officer's insignia.

Mad Rush.

There's a mad rush for the train and by the time you get on there aren't any more seats. You're perspiring from head to foot. It's a WINTER uniform you've got on. You've heard somewhere that you've to keep it buttoned. The train's so crowded you can't take your blouse off and put it anywhere.

For several hours you stand between the cars and finally you're tempted to offer a soldier five bucks for his seat. But you don't.

On the train I chatted with a pleasant young officer—a Catholic chaplain. Ultimately I explained my status to him.

"Oh, I thought maybe you had a hangover and forgot to put your bars on this morning," he said.

Later I ran into a man whose immediate destination was the same as mine—a man in the diplomatic service returning to his post.

The diplomat is a friendly fellow but easily irritated. The complaints (not too audible) of a young child were most annoying to him and, when we got off at our station and another train came down the track with its whistle screeching as he sought to instruct a WAC about his luggage, he turned toward the howling locomotive and shouted:

"Oh, shut up!"

You should have heard him when he found there weren't any sheets in the barracks where we are billeted.

REGISTER, OCTOBER 11, 1943.

PORT OF EMBARKATION, ATLANTIC COAST (DELAYED)—Before men board ships to cross the Atlantic they enter what is called a staging area.

If you think, as I did, that when you reach your destination you'll be whisked away to the waterfront and up a gangplank, you are sadly mistaken.

I have been here three days and I have no more idea what the actual port or the boat I am to travel on looks like than if I were walking along Locust st. in Des Moines.

The only water I have seen has been in the latrine, the mess tables and in the ditches along the roads of the camp.

You enter this staging area, which is actually an army camp, and once you are in you are part and parcel of a vital military secret and you are locked up with it.

There's something exciting about that, too. You are shut off from what is left behind you and from what lies ahead.

Men who have to stay here long don't like it. They become restless, itching to move, and they try to guess when they will go, but until the last few hours it is strictly a guessing game.

Most of the soldiers here don't know where they are going. Officers who know where they are going are under secret orders and they don't discuss their destinations. Civilians usually know where they are going but they are told to keep their mouths shut.

Throughout the camp there are posters that say:

"If you tell where you are going, you may never get there."

In the military intelligence office there is another poster with a unique touch. Originally the poster showed a sailor with his head sticking out of a porthole and the warning is: "IF YOU TALK, THIS MAN MAY DIE."

But one of the intelligence officers cut out the picture of the sailor and plugged the hole with a mirror.

If you are kept at the staging area for only a short while, there is plenty to do. At first you are billeted in a barracks and you visit the military intelligence office where your credentials are checked.

As soon as you are settled, you are handed a sheet with a fat list of things to do and you start the rounds. The dispensary checks your immunization record and then you go to the dental clinic for a dental check-up.

The battle-bound troops file through the clinic by the dozens. The numerous dental chairs always are filled. Our soldiers are going overseas with their teeth in good shape.

No time is lost in this clinic. A soldier sits in the chair and opens his mouth. A dental officer goes to work and when the work, ALL OF IT, is done, the soldier gets to close his mouth again. There's no talk about the weather—or anything else. There are even metal gadgets to keep the soldier's mouth open in the desired position. Desired, that is, by the dental officer.

One officer awaiting shipment, a physician by the way, said he had eight cavities filled in 30 minutes.

"At home," he said, "the work would have dragged out for weeks."

Emergency Address.

You proceed to another office where you leave your emergency address and from there to the military intelligence office where your credentials are re-checked and where you are told in more detail about what not to do and what not to say.

Then, from another intelligence officer, you receive a censorship lecture. Much of this is for the benefit of officers who will have to cope with the problem of supervising the censorship of soldiers' mail.

"One thing that happens is that soldiers being subjected to censorship for the first time are afraid to tell their wives and sweethearts that they love them," the lecturing officer says.

They are afraid that if they write "I love you, darling," it will get back somehow to their comrades and they will kid them about it. So, the intelligence officer reports, soldiers frequently place their message of love underneath a stamp and hope the censor won't spot it.

"After about a week the boys stop feeling shy about writing what they feel," the officer says.

Now you start getting loaded down with equipment and that entails going the rounds from one building to another, first receiving authorization to obtain the stuff and then getting it.

Among the things you receive are blankets, eating utensils, gadgets to attach various articles while you're carrying them, a heavy steel helmet, first aid package with sulfa tablets, gas mask, barracks bags and other articles, the listing of which might tip the destination.

Then you have the job of sorting your belongings, putting in your "A" luggage what you'll have with you on the ship and in the "B" luggage the stuff which will be stowed away and returned to you on the other side.

For a novice, getting some of the equipment correctly adjusted is not exactly a cinch. Some of us wrestled quite a while with our helmets. Experienced officers gave us a hand.

There's always an atmosphere of mystery in this staging area. Soldiers are here today and gone tomorrow. Officers sometimes can't understand what's delaying their departure and as they see shipments come and go, they get restless and fidgety.

You may be told that it is urgent to get to the staging area RIGHT NOW but once you get there, you may stay a week or a month.

Soldiers always are in evidence at the camp. You hear their marching, sometimes running, feet from the crack of dawn and they chant rhythmically "One, two, three four," as they march along.

Swingy Trick.

A Negro detachment catches your attention with a swingy trick of injecting melody and fancy rhythm into their "one, two, three fours." They do it with jive.

At intervals chimes from the camp chapels ring out with "Onward Christian Soldiers" and other hymns.

Rumors always are being kicked around and invariably they hinge around the departure time of someone or some group. Things happen which make men think the embarkation time is near. But often they mean nothing at all.

You think you sense something in the air but imaginations work overtime here.

One thing you do know. Within 48 hours of your departure, you receive a once-over physical examination. And you receive a 24-hour "alert."

Then you go.

REGISTER, OCTOBER 12, 1943.

ALLIED HEADQUARTERS, NORTH AFRICA—When you have to ride across the Atlantic in these days of war you find yourself aboard whatever is going your way, and in my case it was a slow, ugly freighter jampacked with troops and cargo.

After four days of preparation at the staging camp near the Virginia coast, we received orders that we were ready to move and everywhere excitement began to mount.

The night before we left we had a last-minute physical examination which took about 15 seconds per person.

On the day of embarkation we wrestled with the intricacies of getting harnessed up with blanket rolls, gas masks, canteens, musette bag and battle helmet. Then we headed for a troop assembly point.

I was struggling along accompanied by a friendly army intelligence officer and feeling as if I were giving Babe Carnera a piggy-back ride when something happened I'll never forget. Hundreds of soldiers were moving along the camp road. There wasn't much animation among the men. Some groups counted cadence, "One, two, three, four," as they marched.

Then we heard one man's feet and one man's voice behind us. We looked back and saw a little fellow who weighed 125 pounds at the most. He was having a helluva time with all his gear.

A bulging barracks bag was his biggest problem. He was holding it by the rope and he kept trying to hitch the bag up on his back. Every time he gave a hitch he got out of step.

It dawned on us that the lad was carrying on a conversation with himself—his buddies were 30 yards in front of him—and it went like this:

"One, two, three four—one, two, three four—Get in step you no good private—One, two—dawgone you, get in step—now you got it, one, two, three, four."

But then the boy gave the bag another hitch and out of step he went with his own count. He began to get mad.

"Didn't I tell you to get in step—one, two—listen you dumb, ornery hillbilly, get the lead out of you—one, two, three—I'm tell you damn private, get the hell in step—one, two, three, four—now you're talking."

The intelligence officer smiled and commented:

"What couldn't you do with 10 million men like that?"

At the assembly point the solders were lined up. They were tired. They put their helmets on the road and sat on them. Some planes roared by overhead.

"Boy, I'd like to be in one of them headed for Indiana," said a soldier with a longing look in his eye.

A Cheer.

The soldiers cheered when the order to move to the embarkation train was given. They marched a mile in double file and you could look between the lines and see endless rows of rifles bobbing up and down with the rhythm of the movement.

A pretty WAC walked by smiling and waving goodby to the boys. The soldiers stared at her admiringly.

"Keep your eyes ahead of you or you'll get a rifle in your face," shouted a lieutenant, but he too was staring at the WAC and smiling.

There were 18 cars in the embarkation train and the troops were moved into them quickly and efficiently, each man receiving a packaged lunch on the platform.

The train whistled and started the 12-mile trek to the dock. The soldiers seemed neither elated nor depressed, although the everyday chatter quieted when we passed a Red Cross hospital train.

When the ships came into view there was nothing to cheer about—two ugly freighters and the stories we had heard about riding on them were not encouraging.

Each Man Checked.

The troops moved up the gangplank and each man was checked as he boarded his ship. White soldiers boarded one ship while Negro troops, their officers, six office of war information (OWI) men and I boarded the other.

There was a band on the pier. The music put life into the boys when the band broke into "Jersey Bounce." The soldiers cheered and, forgetting the weight of their packs, stamped their feet and whistled and hummed.

A Negro soldier grabbed his rifle, held it as he would a dancing partner and started dancing around the pier. Another Negro started jitterbugging and their comrades clapped the rhythm.

The troop loading took only a few minutes. The soldiers moved down to their quarters. Smoke drifted lazily from the single stack of the ship. The officers who checked the troops left. The band departed.

And with dusk falling, quiet settled over the pier.

REGISTER, OCTOBER 13, 1943.

On the second night at sea Capt. Clayton E. Johnson of Jamestown, New York, talked to the troops in their quarters. He told them the probable length of the voyage.

For several seconds there was a dull silence. Finally a soldier broke the silence by saying:

"Why Captain Johnson, sir, we're going to sail right out of this world."

One of the soldiers was a former night club singer from Chicago. In army camps back home he always had been quick to give the boys a song whenever they asked it, but at sea he became voiceless.

"No sir, I'm seasick; I'm waterbound," he said when someone asked him to sing.

The rolling and pitching of the ship was a new sensation to almost all of the soldiers and an unpleasant one to most.

"I feel like I drunk all the likker in town," one of them said as he struggled along the deck of the heaving ship.

Another soldier pointed to a raft and asked: "Are these the things you get into if we get blowed up?"

Dice Games.

During the first three days of the trip the decks and the troops' bunk rooms were cluttered with troops playing poker and shooting dice. In some of the games the stakes were plenty high. The boys may not be mathematical wizards but surely they know how to handle money and make change in these fast moving games.

After a while the games subsided. The money was gobbled up by a lucky few, one of whom gave an officer 560 dollars to keep for him.

It was amazing to see how easily the soldiers could grab a nap. They snoozed everywhere. One boy slept out on the hard deck and rested his head on a block of wood while a group of soldiers went through noisy calisthenics a few feet away.

Others stood on catwalks and slept with their arms and heads draped over the rails. One soldier nestled his body around the turret of a tank and dozed.

The officers have a high regard for Negro soldiers. They say they are as good as any, that they are faithfully obedient and interested in their work.

Lieut. Bill Adams of New York said one weakness of Negro soldiers is their disinterest in classroom work but they're swell, he said, at getting out and doing a job. They're always asking questions and are curious as to why this or that is being done.

The Negro soldiers have varying moods. Sometimes they sing cheery, lovely songs. On other days their songs are "blue." Or they don't sing at all. Whatever the mood, it is contagious.

Every night aboard ship they sang in their bunk rooms.

One night they had a boisterous "jam" session. Eight of them sat on two benches facing each other. One was the leader and at first he sang alone while another soldier beat a rhythmic tap with a fork on a messkit.

Then they all joined in the chorus which became louder and louder. Four tapped lustily with their forks, spoons and messkits. Two formed the bass section by tooting through paper funnels into their field helmets, and the other two carried the lyrics as dozens of boys in their bunks hummed the melody.

The night before that the soldiers sang spirituals. The stairs leading down to the bunkroom were jammed with soldiers sitting on the steps and standing by the rail.

Their favorite song was "Ain't gonna study war no more."

The Same Mess.

The officers in charge of the group throughout the trip neither asked nor accepted more than their men received. The steward staff arranged to add soup and salad to the officers' mess but Lieut. Vincent M. Sczupauk of Fulton, N.Y., the mess officer, ordered that nothing be served the officers that was not served the troops.

Despite the fine morale of the troops, tempers got the best of the boys on a few occasions and fists flew. One night the officers supervised a fight. A Negro sergeant came to the officers while they were reading and playing cards.

"Where are the gloves?" he asked. "Two of the boys have been at each other all the trip and I'm going to get it out of their system."

The gloves were taken from a box of recreational equipment and we went into the troop bunkroom to watch the fun.

It was a scene of excitement and hilarity. In front of the rows of bunks there was a tarpaulin-covered open space about the size of a fight ring and it was spotlighted by a searchlight.

The soldiers, shouting and laughing, sat on the edges of the bunks facing the ring on three sides and reaching almost to the ceiling. It easily could have been a dingy fight arena back home.

The ring was cleared. Volunteer seconds helped the fighters on with the gloves. Lieut. Dick Prophet of Detroit, Mich., moved in to referee and blew a whistle for the boys to start slugging.

The gloves began to fly, the troops yelled themselves hoarse and then began laughing when one of the fighters decided he'd had enough and after one knockdown retired to the background.

A buck private, Smith by name, is one of the characters among the soldiers. One day back home he came to Captain Johnson with a problem.

He'd been married once in Mississippi under his mother's name and again in Michigan under his own name. Now he wanted to get married a third time and he wanted Captain Johnson to tell him what name to use and how he could get an army allotment for each wife.

"For goodness sake, Smith," said Captain Johnson, "that's against the law. The F.B.I. will be after you."

"No kidding, sir?" replied the surprised soldier, "I thought it was all right so long as the women didn't make no fuss."

Smith's officers said he's a darn good soldier, an excellent truck driver. When he was inducted he couldn't read or write but he studied hard and constantly has a spelling book with him now.

After arriving in Algiers, Gammack spent two weeks waiting for passage to the front. One week was taken up in getting permission to join the 34th Division of the Fifth Army in Italy. Then the plane on which he was booked turned out to be full of army officers whose business, he conceded, "was considerably more important than mine." Ultimately Gammack hitchhiked air passage into Italy.

With the 34th Division at the Italian front in November of 1943, Gammack was profoundly impressed by what he heard General Eisenhower call the "unsung heroism of the foot-slogging soldier in the foxholes, the rain, mud and dust of battle." The Iowa men he found and talked with provided a direct and personal account of the common ordeals of the front line. His interview with Sergeant Wayne Seastrom is a case in point.

TRIBUNE, NOVEMBER 3, 1943.

Gammack Talks to Fighting Sergeant

AT THE 5TH ARMY FRONT IN ITALY—The only unusual thing about this story is that it is happening every day to hundreds of American soldiers on the front in Italy.

It is perhaps what Gen. Dwight Eisenhower had in mind when he spoke at a press conference of the unsung heroism of the foot-slogging soldier in the foxholes, the rain, mud and dust of battle.

Sergt. Wayne Seastrom, 25, who lived and worked on a farm near Coon Rapids, Ia., before he went to war, has just pitched his pup tent in a rest area behind the front lines after eight straight days of bitter, nasty fighting against the Nazis and German artillery, machine gun and mortar fire.

The easiest times during the eight-day attack were when he could rest, with danger on every side, in a foxhole.

During those eight days, Wayne marched between 50 and 60 miles—although only a portion of that distance in actual advance—and by catching 15-minute naps from time to time averaged about three hours' sleep each 24 hours.

"We went up hill and down through ditches, water and what have you," he said.

The Italian hills are bitterly cold at this time of year, yet the sergeant and his buddies have nothing but raincoats to keep them warm.

"It has been all I could do to keep warm with four blankets.

"We slept in pairs, lying up against each other to keep warm," he said. "When we could, we'd get up and run around to try and warm up some."

Close Calls.

Dozens of times during that attack bullets and shrapnel missed Seastrom by inches and he saw men drop only a few feet from him.

"One of my pals got it in both ankles and there was a small wound in his head," Wayne recalled. "There was a hole the size of a half dollar through his helmet; that's the only thing that saved him."

I tried to get Seastrom to tell his story in a day-to-day narrative but days and nights have little meaning in themselves to men who are fighting for their lives, clinging to the principle of kill-or-be-killed.

He started out with his battalion on a Tuesday and marched 10 miles with rifle and 30-pound battle pack. Most of the time Nazi shells dropped around him. Three times during the day he had to dig a foxhole like mad and hole in against the fire.

"We didn't stay in the holes all the time but we stayed right handy to them," said Wayne.

Seastrom had his closest call on Wednesday. The Nazis threw an artillery barrage and he started running for cover.

"Lucky, there were quite a few duds in the bunch they threw but a piece of shrapnel came between my legs and ripped a hole in my pants," he said.

"I got a little scratch out of it but it wasn't much."

Outflank Nazis.

On Thursday after a night crossing of a river Seastrom's gang was plastered again with machine gun, mortar and artillery fire as they advanced against a German position and outflanked it.

"On Wednesday and Thursday everything was coming close to us and we had some casualties," Seastrom related.

The doughboys made an attack Friday morning and wiped out some Jerry machine gun nests.

"We got shelled five or six times that day and it was plenty hot," he said.

"We attacked on Saturday but our job was mostly to hold a position. Saturday at 3 a.m. we attacked a steep hill.

"We took the town but it took us all Monday and Tuesday to clean up machine gun nests and snipers."

On Wednesday night Seastrom and his men were relieved. In two or three days whenever the situation demands it, they go out for another dreary spell of marching and fighting.

They will fight and stay in their foxholes in cold and wet weather. They'll get by on their field rations—one can "wet" and one can "dry" for each man.

The wet cans will contain stew or some such concoction while the dry cans will have biscuits, sugar and coffee.

Each squad carries one small stove but they can use them only by daylight when the glow won't betray their positions.

As Seastrom talked, he ran his right hand, bandaged from some sort of an infection, up and down the barrel of his rifle. He looked tired and he told his story undramatically.

Even in a rest area only a mile or two behind the front lines there is no real peace.

Artillery fire is booming all around.

Shells can suddenly crash in the midst of resting men.

"We were always on the lookout for those booby traps. You never know when you're going to step into one during those days. They killed one of our fellows and wounded two others."

Such experiences told sketchily and minus the detail show what the fighting men take as a matter of course. Such is the proud existence of the men General Eisenhower spoke of when he said he wondered whether the postman in a town like Emmetsburg, Ia., and villages in Britain appreciate the heroic if unspectacular fighting of men like Sergt. Wayne Seastrom.

But gasoline rationing is a nuisance, isn't it?

Shortly after he arrived in Italy, Gammack focused his attention on some aspects of American morale. His first impression was of the terror that was routine at the front. And he was intrigued by the emotional and psychological changes demanded of fighting men. With large numbers of soldiers he encountered he probed the question of how they felt about the job they had been given to do.

TRIBUNE, NOVEMBER 19, 1943.

Not Afraid at Front? Somebody's Kidding

AT THE FRONT IN ITALY.—Just in case anyone wonders whether you get scared at the front, the answer is, "Hell yes," and as far as I'm concerned, anyone who claims otherwise either is a liar or should be sent without delay to the nearest insane hospital.

There are, of course, varying degrees of fear in surroundings where folks are living lives of trying to kill each other. Usually the veteran at the front gets scared only when there are very good reasons, but the newcomer is frightened all the time—or certainly most of it.

The veterans don't fret about what might happen or what just doesn't happen, but wait until something dangerous comes along before getting the shivers.

Now that I know a few more things about the front than I did (and they aren't many), I know that I've been scared silly at times when there was no reason for it and comparatively at ease when through blissful ignorance I just didn't know what was going on.

I was like a babe in the woods the first day. Our jeep was bouncing along slowly, and one didn't think we were anywhere near the front despite the grim expressions on the faces of drivers hurrying along the road.

About this time we passed an intersection which I learned later the Germans had been shelling persistently.

The first night, which I'll never forget, a colonel in command of a regiment invited me to ride with him to a new regimental command post near the front lines.

It was dusk when we left and we had gone only a short distance when we got caught in a traffic jam at a point near a bridge and had to wait until a convoy rumbled along toward the battle line. Soon it was pitch dark. We could see dozens of vehicles behind their pinpoint headlights and there were many trucks and jeeps ahead which we could see by their dull red tail lights. White tapes along the road shoulders led the way.

An M.P. came running along the line of vehicles. "Out with all lights," he warned. "There are plenty of Jerry planes above."

Then we heard the uneven drone of the German planes. The colonel's bodyguard was sitting with me in the back of the jeep. He is from Cherokee, Ia., but I never did get his name. He nudged me.

"Look back there," he said, and back of us the sky was alive.

Naples was being bombed and the blue starlight was full of our bright red ack-ack. It was a silent and beautiful spectacle. Our barrage could be seen but not heard.

Thousands of the red tracer bullets were in the air all at once, flying in all directions, as our gunners sought to throw up a deadly curtain of fire. The tracers shot up high into the air, then arched and started their downward course. They crisscrossed against the blue background.

A Gorgeous Show

We knew, of course, that the ack-ack was sent into the skies to kill, but out in the valley it looked like a harmless and gorgeous show—far more beautiful than any display of fireworks.

"There's no more beautiful sight in the world," the colonel commented.

It seems hard to understand that in Naples itself, scared people were running for cover, men and women were dying and at least a few of the German planes were plummeting to destruction in bursts of flame.

When we reached the new regimental command post, supper was ready. I had little trouble finding a few officers who knew me so that I could find out how to go about getting something to eat. It was really dark.

After supper, the colonel invited me into the command truck which had lights inside and is blacked out from the outside. We passed around small portions of cognac to the staff officers. A noncom had obtained the bottle somewhere.

The colonel glanced at the map outlining the German defense positions. In another 24 or 36 hours his men would go into an attack. "We might try the old center buck," he said. "Sometimes it's good for nine yards."

"I have an idea we'll get the end run," commented Maj. Kermit Hansen of Omaha, Neb., the best thinker in the regiment.

Just then there was the most terrific explosion I'd ever heard. The concussion literally rocked the truck. I felt a puff of wind hit my legs. I jumped off my chair a good few inches. The colonel smiled.

"That sounds good," he said, "That's like the bass drum in your band when that shell hits its destination. I wonder if it won't be a little disturbing to the people at the other end of the line."

All this talk was about a shell which had been fired from one of the biggest guns we have on the Italian front. The terrific blasts in themselves are shocking enough, but they come with such awful suddenness. Of course it wouldn't be the thing to do in war to send around messengers for the artillery who would drop in at each place in the neighborhood and say:

"We've put a big gun near your area and we're going to shoot it every few minutes for six hours starting at midnight, so don't let it alarm you."

But sometimes I've wished they could do that and I'd be sure to have my watch right all the time if they did.

The officers in the command truck started mimicking the various noises that accompany artillery fire—ours and the Germans. They do a very good job of it; also of describing graphically the mental and physical things that happen to you when an enemy shell comes close.

All night the big gun nearby blasted away at the Germans, not only to do damage but to make sleep for the Nazis more difficult. Harassing fire they call it—and it harassed me plenty.

Lying on the ground between blankets in a tent with several officers, I felt sure each blast actually shocked me an inch or two.

I thought about the colonel's remark about the gun being like the bass drum in your own band and decided it didn't lull a fellow to sleep.

"Pretty lively tonight, isn't it?" I asked the officer next to me.

"Oh, no," he said, "this one's pretty quiet."

I may have slept a few minutes that night but I doubt it. At 4 a.m. there was another loud explosion but this one was different from the wham from

MARCH 16, 1945. Infantrymen of Co. B, 339th Infantry, 85th Division, march up to take position in the line at S. Clemente, Italy. Troops pass smoke pots, fogging the area to hide troop and vehicle movements from enemy observers. *(Signal Corps)*

our big guns. I thought everyone else was asleep, but Major Hansen called out.

"Gammack, that one was theirs," he said with emphasis on the "that" and he explained that it was a German flat projectile which is fired on a straight line rather than on the arc and for that reason doesn't whistle as it nears its destination.

There's No Place Like . . .

By the time it grew light my thoughts were very strong on Des Moines, Ia., and how badly I wanted to be there. The colonel suggested a number of units I might like to visit but I was not in the mood.

Since then I've seen jittery soldiers run for tents when enemy planes came over, and in front line hospitals I understand nervous patients pull blankets over their heads at the sound of planes.

But the feeling of desperation subsides. At first, I shivered mentally at the sound of an airplane motor, but after a while I waited for the sound of our own ack-ack before looking for the nearest ditch.

That's followed by a period when if the enemy planes aren't too close you want to watch the shooting, hoping that you'll see one of the Jerries shot down. But when the Jerry planes are near or when they start strafing or diving anywhere in your vicinity it's a different story and, like a lot of people, I always get the feeling that one of those bombs surely is headed my way.

Around the front there's often some chaff about the people being the farthest from the fighting being the most scared. An army division has what is known as a rear echelon which handles the paper work if the outfit is anywhere from 20 to 50 miles from the front lines.

There the foxholes are deeper than I have seen elsewhere and there's considerable scattering of men when planes are seen or heard in the distance.

However, most of the officers, like Lieut. Col. D. M. White of Marshalltown, Ia., the ranking officer at the echelon area, are amused by this consternation and he is said to have warned some of them they are likely to be hurt in the rush for foxholes.

Not Only the Newcomers.

Nervousness at the front is not reserved exclusively for the newcomers. Soldiers who have been in and near the lines for a long time begin to show the strain.

"I jump every time I hear one of our own guns," said an Iowan who has been overseas more than a year and a half. "I know they're ours, but I jump just the same."

Men who have been wounded or who have had a bomb land terribly close reach the point where they can no longer stand the strain.

I know one boy who saw his two brothers killed in action and then was assigned to the job of going under fire and evacuating our dead.

The lieutenant in charge of this assignment couldn't stand the idea of letting the soldier do that work under the circumstances, and rather than have the soldier do it, he took on the work himself.

In most cases, consideration is shown men whose nerves have been shattered by war and they have been given jobs where, as the saying goes, "It isn't so noisy."

I was talking to Don Whitehead, whose Associated Press dispatches you've read, about this story and he made the good suggestion of mentioning the distinction between fright, which is normal and natural, and cowardice.

While fright is common, in American soldiers cowardice in the front lines is usually nonexistent. No matter how great the fear, the overwhelming majorities of the American soldiers do the jobs they have to do and are ordered to do.

REGISTER, NOVEMBER 28, 1943.

Iowans Learn to Kill, without Lust for It

AT THE 5TH ARMY FRONT—This is a story on how Iowa and Minnesota soldiers feel personally towards German troops.

Sergt. Ralph Garthwaite, a scrappy front line soldier from Sheldon, Ia., had been harassed for several hours by a German with a machine pistol.

He saw men from his squad wounded by the German's fire, but finally the Jerry ran out of ammunition, threw down his gun, yelled "Kamerad," and Sergeant Garthwaite took him prisoner.

"Why didn't you shoot the — — — — —," a soldier asked the Sheldon man. "I don't know," Garthwaite replied. "I just couldn't bring myself to killing a guy with his hands in the air."

That story comes as close as any to what I feel is the prevailing attitude of soldiers from Iowa and Minnesota towards the Germans. The soldiers give you different answers when you ask about their personal feelings toward the Jerries.

Intense Hatred.

A lieutenant colonel who is a division intelligence officer told me that the hatred of the doughboys for the Germans is intense and that they hate them more than they do the Japs.

But the talks I have had with our fighting men do not bear out that contention. The American soldier is a forgiving guy at heart and while he may go through periods of fighting when his anger becomes great, he has not acquired a lust for killing.

Killing does not bother the veteran soldier. If he kills a half dozen Germans in one day he is apt to feel good about it although the idea of it doesn't weigh on his conscience.

But he is guided primarily by the thought of "kill or be killed."

Most officers agree that men with unemotional attitudes toward the enemy are more efficient fighters and they think that the lack of lust for killing is an aid rather than a detriment to our campaign.

I have seen German prisoners brought in and American soldiers continue to gape at them with far more curiosity than hate. A German prisoner had dinner with us one day and when he asked for seconds he got them. If a prisoner wants a cigarette he usually gets one.

Learn to Hate.

Americans who have been fighting the Germans a long time do feel more bitter toward them than they did at first. They have seen their buddies killed and wounded by booby traps and mines and they have seen Germans pull fake surrenders.

But I doubt that the bitterness is lasting.

"The Germans have been misguided," said Corp. Orville Pedersen of Minneapolis, Minn. "You can't really blame them for believing what they've been taught so long."

Pvt. (f.c.) Arthur Carlson of Cedar Falls, Ia., said that "At first it was kinda hard for me to kill Germans but when you see your buddies getting killed you don't mind any more. It gets like shooting rabbits."

"I don't feel like I'm killing a human when I shoot a German," said Corp. Ernest Thompson of Spencer, Ia. "It gets sort of mechanical."

I had the feeling that when soldiers said they harbored real hate for the Germans they didn't say it with much feeling. Certainly they talk with more emotion about other matters that irritate them.

The soldier from Iowa and Minnesota is physically hard and tough and he's a hell of a scrapper but when the smoke of battle clears away he is still a pretty soft-hearted guy underneath.

I don't think war has changed his character much. In fact, I think he is a very grand and sweet gent.

Gordon Gammack stayed with the 34th Division long enough to understand the weariness that came with prolonged privation and danger and the gradual erosion of morale. He was conscious throughout of the relatively privileged status enjoyed by correspondents, although he experienced the accommodations and, in some measure, the perils of the fighting men he accompanied. As service at the front lengthened from days into weeks and months, the soldier's devotion to his comrades became a major source of emotional sustenance.

REGISTER, DECEMBER 26, 1943.

Valor Based on Devotion to Comrades

WITH THE 34TH DIVISION IN ITALY—Nothing at the front transcends devotion of a soldier for the men with whom he has been dumped into the whirlpool of war—his buddies.

A soldier's devotion to his country is an intangible, vague thing. Basically he fights for his country because he has to, but he fights for his buddies because he wants to.

When I hear of a soldier who does a very brave and courageous thing, who risks his life with great abandon, I can usually trace it to an urge to help his friends who are in trouble.

A few nights ago, I was sitting in front of a fire in an Italian farm house with Lieut. Col. Lloyd Rockwell of Council Bluffs, Capt. John Agnes of Sioux City and several other officers and we were talking about this.

"You ought to get a story on Stan Davis," suggested Colonel Rockwell, referring to Sergt. Stanley Davis of Kingsley, Ia. "He's a mess sergeant. He doesn't have to get in there and shoot with the boys, but he does every time there's a fight on. He grabs his rifle, tells his assistant to take over the kitchen, and goes into the line with the boys."

That led to mention of two other soldiers in the colonel's battalion who do the same thing—Sergt. Floyd Drake of Sioux City, and Sergt. Nenzo E. Hatter of Davenport.

They are supply sergeants and they could stay back of the front lines and do their routine jobs, but when they think of their friends in trouble they, too, grab their rifles and join them.

I didn't get a chance to talk to Sergeant Drake, but Davis said, "He's never out of it when his company is in the line."

Several weeks ago, Sergeant Hatter took rations up to his buddies, found they were having a tough fight, "and just couldn't get back."

Behind the Lines.

"It gets to working on you when you are sitting back away from the real fight," said Sergeant Hatter. "When reports come in that the boys are getting it, a man feels he must do something, particularly when they are his buddies. You sweat it out more in the rear areas in a mental way. It's harder than being up there."

"There are so few of the old men left," interjected Sergeant Davis. "The new men kind of like to see an old man out there."

"And then I saw a friend of mine whose feet had been frozen. The pain was so great tears were just running down his face, but he put on his equipment and went in fighting."

"I asked one man in pain why he stayed in there," added Sergeant Hatter, and he tells me, "damn it, someone's got to stay. If I leave, there would be a hole in the line."

Then Sergeant Hatter told a story about Second Lieutenant Dennis Neal of Villisca.

"Four of our men were injured at a command post," he said, "Lieutenant Neal took the men into a shelter. The water was up to his boot tops. Two of the men were hurt bad, and one was in awful pain. Lieutenant Neal stood in that water for 12 hours caring for those men and he didn't leave until the men were evacuated.

There are so many soldiers with such great character that it stuns a civilian like myself coming among them. I keep on saying that they're the finest men I've ever known.

They complain bitterly about this and that—and

often they complain with the greatest amount of justice. War is repellent to them. They long for peace and quiet in their homes.

But they're great fighters, those men from Iowa. They're the best. There's a lot of poppycock about soldiers in noncombatant jobs itching for combat, about wounded soldiers restless to get back into action.

But one thing about an Iowan in war is true. Almost everyone of them will sacrifice his life for his buddies and heroes are made through this devotion.

Admiration for the foot soldier at the front was balanced, in Gammack's coverage, by a desire to quiet unnecessary anxiety amongst his readers and to suggest the diversity of the American soldier's experience. He observed: "There are many jobs at the front well within the range of enemy guns that aren't much more dangerous than the jobs our soldiers had before the war. The vast majority of casualties occur in the heart of the very front line.

"Awful as enemy artillery fire is, the shell must make virtually a direct hit to kill or wound a soldier who is in a fox hole, or who has adequate cover. There aren't many direct hits. And in the theater of war, there are more soldiers behind the line than there are in the line."

That having been said, Gammack moved into the heart of the very front line. He joined the fighting edge of the 34th Division and wrote about its struggles in crossing the Volturno and engaging the enemy at Salerno and Benevento.

REGISTER, JANUARY 2, 1944.

Smashed over Volturno Line in Hail of Fire

WITH THE 34TH DIVISION IN ITALY—No American division has fought harder or longer in Italy than the hardhitting 34th.

When the division left the shores of the United States in February, 1942, after a rigorous training at Camp Claiborne, La., its membership almost exclusively was of national guardsmen and selectees from Iowa and Minnesota.

Not many of the old boys are left. Many are dead. One battalion of one regiment has not been in combat, being assigned to security duties with Allied force headquarters at Algiers and replaced at the front by a battalion of Japanese Americans until recently commanded by Maj. James Gillespie of Des Moines.

In one regiment there are only about 250 men who left the United States for training in Northern Ireland nearly two years ago. Replacements in the other two regiments are comparable.

The division fought gallantly in Tunisia, climaxing the campaign by playing the key role in the capture of Hill 609.

It then trained hard near Oran, Algeria, and landed in Italy Sept. 21. The 34th had its first contact with the enemy in Italy Sept. 28, at Montemarano, although one battalion of artillery took part in the initial landing at Salerno, possibly saving the beachhead.

The division's first full scale action came Oct. 3 when a battalion led by Lieut. Col. Lloyd H. Rockwell of Council Bluffs, Ia., took the Nazis by surprise and captured the key road center of Benevento.

Crossed Volturno.

That was not a very bloody affair, but the division's next major action was the crossing of the Volturno river south of Caiazzo, and from there the division moved ahead from Dragoni, crossed the Volturno a second time and captured 'd Alife.

From there the division moved north to a beautiful valley, engaged in the fierce Hill 235 battle near St. Angelo and continued the slow movement through Pratella and Pratta to Capriati.

At Capriati, the division felt the first full effects of the so-called German winter line.

There the troops of the divison were subjected to intense artillery fire from positions the Germans had forged into the mountainous rocks ahead.

But the division still was on the move, and in a major battle crossed the Volturno a third time, marched with fear in every step through treacherous minefields and captured high ground north of the crossing at St. Maria Oliveto to hold Roccaravindora. There followed a period of nearly three weeks when the divison held defensive positions.

Then came the terrific battle of Montepantano.

Within a few weeks after the division landed in Italy, it encountered two enemies in addition to the Germans, and they were almost as devastating as the Nazis.

One of these was the terrain and the other was weather. The Germans almost always held the high ground. The American soldiers longed for a chance to fight on even terms.

The problem of supplies became acute in the mountains and supply officers in the division had to overcome inadequate planning in higher command by scouring the countryside for mules, packs and shoes for the animals.

140 Mules.

At one point Capt. Russell Mann of Iowa City, Ia., was sent out on exclusive mission of obtaining mules and when he rounded up 140 of them, he won the acclaim of the division staff.

The weather was awful during most of the 34th Division's fighting.

It rained for days at a time and turned roads and bivouac areas into miserable quagmires. The ever-present and damnable Volturno raged and swelled.

The weather was cold, and the soldiers suffered. The farther the troops climbed into the mountainous region the colder it became and the troops fought most of the time with inadequate clothing.

Even more so than in Africa the division was harassed constantly by German mines and booby traps in Italy. The Nazis used them in wholesale quantities and used them as effective weapons against anticipated attacks.

The Germans used the mines and booby traps devilishly.

In one vineyard, the most luscious looking bunch of grapes was attached to the tripline of a mine. Tempting apples hanging on trees would have meant instant death to an unwary hungry soldier.

At the entrance to one town was a sign reading, "WELCOME AMERICAN SWINE." If the American soldiers had given in to impulses and knocked down the sign, they would have set off a mine.

REGISTER, JANUARY 3, 1944.

34th Gunners Played Vital Salerno Role

WITH THE 34TH DIVISION IN ITALY—Whether the Allied landing at Salerno would have ended in a disaster without the sure shooting of the Minneapolis artillery battalion is certainly a matter of conjecture, but the Iowans and Minnesotans in the battalion believe they saved the beachheads.

The battalion under the command of Lieut. Col. Gerald E. Du Bois of Boone, Ia., was the first American artillery unit to land at Salerno, and on the day of the invasion, Sept. 9, it knocked out nine German tanks threatening to push the invasion forces into the Mediterranean.

Maj. Eugene E. Surdyk of Minneapolis, operations officer of the battalion, tells the story:

"Toward the end of our training in North Africa we were told that we were being assigned for a special mission. We had a pretty good idea that it was an invasion of some sort.

"But it was not until after we had been at sea two days that we were told what the mission was to be, that we were assigned to the 36th Division for the invasion at Salerno. Then we were shown maps, photographs, and sketches outlining the operations.

"We were scheduled to come in with the fifth wave of infantry. We disembarked at 1 a.m. It was pitch dark, and we could barely see the glow from Mount Vesuvius as a rough guide.

"There was a mixup, and instead of coming in with the fifth wave, we came in with the second wave. We were supposed to land on 'Green beach,' but it was under very heavy machine gun, mortar and artillery fire, and we couldn't make it.

"So we switched to 'Red Beach' where the enemy fire was not so great. We made the landings at 7:25 a.m. and immediately sent out observers."

Capt. Harold H. Holleran of Minneapolis set up one battery on the battalion's right flank in a grove near the south wall of the ancient ruins of Paestum, and at 9:30 a.m. seven German Mark IV tanks attacked the position.

The batteries scored direct hits on two tanks within 300 yards and forced the enemy to flee, but heavy machine gun fire forced the gun crews to take over.

Stayed with Guns.

But Captain Holleran and a lieutenant stayed with the guns, and after the machine-gunning, which came from concealed tanks delivering parting shots, the men returned and the battery began firing in direct support of the infantry.

Later in the morning Lieutenant Colonel Du Bois received word that the Germans were about to launch an enveloping attack with 20 to 25 tanks. The colonel sent two batteries up the Paestum road. One of these batteries was commanded by Capt. Carl Constant of Minneapolis. The trails of the 105 mm. howitzer guns were dropped hastily, and a battle developed near the command post of the 36th Division.

The batteries knocked out six of the Nazi tanks and forced the others to flee. If the tank attack had not been stopped, the consequences could easily have been very serious.

It was during this battle that the commanding general of the 36th Division's artillery worked like a doughboy for nearly an hour, helping one of the gun crews hold a shift on the trails of the gun.

"He was the highest priced No. 5 man I ever commanded," Sergt. Thomas J. Ahr, Minneapolis, commented later.

During the fighting, Capt. Edward Stewart of Boone, Ia., battalion liaison officer, went forward with infantry units to call fire for the artillery batteries and at one point even assisted in the direction of an infantry platoon.

[*Captain Stewart, 32, was killed in action Nov.*

29, according to war department notification to Mrs. Stewart.]

At 4 p.m., on the day of the invasion, Major Surdyk, operating the fire direction center, spotted an enemy infantry column retreating around a hill.

He called for fire on the column. The artillery crews saw black columns of smoke climb skyward, and the next day it was learned that the shelling knocked out one tank, one staff car and five motorcycles, forcing the Jerries out of a command post.

Covered Retreat.

When the Germans later forced the 36th Division to retreat temporarily out of Altavilla, the Minneapolis artillery battalion covered the withdrawal and pulled out of its own position just before the Germans took it over.

During the first week of the Italian compaign the battalion fired more rounds than it did during the entire Tunisian campaign.

It always has been the aim of the battalion to beat the record of 90 days in steady combat with the enemy attained by the battalion in World War I. The battalion now has achieved that goal.

Sergeant Ahr's father was a corporal in the battalion in the last war.

After the battalion became a combat contingent of the 34th Division and took part in the push on Benevento, the battalion worked night and day in the hard push against the Germans.

In the midst of the Salerno fight, Sergt. Francis Uran of Excelsior, Minn., and Corp. Ted Guzik of Minneapolis went into the midst of a mass of burning ammunition and bursting projectiles to drag wounded buddies from a gun pit.

In the last analysis it has been the artillery that has exerted a pressure sufficient to force the Germans back slowly in Italy.

It's difficult to write about the artillery except in such engagements as the Salerno affair because most of the artillery work is unseen. The batteries rarely have direct contact with the enemy. Moving these guns every day or so to new positions is a hard, thankless job, and the firing process provides scant variety.

The artillery barrages fired by American units in Italy have been terrific.

Generals who were in World War I say that some of the barrages exceed anything they ever saw in France.

It was constant, dreadful artillery blasting that caused one German to write in a letter, which was taken from him, "Those of us in Italy have learned to love Russia."

One of the artillery battalions attached to the 34th Division took a severe pounding from the Germans several weeks ago. The Germans spotted their gun positions and their counter battery inflicted many casualties.

But when it was over, Col. Edwin R. Bodey of Duluth, Minn., said that the gun crews had gone through the ordeal so splendidly and with such a lack of panic, always carrying out orders to the letter, that "I know I can always have the utmost confidence in those men."

Capt. William Lind of Duluth, operations officer, said that the infantry had advised the battalion that its accurate firing "probably saved an infantry battalion" in one action.

The artillery battalion, commanded by Lieut. Col. Joseph Kelley of Minneapolis, has been in the thick of the Italian fight. The battalion several times encountered action so hot that the gun crews left their guns and fought the enemy with rifles.

One of the chores of the battalion in Italy has been to fire the shells that send propaganda and small newspapers in German scattering over the Nazi lines.

The propaganda leaflets are fired at the discretion of battalion commanders, but the small German language newspapers must be fired over the enemy lines within 48 hours after publication.

It has been found that a heavy barrage of field artillery is a good time to scatter the propaganda because that's when the Jerries are in a receptive mood for it.

REGISTER, JANUARY 4, 1944.

34th Troops March Hard, Fool Nazis at Benevento

WITH THE 34TH DIVISION IN ITALY—The story of the capture of Benevento is a pleasant one to write because it is a tale of success through speed and surprise, and it was completed with a minimum of American bloodshed.

The 34th Division moved north from Salerno and had first contact with the enemy Sept. 28, near Montemarano. The Germans were trying to fight a delaying action, firing harassing fire with self-propelled artillery.

What the Jerries did was to fire a few shots and then back up.

But it was a good guess that the Germans would defend at Benevento, because it is the center of a large network of highways. The job of seizing the city fell to the battalion led by Lieut. Col. Lloyd H. Rockwell of Council Bluffs, Ia.

The battalion chased the Germans from Montimilleto to St. Georgia and toward Benevento. It was a gruelling chase. Roads were narrow; bridges along the line of march had been blown up and the mud was thick.

"Most of it was cross-country," Colonel Rockwell

recalled. "We went 27 miles in a continuous march night and day. The men were dead on their feet. They carried mortars and machine guns in their arms all through the mud.

"Men fell into the muck and looked like lolling pigs.

"But the Germans didn't give us credit for making such a speedy advance."

On Oct. 3 Rockwell's battalion swept into the city. The surprised Germans responded with three stiff counterattacks, one with armored vehicles.

Only Light Arms.

"We hadn't had any way to bring anything heavier than machine guns, but we beat them off with machine guns, rifles, pistols and grenades."

Colonel Rockwell said, "If Jerry had known how little we had, he'd sure have shot hell out of us."

Company L, which came originally from Sioux City, Ia., established a command post in a house at the edge of the city.

A group of German tanks came by, and a German kicked on the door. Although a radio was blaring inside, the men in the command post did not answer the knock.

Meantime, Pvt. George Rutka of Muscatine, Ia., came along the side of the house and saw the light shining on one of the German vehicles.

"Turn out those damn lights," shouted Rutka, watching the length of the vehicle.

But for some reason the Germans didn't realize what the situation was, and a few minutes later four soldiers, including Sergt. Lewis F. Collins of Sioux City, Ia., chased out three German staff vehicles and a truck loaded with TNT with two pistols, a carbine, a rifle and two grenades.

The Germans had intended to finish blowing up a bridge that hadn't been completely demolished.

Colonel Rockwell's battalion seized the truck. There not only was TNT in it, but also silk stockings, several bottles of American bonded whisky, some Luger pistols, a good radio and quantities of sauerkraut and beef.

"What we got away with at Benevento was tactical bluffing," said Colonel Rockwell. "Our battalion was spread out, and when the Germans felt fire coming from every direction they thought we were really loaded for them and moved out."

One serious mishap occurred when a German shell landed in the middle of a column of American soldiers who, because it was so dark they couldn't have stuck together otherwise, were bunched closer than military procedure devised. A number of deaths and wounds resulted.

When the news of the capture of Benevento was relayed to 5th Army headquarters, it was announced by the British Broadcasting Co. that "Benevento has been taken by the 5th Army."

This was true in a way, but actually the important capture was made only by Colonel Rockwell's battalion.

"That 27-mile forced march was tough, but it was more than worth it," said Colonel Rockwell.

Sheldon Boys.

Two Sheldon, Ia., boys, Sergeants Thomas P. Downes and Ralph Garthwaite, pulled a coup against the Germans at Benevento.

They took a 10-man patrol with Downes as leader and Garthwaite as assistant leader to go after a German patrol forming 100 yards away. Downes decided to split the patrol, taking four men with him and directing the other four to go with Garthwaite.

Downes yelled for the Germans to surrender, but the Germans answered with fire. The patrol captured a machine gun, killed the gunner and three other Germans.

Garthwaite's patrol went to the left, walked into enemy fire, destroyed a machine-gun and drove the Germans from their position. The five men accounted for three German dead.

With the fall of Benevento, the stage was being set for the first full-scale engagement in Italy of the 34th Division. The division for the first time, but not the last, was to storm the Volturno river.

REGISTER, JANUARY 6, 1944.

How Men of 34th Walked into Death

WITH THE 34TH DIVISION IN ITALY—The Volturno river became a dreaded thing for the soldiers of the 34th Division.

They knew that it must be crossed again near Capriati, and they knew that the Germans would resist the crossing fiercely. They knew also that after they had made the crossing they would be making a direct stab at the German "winter line."

Across the river the snow-covered peaks towered. Here the Germans had entrenched themselves. Venafro could be seen on the left, at the base of the mountains.

The crossing was made the night of Nov. 3-4. From 11:30 p.m. to midnight every gun attached to the division roared, and shells saturated the ground across the river. Then the infantry started across.

Commanding officers saw indications of slight German resistance.

The Germans didn't seem to be doing much shooting, but the ambulances streaming back told the grim story that casualties were heavy.

The answer was mines. The attack had been launched several days ahead of schedule, and it was a fortunate thing because otherwise the minefields would have been even more thick.

Most of the mines were booby traps; "Bouncing Bettys" that hop up when touched and spray a deadly blast of shrapnel.

It took real courage to go through the minefields, but the 34th had that courage.

"The beauty of the story," said an officer, "is that men will go wherever officers lead them."

Lieutenants, sergeants and corporals said, "Follow me," and while many paid with their lives and others with wounds, they blazed paths through the treacherous minefields.

The Iowa regiments suffered the most from the mines. Iowa Regiment B made the crossing abreast of Iowa Regiment A, while the Minnesota regiment supported them. The crossing was made by wading.

On the other side of the river Iowa Regiment B struck out for high ground at Santa Maria Oliveto; Iowa Regiment A for Hill 400 at Rocca Ravindola, while the Minnesota regiment struck for Montaquila.

Each of the three regiments got into fierce battles.

At one point the 1st Battalion of Iowa Regiment A moved up a hill only to find that the men were in the middle of a German company's position.

The Americans drove the Germans off with bayonets.

Capt. Warren E. McBride of Red Oak, Ia., was leading an advance company and was at a road near Rocca Ravindola when he heard vehicles. He yelled for them to halt. They were enemy vehicles, and they tried to get away. Captain McBride shot a German battalion commander and seized some valuable documents.

Germans in Foxholes.

When the regiment reached the top of Hill 400 it was nearly daylight and against the skyline the Americans could see the Germans emerging from their foxholes and shaking their blankets. A terrific battle followed and the Germans were driven from the hill.

But meantime, Iowa Regiment B was having a tough time taking Santa Maria Oliveto, and from there the Germans pummeled the troops on Hill 400 with everything they had.

Lieut. Col. Lloyd H. Rockwell of Council Bluffs, Ia., had one of the closest calls of his fighting career. He was hurrying up to the foot of a hill when Capt. Washington Carter of Montgomery, Ala., screamed a warning and made a desperate grab for the colonel's leg. Colonel Rockwell's foot was tangled in the trip wire of a mine.

One false move and the mine would have blown him and the men around him to bits.

"I never held myself so still in all my life," he recalled later, as Captain Carter got the wire away from his foot.

Five hours after Colonel Rockwell's battalion had crossed the river, it arrived "square at our objective" of Santa Maria Oliveto. The town is perched on the top of what amounts to a cliff.

Company I got into the town at daybreak. At one place the troops surprised Germans cooking breakfast.

Enemy Counterattack.

On the second day the Germans counterattacked, and our men saw the Jerries coming along the streets. Standing in an archway, Sergt. Norbert Rowenhorst held them off with a Tommy gun.

The Germans were firing from a house on a hill. Across a small valley from the town, Sergeant Garthwaite sent Reynolds Gorman of Mason City, Ia., and Corp. Russell Smith of Des Moines to get rifle grenades, and blasted the Jerries out of the house. Later they found a trail of blood where a machine gunner had been.

Within several days after the crossing of the river all three regiments had their objectives firmly held.

Censorship prevented Gammack from immediately dispatching his story of the 34th Division's fierce struggle at Pantano and the report was not published until March. In proper sequence, the articles document the long and desperate ordeal of the 34th Division, climaxed in the early weeks of 1944 by the battle for Cassino.

In presenting the story of Cassino, the Des Moines Register *made the following observations:*

"It is a great story, but a sobering one. Never before had the men of the 34th been thrown into such terrible fighting, never had they acquitted themselves so bravely. In the face of abject physical misery, in the face of ever-present death, these are truly the men who have been willing to fight and to die, that America might live."

REGISTER, MARCH 8, 1944.

Iowa Outfit Grimly Held Peak in Italy

WITH THE 34TH DIVISION IN ITALY—The battle of Mount Pantano, fought up high above the clouds in December, was one of the fiercest battles of the bitter Italian campaign.

It is hard to find words to tell the gallantry of the veteran Iowa and Minnesota soldiers and the many men from the other states who fought with them.

They were all but defeated at some stages. But the soldiers, dazed and wet, elected to die rather than quit the fight.

They withstood one Nazi thrust after another and

FEBRUARY 26, 1945. Vistor Jones (right), Boston *Globe* war correspondent, and Gordon Gammack (center), confer with jeep driver Pfc. Ralph Gurt, Davenport, Iowa, on a road "somewhere" on the western front. *(AP)*

held their ground. The price in blood was high, very high.

The brunt of the battle was borne by the regiment that suffered disaster at Faid pass in Tunisia. The Minnesota regiment helped toward the end, while the other Iowa regiment was locked in another bloody mountain battle with the Germans several miles to the right. Still later fresh troops carried on with the Pantano fight.

The Mount Pantano battle was fantastic. The mountain is approximately 4,000 feet high and on top of it are four knobs, each about 100 feet high and each from 250 to 500 yards apart.

Germans and Americans hurled hand grenades at each other when they were no more than 10 yards apart. When clouds hung over the crest of the mountain, Americans suddenly saw enemy helmets looming out of the mist only several feet away.

The attacking regiment threw 2,400 grenades in four days.

When one battalion ran out of ammunition, the doughboys grabbed rocks and hurled them at the Germans. They even threw their shining canned C rations in a desperate attempt to frighten the Nazis.

The Germans gave our men no rest day and night. They saturated the rocky knobs with intense mortar fire. They followed one barrage after another with vicious counterattacks. The enemy's fire was so intense that many shells landed directly in foxholes and killed Americans huddling in them.

The history of the battle states officially: "At the beginning of the fight the mountain was wooded. When this regiment was relieved, the slopes were bare."

The weather was frightful. The men suffered through rain, snow, hail and sleet. The rain came down in torrents. The soldiers were soaked to the skin, and their wet clothing froze. Overcoats became stiff as boards. The soldiers shivered in foxholes with six inches of water.

Cried with Pain.

The cold and dampness were so intense that strong, tough men lay in their foxholes and cried because the pain in their freezing feet was so great. Sometimes the men's water froze in their canteens.

But they would not come down off that mountain because they knew any gap in their lines would be disastrous. One man took off his shoes and his feet became so swollen that it took him 10 minutes to force the shoes back on them. He trudged off to fight again.

Another man could not walk when the fight was over. He skidded down the mountain on his back. Another soldier had to discard his shoes, wrap his feet in his leggings and hobble down the mountain. Later amputations of toes and feet were necessary because the men refused to quit. The ailment known as "trench feet" began to worry the medical officers.

In one regiment all three battalion commanders were wounded, and two of them were Iowans. Lieut. Col. Edward Bird of Des Moines, one of the great leaders and heroes of the 34th, was one of them. He's back in Iowa now.

[*The other Iowan is no longer here, but it is not known whether release of his name is permitted as yet.*]

Of the men in actual combat from the attacking regiment, every other man was a casualty.

Among the officers there were 41 casualties, and they included nine company commanders. Every available man was pressed into the fight. Cooks, drivers, clerks and soldiers in the anti-tank platoons joined in the frantic task of keeping the troops supplied with ammunition, food and water.

Too Steep for Mules.

The mountain was so steep that mules could go up only part of the way and the men had to carry supplies the rest of the way.

The battle started at 6 a.m. Nov. 29 with Iowa "Regiment A" making the frontal assault. By 8:40 a.m., Hill No. 1 to the left of the knobs was taken by the 1st Battalion.

A platoon led by Lieut. Thomas B. Dunn of Villisca, Ia., made the first attack, and Corp. Martin J. Anderson of Imogene, Ia., led the first squad.

"We got to the top of the knob, but when we did we saw machine guns looking down our throats," said Corporal Anderson. "We chased them with grenades, but right then I knew it was going to be a tough fight."

The assault troops did take the Germans off guard. Lieutenant Dunn pulled the blanket off one German, woke him up and shot him. During the first day the Germans made one counterattack. There was sniping and a small amount of mortar fire, but the first determined Nazi attack came at dusk.

The Germans broke through momentarily on the right flank, but the Americans, letting loose with a weird yell, fought back with bayonets and drove the Nazis back.

"Fog had come over the hill, and sometimes you couldn't see 10 feet," said Capt. Ben Butler of Milton, Ky. "All of a sudden we would see German helmets in our midst. We fought that attack off with bayonets.

"Finally I had to order all the men to stay in their foxholes and shoot anything that moved."

At daybreak on Nov. 30 the Germans started shelling the mountain which still was blanketed by clouds.

Nazis Attack.

"About noon they came up the hill again," the captain continued. "First they'd mortar us and then attack with automatic weapons. Then a red flare would go up. That was the signal for them to drop back. Then we'd get more mortar fire and another attack.

"By dusk the hill was as barren as a plowed field, and they began letting us have it with short range artillery. The stuff sounded like freight trains, but thank God it went by.

"Then the Heinies attacked again. They came like a herd of cattle. I heard awful screams, and I thought our men had been hit hard, but it was the Heinies. We must have killed a lot of them. They kept on attacking until 1 a.m. Our artillery was coming in on the Germans so close that we were getting the bursts, too."

At daylight on Dec. 1 the Germans attacked again. It was snowing, and the hill still was covered by clouds. The Americans were mortared heavily again in the afternoon.

"We sniped some of them," Butler said, "and heard them calling to their medics, and damned if they didn't have an aid station closer to us than our own aid station.

"On the fourth day of the battle it was pretty quiet until about noon," Butler said, "and then we got more mortar fire. They threw about 80 that hit our position right on the nose."

"I could hear the German mortarmen talking and also the flump of the shells going down the mortar chute. If they cut our communications once, they did it 50 times and then we couldn't call for artillery or for supplies.

"Their small arms fire was so terrific that everyone, or almost everyone, who got up from his foxhole was hit.

Relief Comes.

"That night we were relieved. During the whole time our feet were never dry. Our clothes were froze on us, and we couldn't get our dead off the mountain because the shelling was so heavy. At times we couldn't even get our wounded down the mountain."

Despite the awful beating that the 1st Battalion took, the worst crisis of the battle was on Hill No. 2 where the 3rd Battalion had to withdraw at one time to the base of the knob because its ammunition had run out. The battalion took the knob, but got into trouble when it tried to take Hill No. 3 also.

"We got the worst mortar concentration I've ever seen," said Lieut. Glenn Bowen of Iowa City, Ia. "Shells landed by the hundreds, but the men just stayed there and took it."

On the night of Dec. 2 the 2nd Battalion relieved the 1st Battalion, and it had to fight off the same kind of attacks.

"The Germans came at us in waves," said Lieut. Dolliver Zaiger of Audubon, Ia. "The air was thick with grenades, and the battle kept on and on. One man had three rifles shot out of his hand.

"At dusk the Germans tried one of their tricks. One Jerry came into the open yelling, 'Kamerad, Kamerad.' I yelled for him to put his hands up, and he said, 'Ja, Ja,' but he was slow in doing it. Then I saw a squad of Germans coming in on each of our flanks, and so I ordered our men to fire. We killed a bunch of them.

By Dec. 14, all of the 34th Division was relieved and went back of the combat zone for a few days of rest and then training for a new battle. Replacements were received. On Christmas eve the order came through to get ready for action.

REGISTER, MARCH 12, 1944.

The Story of Cassino Is Glorious, but Sad

WITH THE 34TH DIVISION IN ITALY—New and great glory came to the fighting 34th Division in the first six weeks of 1944 when the infantry regiments and artillery battalions that were born in Iowa and Minnesota added pages of triumph and blood to the history of the fierce Italian campaign.

In its drive that started last fall with the capture of Benevento and forged ahead to the fantastic battle of Mount Pantano, the division was in combat for 79 consecutive days.

Relief finally came Dec. 14, but on Christmas eve the order came through to return to combat.

Division officers abandoned their Christmas plans, prepared for the new drive, and then the division proceeded to:

Capture San Vittore and the high ground adjoining the town.

Storm and capture Mount Chiaia, Mount Trocchio and other heights dominating the approaches to Cassino.

Drive ahead to capture Cervaro, a village that overlooks Cassino three miles away.

Break with the vital aid of tanks the famed Gustav line whose defenses made the German defenses of World War I look puny.

Fight through to Hill 593 overlooking the famed abbey of Monte Cassino.

Break into the city of Cassino itself—capturing the barracks, the city jail and the city square—and engage for days in house-to-house, room-to-room fighting whose intensity has not been surpassed in the Italian campaign.

Decimate the famed German 44th Division and batter elements of the tough Hermann Goering Division.

Never before had the 34th been thrown into such terrible fighting. The battle casualty chart alone shows clearly that the most severe battles in Tunisia—Foundouk and Hill 609—were trivial affairs compared to the slaughter from San Vittore to Cassino.

"Tunisia was a maneuver with small ammunition compared to this," said the division's commanding general.

Iowa and Minnesota should be more proud than ever of their famed 34th, but the pride should be reverent because many have died, many have been maimed, many have shrieked with pain, thousands have suffered from the biting cold of the Italian mountains.

The story of the 34th is a great one—but a sad one, too.

But what was terrible for the American soldiers was far worse for the Germans. The Nazi artillery buttressing the Cassino line became far more intense than ever before in Italy, but the mass shelling from our thundering guns was vastly more terrible and devastating.

The Germans feared our men—we learned that on the night before a Nazi counterattack near Cervaro the soldiers of the Hermann Goering Division, many of them fanatical followers of anti-God Hitler—gathered in a church in Cassino and prayed.

But many of the enemy fought desperately to the finish. One dying German rallied his last bit of strength to throw a grenade. Another, with a fatal wound, kept firing his machine pistol until he died.

And there was sometimes desperation, too, in the fighting of the 34th, because time after time the order came down the line that objectives must be obtained "AT ALL COSTS." That was how the battle for Cassino was fought.

REGISTER, MARCH 13, 1944.

Had to Carry Wounded Men for 12 Miles

WITH THE 34TH DIVISION IN ITALY—Above the timberline in treacherous mountain snow banks there was established during the first two weeks of January what was probably the longest litter trail for the evacuation of the wounded in the history of the American army.

This was done when one regiment of the 34th Division was ordered to crush enemy resistance in the high mountains running from above Venafro to the approaches to Cassino.

To protect the advance of the rest of the division from San Vittore to Cassino this had to be accomplished.

There were Germans in those mountains, and there was shooting. But the cruelest part of the assignment was living night and day in the freezing, biting weather with clothing that was necessarily insufficient because the men were on the move. There was very little warm food and so little water that the men used melted snow to drink and make coffee.

Iowa Battalions.

Iowa "Regiment B" was the one given the assignment. It included one battalion with companies that originated in Dubuque, Cedar Rapids and Waterloo; another of its battalions led during this period by Capt. John Agnes of Sioux City included companies from Sioux City, Sheldon and Le Mars.

The regiment also included a battalion of brave Japanese Americans—the hard-fighting, uncomplaining soldiers who are trying to prove that they are as good Americans as the self-appointed patriots in the United States ranting that nothing of Japanese origin is good.

The soldiers suffered in those mountains, particularly the Japanese Americans, who are more vulnerable to freezing weather than most soldiers.

The problem of caring for the wounded became serious.

Engineers tried to build a jeep trail, but it wasn't possible. All rations, ammunition and water had to be hauled by mule.

It became apparent that the wounded would have to be evacuated by litter. The regiment didn't have nearly enough litter bearers, so additional ones were drafted from units not in combat. The total grew ultimately to 480 and included soldiers from the antitank and heavy weapons companies in the regiment.

The plan for removing the wounded was devised by Maj. Horace J. Leslie of Brooklyn, N. Y., regimental medical officer, and his administrative assistant, Second Lieutenant Roy Bates of Fairfield, Md.

As the regiment moved across the mountains, relay stations were established. Finally there were 12 of them, each a mile apart. At each station a noncommissioned officer and 36 men were stationed. Each litter team consisted of six men.

At every other station blood plasma, morphine and supplies for changing dressings were made available. The men lived at the stations in pup tents, and the temperature often was just a little above zero.

Long Trek.

A wounded man was taken first to the battalion aid station for emergency treatment. Then he was taken to the No. 12 relay station from which a six-man litter team carried him to No. 11 station. There a new litter team took over, and the process was repeated until the wounded man reached an ambulance at the end of the trail 12 miles away.

It took from 12 to 20 hours to take a man the length of the trail. Most of the work had to be done at night when the Germans could not spot men moving on the trail and shell them.

"If it weren't for the bright moon we had during that period I don't know what we would have done," said Lieutenant Bates.

Ordinarily a litter team consists of four men, but for this work six were needed because the trail was so treacherous the litter bearers slipped and fell frequently. With only four bearers, wounded men would have been dumped on the icy, rocky path.

Four men died while they were being taken down the trail. One was a major who was given blood plasma all along the way. He died as he was being placed in an ambulance at the end of the trail.

Only the seriously wounded were carried. Men with trench feet or wounds in such places as in the shoulder, hip or arm had to walk.

Slow Work.

"There were two nights when everyone had to keep going without a letup," Lieutenant Bates said. "One litter team had to make eight trips one night. It was awfully slow work. Sometimes the trail was so treacherous the bearers had to crawl.

"One wounded man weighed 230 pounds, and it took 12 men to carry him. It was tough on all the wounded men, but there was no alternative. We doped them up with morphine as much as we could."

Part of the mountain was 5,000 feet in height. The snow was often four feet deep. The men had to live for two weeks under conditions like that. They got a little water that was carried up the mountains and rationed, but mostly they ate cold snow with their K and C rations. And they had to fight the Germans.

Finally the regiment came down from the mountains, and then its soldiers joined their buddies in street fighting in one of the fiercest battles of the war—the battle for Cassino.

REGISTER, MARCH 14, 1944.

San Vittore Captured by Minnesotans

WITH THE 34TH DIVISION IN ITALY— Bitter street fighting marked the capture of San Vittore, a little town blocking the path to Cassino.

The fall of San Vittore, which made headlines throughout the Allied world, was accomplished by the Minnesota infantry regiment of the 34th Division.

Although the other two battalions supported the attack on the town, it was the 3rd Battalion of the regiment that actually went into the steets and drove the Germans out of the buildings.

This battalion is commanded by a rugged regular army officer, Lieut. Col. Fillmore Mearns of California. The executive officer is Capt. Emil Skalichy of Owatonna, Minn.

The attack on San Vittore started Jan. 4 and lasted through Jan. 6. The Americans took 124 German prisoners in the town.

"We were assigned to take the town, clean it out, organize the west end and open the road for the regiment to move to Mount Chiaia and other high ground in the area," related Captain Skalichy. "One company was to take one half of the town, and another company the other half."

House-to-House Fighting.

The companies jumped off at 11 p.m. Two sergeants from Madison, Minn.—Galen Groff and Henry Kremer—were among the first in the town. When daylight came, house-to-house fighting got under way.

"We were going through the streets," said Sergeant Kremer, "when a Jerry stepped around the corner and we opened up on him. The guy started throwing grenades at us, and we let him have it again. Two more Jerries showed up. We fired some more, and all three of them took off."

"We got seven of them in one house," said Sergeant Groff. "First they gave up to an Italian civilian, and the Italian came and told us. We went in and found six of them. Then we found the last one hiding in a box and dragged him out."

Sergt. Donald R. Johnson of Madison, Minn., led a platoon assigned to make a junction in the town with another platoon.

"On the outskirts we got 14 Germans out of the buildings," he recalled. "It wasn't much of a scrap. They just came out one by one with their hands up. The first one had a white flag."

Sergt. Leonard Holtegaard of Peterson, Minn., led one squad through the main entrance of the town and encountered some trouble.

"They were sniping at us, and it was hot," he said. "We threw grenades into the building where we thought they were. The Jerries threw grenades back at us. Then we fired a bazooka into the building, and that made them holler uncle.

"First 12 came out, but we heard a noise in the basement. We went down and got six more. Two blocks farther we got eight more. My squad and another one got 28 Jerries between us."

As usual the medical aid men performed heroically in braving enemy fire to give first aid to the wounded and get them to aid stations. One night they got through the German lines when it was pitch dark and there was so much wind and rain the Jerries couldn't hear.

REGISTER, MARCH 15, 1944.

Iowans Tell Bloody Scrap for Hill 396

WITH THE 34TH DIVISION IN ITALY—After the fall of San Vittore, the 34th Division took over the rugged job of forcing the enemy from the high ground stretching north and west toward Cassino.

The capture of Cassino could not be attempted until five strongholds were stripped of Germans.

Mount Chiaia was the first big obstacle, and Hill 396 was an integral part of Chiaia. The next major objective was Mount Trocchio. Between Chiaia and Trocchio was a stretch of rolling ground to be taken, and there was bitter resistance by the Germans on another ridge, Hill 289.

The village of Cervaro, to the right of Highway 6 and on a slope that looks directly down on Cassino, also had to be taken.

Mount Chiaia itself was taken by the Minnesota regiment, while Iowa "Regiment A" took Hill 396 after a bloody scrap. The Minnesota regiment cleaned out Hill 189, and then both regiments took possession of Mount Trocchio.

The main reason the Iowa regiment had such a severe ordeal in taking Hill 396 was that military expediencies demanded that the attack be made on short notice. The 2nd Battalion was given three and a half hours notice, and only the battalion commander, Lieut. Col. John L. Powers, and a scout had seen the ground in the daytime.

Tough Climbs.

It was rugged enough to even get in position for the attack. Capt. Russell Mann of Iowa City, Ia., executive officer of the 3rd Battalion, tells it this way:

"We started moving after dark on Jan. 3. We made it with 110 mules that carried ammunition and weapons, and then started up the darnedest mountain you ever saw.

"The mules would rear up and fall over backwards it was so steep. Stuff would fall off the mules, and we would have to repack.

"It snowed, and it rained. The trails were icy, and there were some places where a man would drop 1,000 feet if he fell.

"We went over the top of the mountain and spent the next day in a gorge. We had to keep the men quiet because if the Germans had found out we were there they could have slaughtered us with artillery."

The attack on Hill 396 started Jan. 6. All three of the battalions in the regiment were called to crack the intense German resistance, in such fighting as this told by Pvt. (f.c.) Roy J. Neufarth of Newton.

"I was hauling ammunition for mortars at night and was on the end of a column. Suddenly I realized we had worked into a trap and were being fired on. A German officer called out in perfect English, 'Company X come out with your hands up.'

"They captured quite a few and they went around with flashlights trying to find us. They found some men in caves, and our boys fought it out as best they could. I was hiding with some fellows behind some rocks. German officers were standing right above us at one time.

"We were completely surrounded, but some of us were lucky enough to slip back gradually and get out."

Sergt. Vincent Conners of Imogene, Ia., recalled that during the Hill 396 fight the communications were so complicated that in calling for artillery fire on German positions the messages had to go through three walkie talkies, one large radio and two telephones.

REGISTER, MARCH 16, 1944.

Nazis Pray, Defeated by Iowa Outfit

WITH THE 34TH DIVISON IN ITALY—All the way up from San Vittore, the Germans contested almost every yard of ground, but the fighting became more and more severe after the citadel of Cervaro was pierced.

When Iowa "Regiment A" took the town itself, there were signs of German disorganization. Twelve of the prisoners captured were from eight different companies and three different regiments.

But then the Germans called up a battalion of the crack Hermann Goering Division. Many of the men were fanatical Nazis who had been party members for eight and nine years.

For all their Nazism, however, they feared the Americans. They gathered in a church in Cassino the night before they counterattacked the Iowa regiment, and most of the prisoners carried testaments of some sort.

While the 2nd Battalion took Cervaro and beat off the Hermann Goering Division counterattack, the 1st Battalion moved ahead through the hills to the right of the town. There was a spectacular battle on Hill 552.

"We caught a German pack train up there and really gave it hell," said Sergt. Warren E. Huffman of 1345 E. Williams ave., Des Moines.

Officers in Huffman's company said that during the fighting on Hill 552 Sergeant Huffman "did an outstanding job" of getting ammunition and rations up to the front line.

"He even helped direct fire," one officer said, "and he was being shot at all day."

Stage Set for Cassino.

With the capture of Cervaro, the stage was set for the terrific Cassino battle. The 34th Division first made feints and "demonstrations" while the 36th Division attempted a frontal assault at Cassino across the Rapido river to the left. The 36th Division was repulsed with very heavy casualties.

Meanwhile, Allied forces were invading the Anzio-Nettuno beachhead, and the 34th Division was ordered to throw its full might at Cassino, the Gustav line and Monte Cassino.

Repeatedly came orders that objectives must be taken "at all costs."

The battle for Cassino was to become one of the greatest and bloodiest for American forces in World War II. There has been nothing like it in Italy.

REGISTER, MARCH 19, 1944.

Long Days of Bitter Battle inside Cassino

WITH THE 34TH DIVISION IN ITALY—A soldier from Iowa leaps into a building along a street in Cassino being raked with machine gun fire.

He knows Germans are in the basement of the building and that they have fortified their position with bunkers.

The Iowan looks out the window from the room he is in and sees an American tank 50 feet away. He waves his arms wildly to attract attention of the tank crew.

The tank men see him. He signals again, pointing a finger toward the basement window three feet below him. A gunner in the tank trains the barrel of the tank gun squarely at the basement window.

Tank Fires.

The Iowa soldier throws himself against the wall beside the window and sticks his fingers into his ears. The tank fires—and that is the end of the Germans. Those who aren't killed run out of the house with their hands up.

That was what the street fighting in Cassino was like. The Iowan who directed the tank's gunfire later was captured, so according to censorship regulations his name must be withheld.

There was another fantastic story. On the outskirts of the city there is a rock fountain. Maj. Warren C. Chapman of Nevada City, Cal., commander of a battalion of an Iowa regiment whose companies originated at Sioux City, Le Mars and Sheldon never will forget what he saw on that terrace.

"Round and round that fountain one of our men chased a German," he said. "The fountain wasn't any bigger than an average dining room table and it was just like two kids chasing each other around a table.

"Our man finally caught up with the Jerry and shot him. I don't know why he didn't shoot at him before he caught him. A man gets a little excited in a situation like that."

The daily report of the regiment starting with the capture of the Italian barracks on the outskirts Jan. 31 reads like this:

"Nineteen prisoners of war . . . continued mopping up barracks area . . . some advances of patrolling . . . 33 prisoners of war . . . 12 prisoners of war . . . continuing attack on Cassino . . . battalion continues to mop up resistance in northwest Cassino. . . .

"Located machine gun and self-propelled position by patrols . . . small advances . . . slight advances against determined resistance . . . position strengthened . . . slight gain . . . slight gain in Cassino . . . gained in north Cassino. . . .

"Consolidated positions and maintained pressure on enemy in city . . . held assigned sector . . . held assigned sector . . . held assigned sector . . ." (in all 122 prisoners were taken in Cassino by the regiment).

Some of the time Americans and Germans were in the same building.

The Iowa "B Regiment" captured both the jail and the city hall.

The start of the attack is related by Sergt. Bud Van Steenbergen of Sheldon, Ia.

Through Mine Field.

"Our orders were to take the barracks," he stated. "We started out about 2,000 yards from them and moved through a mine field under a smoke barrage. We tried to get at the barracks from a road running along a hill, but the sniping and machine gun fire were too hot.

"Then we crawled under some barbed wire and tried another way. Our men sometimes shot Germans with rifles and automatic rifles from two or three feet away.

"We were harassed by German artillery, but we got the barracks cleaned out the next morning. Another company (one originating in Sioux City) came across the flats. We had tanks supporting us, and we started the main push.

"The tanks fired on spots as our men signalled to them.

"We ran into a dugout on a plateau and captured a German officer and three men. We were in a hurry and were cussing and telling the Jerries to get a move on. The German officer all of a sudden said in perfect English, 'Just a minute, please. I'll be right down.' That happened about 600 yards from the town.

"A little after noon we stopped and reorganized. The men followed the tanks, six of them, into town. The tanks chased three snipers. We were rolling along pretty good until we got about two blocks into the town. Then the tanks withdrew a bit and we did, too.

"You see whenever we took a building we had to leave two or three men in it and we began running low on men."

That's how the wild street fighting started. It became so hectic that the men lost track of time and days and nights.

Corp. Glenn Moen of Fort Dodge, Ia., tells this story:

"We tried to go from house to house, but the entrances were covered by machine gun fire. So we got tanks to blow holes in the backs of the buildings and got in them that way.

"At one point we only had one house—a long narrow one—and the Jerries knew we were in it. They kept on firing until they knocked down one wall and then they began firing rifle grenades in on us. It was tough.

"We had orders to send patrols into the streets to see if there were any Germans there. Hell, all we had to do was to look out the windows and see them."

The fighting with hand grenades was intense.

"Several Iowa boys got to going too fast," said Major Chapman. "They just wouldn't slow down. Some got captured, and groups would just disappear during the street fighting."

"It got nightmarish," said Sergt. Albert Schiel of Dubuque, Ia. "We'd look out the window each morning and see a fresh body in the street. We didn't know how the bodies got there. Someone must have been trying to bust up our morale.

"Germans were at the foot of one hill. Three of our men went after them, and two didn't come back. The Germans yelled at us: 'Surrender, surrender! You're crazy if you don't surender.' But we were not in a surrendering mood."

After a tank blasted a hole, Sergt. John Trobaugh of Le Mars, Ia., and several comrades got into a house.

Didn't Dare Fire.

"Just before dawn the next morning we saw Germans and Americans in a melee in the street in front of us. We couldn't tell the Jerries from our boys, and didn't dare fire. We lost half a platoon."

Sergt. Robert W. Wilson of Hazelton, Ia., who fired more mortar shells than ever before in Italy and who saw the Cassino jail shot "to bits," tells the story of an American tank going after a German pillbox.

"The tank fired right into the pillbox. Three Jerries sneaked out and crawled behind a rock pile. The tank fired into the rocks. No one came out after that."

Pvt. (f.c.) Gary Byker of Hull, Ia., personally captured eight prisoners.

"There really wasn't anything to it," he said. "I was pretty much on the alert. A German came out of a door with a big white flag that must have been a sheet from one of the beds. I speak a little Dutch, so I asked him in Dutch how many more there were inside. He said eight, and I told him to go get them. They all came filing out, and I turned them over to someone else to take back."

Gordon Gammack had a knack for being in the right place at the right time and he displayed that knack elegantly when be boarded a landing ship tank for the beachhead south of Rome on January 26, 1944. In covering the invasion of the Anzio beachhead, Gammack represented the combined American press. His dispatches were used by the Associated Press, United Press, and International News Service.

REGISTER, FEBRUARY 1, 1944.

A Mammoth Task to Load Invasion Ship

BOUND FOR THE 5TH ARMY INVASION BEACHES BELOW ROME—(DELAYED)—It was about midnight when we arrived at the blacked-out beach to board the LST (landing ship tank) for the beachhead south of Rome.

I was with Ken Dixon of the Associated Press, Jack Foisie of the Stars and Stripes, and Charles Seawood, Acme News photographer.

Through the hole in the bow of the flat-bottomed ship, equipment for an important engineering operation was being loaded. The loading had been in progress for several hours and would not be completed for several more.

There was a loud clanking as the tracked vehicles bumped over the steel lip that drops down from the bow to the beach, and moving the vehicles on the metal deck sounded like a foundry. The soldiers did a marvelous job of backing the complicated vehicles into the ship.

We had to wait almost until the completion of the loading to squeeze our jeep into a small slot.

Here was a long laborious job involving equipment worth thousands of dollars and yet it was comparatively trivial compared to the broad invasion operation.

There's a lot more to one of these amphibious attacks than pointing to a map and saying, "Let's do it here."

When we awoke in the morning, our ship was at anchor in the bay in the midst of other ships that also were going to the beaches up the west coast of Italy. We breakfasted on rations that come in containers like cracker jack boxes and include such stuff as chopped ham and egg yolk (an unappetizing concoction), crackers, powdered coffee and a fruit bar.

The LST was built in the United States but was operated by the British. All the ship's officers were Britons.

One of the first American officers sent aboard was Second Lieutenant Reuben Day of La Porte City, Ia., who quickly convinced me he has no love for ocean travel although he has followed invasion forces into beachheads in North Africa, Sicily and Salerno.

Italians in rowboats went from one ship to another trying to sell things to the soldiers and sailors aboard. Their wares included oranges, apples, nuts, radishes and cognac.

It was almost exclusively a trading proposition. The Italians threw ropes up the decks of the anchored ships and whoever wanted to make a trade would pull up a pail filled with oranges or such. I negotiated a trade of two packages of cigarettes for six oranges and two apples.

On the Way.

The largest deal I saw made was by a British ship officer who turned over a 28-pound tin of bicuits for a large basket of radishes.

Shortly after dark our strictly blacked out convoy moved. One could see nothing but the phosphorescence of the churning water in the Tyrrhenian sea and the quick bright flashes of guns on the main 5th Army front.

I expected a peaceful trip. I had the feeling that we had rigid control of our invasion operations. I didn't know that all hell was going to break loose in the Anzio-Nettuno harbor the next day, or I wouldn't have slept so soundly.

REGISTER, FEBRUARY 3, 1944.

Views Battle from Pit of Ack-Ack Gun

REPRESENTING COMBINED U.S. PRESS WITH THE 5TH ARMY AT ANZIO, ITALY (DELAYED)—Even in the most spectacular air battles you can't get anything like a full picture just watching the skies.

Ever since the invasion here started there has been all kinds of excitement—dog fights by the dozens, descending parachutes, mighty bomb bursts in the sea, blazing doomed planes and even a few ships afire.

Men who were on hand for the invasion of Sicily and Salerno say the fierce air battle over Anzio Nettuno harbor is the most spectacular one yet in this theater.

But you can't see everything. The sky's too big and things which turn the course of battle often happen out of sight.

I think I obtained a far better understanding of the scope of battle and the great efficiency of the air force during the hour I visited an anti-aircraft gun at the edge of the harbor.

If I hadn't been there I wouldn't know there were 11 warnings of approaching enemy planes during an hour. But not one German plane appeared during the time.

Instead, planes would dart across the sky, heading for oncoming Jerries spotted by other gun crews. The crew would look carefully at ships and call out reassuringly: "P-40s and A-36A.", "Flight of Spitfires."

Repeated warnings and the jumping of ack-ack gunners to their stations told the story of the losing game of hide-and-seek the German pilots tried to play.

Sure, Jerries slip in sometimes. It can't be helped. And they can drop deadly loads with more freedom in the darkness of night.

But virtually every day there are attacks, and one of two things happens to German pilots. They either jump or are shot up.

Planes are so harried and hurried when they try to attack that they can't do an accurate job.

That's why so many German bombs plumped harmlessly into the sea.

Ack-ack gunners know this story.

Always After Them.

"Our planes are always after the Jerries," said the sergeant in charge of the crew. "The only trouble is that some times they get in our way."

Ack-ack men have tough jobs. Jerries have been making a practice of dropping their bombs and then zooming low over a gun position and strafing it.

"But frankly," said the sergeant, "we'd like to have the rats come in. Take this deal right now. We're getting warnings every few minutes. This is a dry run. Boys get lax."

While the sergeant was talking to the group, front-bound marching soldiers came by on the street in back of us, whistling "As Time Goes By." Then a jeep drove by with a German prisoner sitting rigidly in the front seat. Two American soldiers were down in the back seat.

"Look! For crying out loud," one of the ack-ack men said, "They're letting him sit in the front seat."

One gunner had read a map of Italy, and darned if it didn't advertise Texaco motor oils.

A telephone in the gun pit rang, and a soldier who answered it quickly relayed this message. "Red alert, eight enemy fighters coming from the northwest."

Gunners jumped to their positions, readied 40-millimeter guns for firing and wheeled their weapons around in the direction from which the Jerries were expected.

Six Spitfires dashed northward across the sky.

We searched the sky for Germans but they didn't come. The telephone rang again. "Yellow," said the man at the phone, meaning "Stand By." A minute later, "White," or all clear came through. Gunners relaxed.

When you don't hear alerts at an ack-ack gun position, you quickly get the habit of ignoring the hum of a plane's engines. You assume it's friendly.

But when ack-ack starts popping, it's a different story. If you haven't got protection you hunt it hurriedly.

From the Italian front, Gammack moved to England. The airmen he interviewed experienced a war different from that of the soldiers at the front. Although it had its own grim aspects, the assignment of the pilots involved a kind of excitement and a personal bravado which had no counterparts on the ground.

REGISTER, APRIL 23, 1944

Fliers Learn the Target; It's Poland!

A BOMBER BASE IN ENGLAND—The daily life of a Flying Fortress bomber pilot in England often starts at 2:30 a.m.

That's when the pilots and their combat crews were awakened the other morning at this base.

The men rub their eyes and stumble unhappily out of bed.

Many of the men have slept fitfully or found it hard to get to sleep with their thoughts on flak,

Messerschmitts, Focke Wulfs, prisoner-of-war camps and the icy waters of the English channel.

I climb out of bed with the combat airmen. It is raw and chilly and outside, on the way to the mess hall, it is very dark and you have to feel your way along with a flashlight.

In the brightly lighted mess hall, the men yawn and rub their eyes and stand in line with plates in hand at the chow serving table, waiting for fried eggs, bacon and cereal. On the tables were tomato juice and coffee.

Only at these early morning breakfasts for men who have long, hard, dangerous days ahead of them are fresh eggs served.

"A couple of ground officers in my barracks get up for these early breakfasts just to get the eggs," a pilot observes.

"They're nuts," says another, and a third adds:

"Anyone who wants eggs that bad ought to get them."

Think of Job Ahead.

Some of the men begin thinking about the mission.

"This is a hell of a time to get a decent and respectable American out of bed," observed a bombardier.

"This one looks like a Tokyo job," comments a pilot who knows that the planes are loaded with extra gasoline tanks for the coming mission—and when that happens it's a "Tokyo" in air force parlance.

"Well, seven more and home for me," says a copilot.

"You hope."

"Don't forget, we only see the guys who don't get to go home after their tour. We don't see the guys who do go home."

"The only trouble with breakfast like this is that back home I'd be eating one like this BEFORE going to bed. I'd be coming home from a dance. Four sinkers and three cups of coffee and then you'd go to bed and the bed would rock. Oh man, fond memories."

One pilot turns to another and asks him if he wears his parachute all the time during a mission. (All combat men have them in their planes with them, of course.)

"All the time, boy; all the time. I know that 50 per cent of the guys who have to bail out get down O.K. So it's all the time for me. And if the plane blows up, there's always a chance that you'll get blown out and can get down."

"I just put mine on in the heavy flak areas," says the other pilot.

"What is this, our third or fourth in a row?"

"Fourth."

"This'll be a long one. Eight hours anyway."

The men start leaving the mess hall shortly after 3 a.m.

Trucks are waiting outside for them. They climb in. Through the darkness in the truck loom the small red glows from cigarettes. Almost all the men are smoking. The truck's motor is drowned out by the roar of Flying Fortress engines being warmed up for the mission.

"This is a hell of a way to make a living," says a voice in the darkness as the truck pulls away.

The next stop is the briefing room. In it are rows of wooden benches. Gradually, the men fill them up. There are pilots, copilots, navigators and bombardiers. The gunners are briefed in another room.

At the front of the room is a huge map, but it is obscured by a white screen just in front of it. Two briefing officers are talking to each other as the men file into the room.

"One kid pleaded with me to let him go on this mission," one of them says. "It's over his own country. If he is forced down, there'll be a lot of people he knows."

In the front row are four full colonels. One is the commanding officer of the base. Another is from another base, but he is going to lead this mission. The other two are visitors; one is the brother of the C.O.

Officers Checked.

The combat officers are checked as they come into the briefing room, which is one section of an arc-shaped Nissen hut. When all the men have arrived, a lieutenant colonel walks to the front and instructs an enlisted man to pull up the screen.

"Here it is," says the briefing officer.

The enlisted man pulls up the screen with a small rope and unveils the map. Stretching from the home base in England is a piece of black tape.

It runs the course that the mission is going to take—to an aircraft assembly plant in Poland.

The combat men gape at the target and low whistles sound through the room. The whistles say "gosh!" "whew!", and "wow!"

"It's a long one, all right," says an officer sitting beside me.

The big map glistens as if it were dotted with tiny electric lights. But that isn't it. The glistening is from pieces of celluloid on thumbtacks stuck all over Germany and Nazi-occupied territory. They tell a vastly important story—the location of Nazi flak guns.

There is a tremendous amount of coughing in the room. At times more than a dozen men cough at the same time. But there is no smoking. That's forbidden during the briefing.

The briefing takes a half hour or more. Maps of the target are flashed on the screen. Instructions about rendezvous are given. A report on weather expectancy is made. The colonel who is going to lead the mission talks briefly to the men, telling them the importance of the mission.

The commanding officer, Col. Hunt Harris, stresses the importance of an accurate bombing job. On the last mission, he says, "You did a bang-up job." And, finally, he adds:

"The best of luck to you, fellows."

The men are told how long they will be in flight and they whistle again. It will be a long flight, all right, some of it under oxygen at high altitude.

Finally, they start filing out of the room. The navigators, who must get additional briefing, go to another room. The rest go to the locker rooms and start putting on their flying clothes—bright blue electrically heated suits, heavy fleece-lined boots, coveralls, Mae Wests, parachute harnesses, and helmets.

The coveralls of one pilot are virtually in shreds.

"Me, I'm not superstitious," he grins.

The locker room seems like a football locker room before the big game of the year. The combat men look pretty grim although some are laughing and joking among themselves.

Men from different ships walk up to each other as they leave the building.

"Good luck, fella."

Some shake hands as they part.

It will be unusual if all the ships come back. Which ones won't? You can sense that question is running through the minds of these fine guys.

"Tom has convinced me I should take my tin hat," says a pilot as he reaches for his flak helmet, a little lighter and slightly different shaped than the infantry helmet.

From the time the briefing of the crews is over, there's still more than two hours before take-off. The men are in no hurry. One by one they start out for their ships, stopping first to pick up the emergency kits issued to them in case they are forced down over enemy territory.

"Man, this is going to be a long one," says a bombardier. "Next thing you know we'll be dropping pamphlets over New York City. Might be a good idea. Tell 'em that the war isn't over yet."

"Take me with you on that one," says a co-pilot.

"I'd burn out all four engines and bail out," adds a pilot.

Tower Room.

After the men have left for their planes, I go to the flying control tower. This is a big day. The mission is a big one and highly important. So the tower is crowded with anxious officers.

The big tower room has large blackboards, listing the planes going on the mission. The crews of each one, and the numbers of the planes are listed, too.

There are huge windows all across the front of the room, but they are covered with blackout curtains because it's still dark.

Reports from several of the planes start coming in. One pilot reports that the ball turret of his ship won't work. He's assigned to another ship, and a change is made on the blackboard. Something is wrong with one or two additional planes, and the crews are moved quickly to other ships.

There is tenseness in the room. The take-off, which will start soon, is one of the crucial parts of the mission. It must go off smoothly.

Colonel Harris, very calm but alert to everything that is happening, walks by and smiles a little.

"Don't know if I'll live through this one or not," he says, and then turns to the officers crowded into the room.

"There are quite a lot of people in here this morning," he says. "I don't mind if you stay, but you'll have to keep quiet in case we have some business. Captain, will you have an ambulance stand by at the control tower?"

"The Old Ladies."

Twenty minutes before the take-off the blackout curtains are pulled back and out over the field is the picture of the huge Fortresses—"the Old Ladies," the pilots call them—moving slowly up the taxi strips and lining up for the take-off.

Their lights shine, and the squeaking of the brakes on the planes sounds like something halfway between the creak of a rusty door hinge and the shrill whistle of a British locomotive.

The ships are heavily loaded with bombs—incendiary and high explosives—and with gasoline. Each ship carries enough gasoline for more than 10 round-trips from Des Moines or Minneapolis to Los Angeles, Cal., by automobile.

Everyone watches intently as the signal is given and the first of the "Forts" starts along the long runway, gradually picking up speed and finally rising slowly from the ground. It still is not very light, and there is haze. So as each ship takes off, there is a blinking signal of identification and confirmation of take-off flashed back to the next ship in line.

Soon the "Forts" will be leaving the English coast. A few hours later an aircraft assembly plant in Poland will be blasted to smithereens.

Late in the afternoon, the roar of Flying Fortresses is heard again. The formations loom into sight. One by one, the ships land.

That morning, 38 ships left the base. Thirty-five are coming back.

TRIBUNE, JUNE 1, 1944.

Fighter Pilots Bare Love of Battle—They're Eager to Take On Nazis

A FIGHTER BASE IN ENGLAND—Finally, at this base of daring Mustang fighter pilots, I have found men who like the war.

Not war in general, because they dislike that as much as anyone, but the kind of war they fight—streaking through the skies at incredible speeds, chasing German fighters they know they can whip, blasting Nazi planes to smithereens and giving dogged protection to their big brothers, the Fortresses and Liberators.

I sat with a bunch of these P-51 Mustang pilots one morning while they were being briefed for a mission deep into Germany. The two pilots next to me were talking.

"Those babies are going to be out today," said one. "I can feel it. I'm going to get five."

"Why not make it six and make a record?" chided the other.

"O.K. Six, then."

"This is a good old day for an air battle. Hot damn."

Lieutenant Colonel Bickel, the young commanding officer of the group who was a clerk in a Wall Street brokerage house before the war, explained the mission, which was to escort heavy bombers to an important target.

You could sense a keen fighting spirit through the briefing tent. Not a bloodthirsty attitude but a competitive and thrill-seeking one. The pilots tossed on their flying togs and went to their planes. . . . The Mustang engines chattered as the planes started to taxi to the takeoff spot and then, suddenly, they returned to their stands.

"Mission's been postponed," it was explained.

When the pilots came back this time, they were mad. They kicked the ground, flung their paraphernalia angrily to the floor and cussed the cancellation of the mission.

"Now we'll probably get a dive-bombing job in France this afternoon," said one. "Not a chance for a fight. Just flak."

With the approach of D-Day, the focus of international attention shifted to Normandy Beach, and Gordon Gammack moved with it. He had reported from behind the scenes in England the experiences of Allied airmen. At Normandy, he witnessed their full effect, both in preparing for the invasion and, somewhat later, in establishing complete air supremacy. Gammack chronicled the massive influx of supplies and manpower and, as soon as the opportunity arose, he traveled to the beachhead by troopship.

REGISTER, JUNE 11, 1944.

D-Day Drama at American Fighter Base

LONDON, ENGLAND, FRIDAY (DELAYED)—Fifteen minutes before American troops were scheduled to storm the beaches of Normandy, pilots gathered in a room at the air base I had just reached and gaped at a huge map that showed the route of the convoys and location of the assault beaches.

They were in flying togs and ready to go on a minute's notice.

An army liaison major, with a pistol hitched to his belt, stood before the pilots and turned the pages of a fat book of mimeographed pages with a light green cover.

He told the pilots the general invasion plan plus the part the air force would play. He pointed to invasion beaches on the map, which had been labeled with code names given beaches or amphibious operations.

There was one set of code names for the American beaches, and another for the British. The American beach names had a distinct American flavor.

"On D-Day," said the Major, reading from the master plan, and proceeded to outline various steps, finally concluding almost casually, "And this is D-Day."

Completing his review, he asked for questions, and a lieutenant colonel from Georgia, executive officer of a Lightning P-38 group, asked many questions he knew the answers to but wanted brought out for the benefit of his pilots.

Although the pilots listened intently to every word, they received D-Day news with surprisingly little emotion. The clock on the wall ticked away minutes until the hands pointed to H-Hour.

Then there was a moment of silence, and I think some of us were breathing a silent prayer.

There was some tenseness in the air, but for the most part pilots were calm and businesslike as they have been during the pre-invasion blitz.

Back in Iowa most people were abed and would not be electrified by the big news for a few more hours.

Above us great masses of planes droned as they lew to and from the stupendous battle scene. Pilots went off in groups to their squadron quarters to await their calls for missions.

A transport plane that had carried paratroopers to Normandy in the darkness of the D-Day predawn circled the field and came in. The co-pilot told the following story, the most dramatic invasion story I have heard personally:

When the troop carrier reached the target the paratroopers jumped—all but two who became panicky with fright and refused to jump. The pilot left his post and talked to the two men, reminding them of their duty. Then they agreed to jump, and the pilot swerved his plane back to the jumping spot.

Great bursts of flak shook the plane, and the rest of the story is that the pilot was dead when he was carried out of the plane at the base.

Puzzling Feature.

On D-Day and on following days accounts of fighter bomber pilots were puzzling. Except for the channel and the beaches themselves they reported very little activity on the ground, few enemy fighters, virtually no flak.

Pilot after pilot has told the same story, yet no one believes the luftwaffe is smashed.

Everywhere there is apprehension about the possible tricks Adolf Hitler has up his sleeve, but it had been taken for granted the Nazis would throw in what is left of their air strength to combat the Allied invasion.

I have witnessed no tendency by anyone in Britain to adopt an overconfident attitude. All know the German as a tricky, resourceful, strong foe. Most observers feel the Hun is planning to strike back furiously somehow, somewhere.

Except for the array of steel helmets and weapons—because the possibility of a German paratroop assault on our air bases is not ruled out—life at fighter bases goes on much as before the invasion.

There are a few other exceptions. At some bases squadrons stand in two-hour shifts with pilots in their cockpits on the alert for immediate takeoff.

Also at all squadron headquarters are snack bars where pilots can grab a bite to eat between rush missions, but I have found no such emergency yet, and pilots eat their meals at regular mess halls. Regular hours though have disappeared, and pilots and planners sleep when they get a chance.

I have a feeling that direct air support is going to be far more effective in this drive than in Italy because improved fighter bomber techniques have been developed.

I recall repeated attempts to bomb out a bridge at Pontecorvo on the Cassino front before success. Yet fighter bombers here have been hitting bridges and other targets with gratifying regularity.

American officers entrusted with invasion plans did a marvelous job of keeping their mouths shut. Within two days of assault time two 27-year-old colonels, who knew the score yet miraculously acted as if nothing was imminent, took one hour away from the office to fly three of us correspondents from one base to another.

I was interested at the tactical reconnaissance group commanded by one of these colonels at the sight of black and white stripes on Mustangs (P-51s), which made them look like flying zebras. He said casually that they were the markings of his group. Actually all planes in the invasion carried these zebra markings to combat possible German use of planes with our normal markings.

Bobby Jones.

On arrival at a fighter wing command late Monday afternoon, Col. Arthur Salisbury of Sedalia, Mo., the commanding officer, talked casually with Duke Shoop of the Kansas City Star and me about his experiences in Africa and Italy. Lieut. Col. Bobby Jones, the golfer, came in with his wing intelligence officer and joined the conversation with an equally casual air.

Then they excused themselves, explaining they had "a little dinner date," which really was the invasion conference.

A few hours later Capt. Rush Shortley of Des Moines and other pilots reported a mass shipping movement in the channel. I aroused Salisbury and Jones, who were catching a little sleep before long hours of work, and said it was imperative that I get to another base if the invasion was imminent.

Colonel Salisbury was noncommittal except to say "if that's where you want to be you better go" and lent me his car and driver.

En route I curled up in the back seat and slept. If I had stayed awake I would have seen the greatest air armada of paratroopers in history flying overhead on the way to France. As it was I just saw the last flights leaving the coast of England.

REGISTER, JUNE 29, 1944

Tells of Trip to Normandy on Troopship

NORMANDY, FRANCE (VIA PRESS WIRELESS)—Thousands of soldiers, among them men from Iowa and Minnesota, are pouring into France, and inasmuch as I made the trip from England much as they are making it, this story will give you (I hope) a general idea how the shift to the continent is made.

Six of us correspondents with Lieut. Col. Jack Harding of the U.S. 9th Air Force public relations office tossed our bed rolls, barracks bags and typewriters into a big army truck, climbed in after them, and took off on a—not too comfortable—trip of several hours to an invasion port in southern England.

Approaching the invasion port we saw large groups of tanks and other armored vehicles and farther on, area after area, filled with troops who will arrive in France ultimately.

We pulled into one of these "staging" areas, which was somewhat similar to those of more temporary nature than Camp Patrick Henry near Norfolk, Va., where I was staged prior to coming overseas last September.

Supplies Issued.

This tent camp is nestled in woods, and we were assigned to our tents. Blankets and overseas rations were issued to us. The rations included a carton of cigarettes, three boxes of K rations, a unit of canned meat, a box of insect powder, a razor blade, gum and two heavy black paper bags into which to vomit during the channel crossing if necessary.

The army makes a special effort to make pre-embarkation hours or days (how long you will be

in a staging area is always a mystery) as pleasant and comfortable as possible.

We had a fine chicken dinner and were told that chicken was served every three days here and steaks also were served often.

In the officers' mess tent there were even vases of large roses on the tables. Radio programs, including the latest invasion newscasts, echo through the camp from loudspeakers, and I heard on a British broadcasting program an account by Donald Grant, (former Register reporter now with Look magazine) of his flight over Cherbourg.

After supper we had our choice of a United Service Organizations show or double feature movie, but both were too jammed with laughing and applauding troops to get in.

We started our trip Friday afternoon. Saturday morning we were told we would leave camp at noon and make the trip in an LCI (landing craft, infantry), which is not ideal for a channel crossing. Our thoughts turned to those black paper bags.

At the designated time we piled into another big army truck and headed for the port and docks. Soon we found ourselves in a large convoy of troop filled trucks, and as we passed through the streets hundreds of children and some adults paused on sidewalks to wave and shout messages of good luck.

There were many stops as the convoy edged toward the docks. We saw a good sized clean looking ship, and one of us commented to Colonel Harding it would be nicer than an LCI. He made no reply, but after he had reported to dock officials he reported with a smile of satisfaction that it would be our ship. In this respect there is of course a variance from the average troop movement.

We got our equipment aboard and were requested to stay in our hot and stuffy cabin until all troops were loaded. Troops were of various types from combat engineers to units to speed mail from the United States to your men at the front.

Military Miracle.

We were told what time the ship would leave, and it pulled away from the berth 15 minutes ahead of time, which I regarded as a military miracle.

British merchant marine officers aboard gave another of their demonstrations of being amazingly calm in embarking on a trip fraught with possible dangers. But at the same time American troops seemed equally undisturbed as they started out on this adventure whose future was completely unpredictable.

One announcement after another came over the ship's loudspeaker as the troops were told when and where to eat, given instructions about battery drills, and repeatedly warned that "safety of this ship depends on absolute co-operation of everyone on board."

Boat drill was carefully conducted. Our little group was assigned to a raft near the stern of the ship, and I am glad there was no emergency because on abandoning the ship our job was to get on top of a high platform, get the raft to the side of the ship, toss it overboard, and then jump in after it.

The troops were told that if there was an emergency "you will walk slowly to your posts and there will be no talking."

With all the warnings about how tough the English channel can be, I was prepared to be seasick for the first time in my life. But we had been at sea several hours before I even knew we had pulled anchor from the convoy spot and had started moving. For this trip, the channel was that calm.

TRIBUNE, JUNE 18, 1944.

Prefers His War Out in the Field

NORMANDY, FRANCE—Most of us war correspondents feel mighty good about being back in a battle zone again.

As long as you have got to be away from home covering a war, the place to do it is in the field, not caring how you look and not caring too much when you had your last bath, and moving ahead as the army moves, living and eating in camp fashion and being thrown in with the grand men you always find in a combat zone.

I must admit, too, there is a certain fearful fascination about war. As much as you hate war and all that it does, it has a tantalizing appeal. When I return from a trip to the front after being scared to death I feel buoyant. The feeling is almost one of intoxication.

How They Live.

Perhaps you would be interested in how we correspondents live.

At present there are two main groups of us attached to the American forces. One is assigned to the ground forces and the other, to which I am attached, is assigned to the air forces. Air correspondents, however, do not confine their reporting to air activities.

Right now my stories go to England by airplane courier which goes thrice daily and are cleared to Des Moines from London. Starting this week they will go direct from Normandy.

Up to now most facilities from here have been reserved for the major press associations and New York and Chicago papers.

Our group is quartered in a three-story house in a small Normandy town. I have a metal cot but no mattress so my bedding roll rests on springs. There is running cold water but if you want hot water

you have to heat it yourself over an open air fireplace we rigged up in the back.

Then you take your helmet full of it to wash and shave.

Some correspondents are more particular than others about keeping washed and shaved.

With the army you are supposed to shave once daily but many don't and I usually wait until I think some officer is likely to say something about it.

Also in the field I grow a mustache for one, simple reason—that much less of my face to shave.

Among correspondents in the field for the first time are a few who probably never will get accustomed to it and seem surprised on learning that there is no one to bring them hot water and are aghast over basic rations, which are about all anyone gets in the early phase of amphibious operations.

About a block from our house is another building where there is the "press room" and correspondents either can write their stories here or in their rooms.

When they are written (censors require three copies of each story) they are placed in a canvas bag on which "Press" is printed in big red letters.

Sometimes in the field you eat out of mess kits but at present we have metal plates and tin cups and sit down to tables in a building for our meals, which consist largely of powdered eggs, a few types of stew, peas and lima beans, bacon, cereal, coffee and lots of graham crackers and jam.

Butter comes in cans and is rather pasty. When the shipping emergency is over, better and more varied foods will come in.

Somehow we had steaks, peas and mashed potatoes for dinner today but that sort of thing doesn't happen often.

Correspondents wear olive drab trousers and shirts and usually are tieless. They wear either field jackets or more satisfactory and warmer combat jackets. Most wear G.I. leggins but I avoid this with combat boots picked up in Italy from a kindly quartermaster officer.

Complaints.

Usually among groups of correspondents, particularly at times like the present when everything is new and there is lots of inexperience, there is considerable complaining.

Our group has been miffed over the lack of direct cable facilities and virtually no transportation, which means we have to hitchhike often to where we want to go.

About the only transportation available to us is a big truck known as a six-by-six and on long trips—such as to Cherbourg—the bouncing gets mighty monotonous.

It looks as if we are going to get some jeeps, though, in a few days.

We are at the 9th air force headquarters now but we are moving soon and I am glad of it because somehow headquarters always are stuffy places, where officers tend to sneer at correspondents, and resent their presence. One sour-faced major referred to us as "damn sightseers."

But nearer the front or at a combat air base, correspondents almost always are very welcome and the officers almost overdo themselves in being co-operative.

Living in the field calls for some initiative, and some enterprising guy always turns up with cases of rations to provide between-meal snacks and to keep fellows who come in late from trips from going hungry.

Although you are always hampered somewhat by army rules the boys also are apt to turn up with eggs and occasional cuts of meat purchased or traded from natives.

Hours.

In the field you are apt to keep long hours. Frequently you spend a full day up to 7 or 8 in the evening and then start writing.

On quieter days there are apt to be card games in the evening. Correspondents form their own little groups and maintain them for news-hunting junkets.

There isn't much to do in the field but work; but we really enjoy working, and, as for myself, it is a hundred times better than London with all its soft mattresses and clean sheets, fine food, movies, theaters and orchestras and bars and smart uniforms.

I'll take the war this way.

TRIBUNE, JUNE 30, 1944.

The Master Race in Allied Hands

ON THE HIGHWAY TO CHERBOURG (TUESDAY)—Every mile of that blacktop road from Bayeux to Cherbourg speaks of war.

There are shuffling lines and truckloads of German prisoners clad in gray green and dead soldiers and dead cattle and towns reduced to massive heaps of rubble and huge bomb craters in the fields.

There are hundreds of poles made from trees stuck in the fields by the Germans to trap gliders, and there are gliders which crashed against them. In other fields there are soldiers pitching their pup tents under trees which deny observation from the air. And the wooden signs on the barbed wire fences enclosing many many fields say, "Achtung, minen" (attention, mines).

There are children who smile and wave and give

JUNE 23, 1944. American soldiers entering the town of Pont l'Abbe, in the Cherbourg area of France, clear away wreckage and rubble caused by shelling and bombing. Man in lead carries a mine detector. *(AP)*

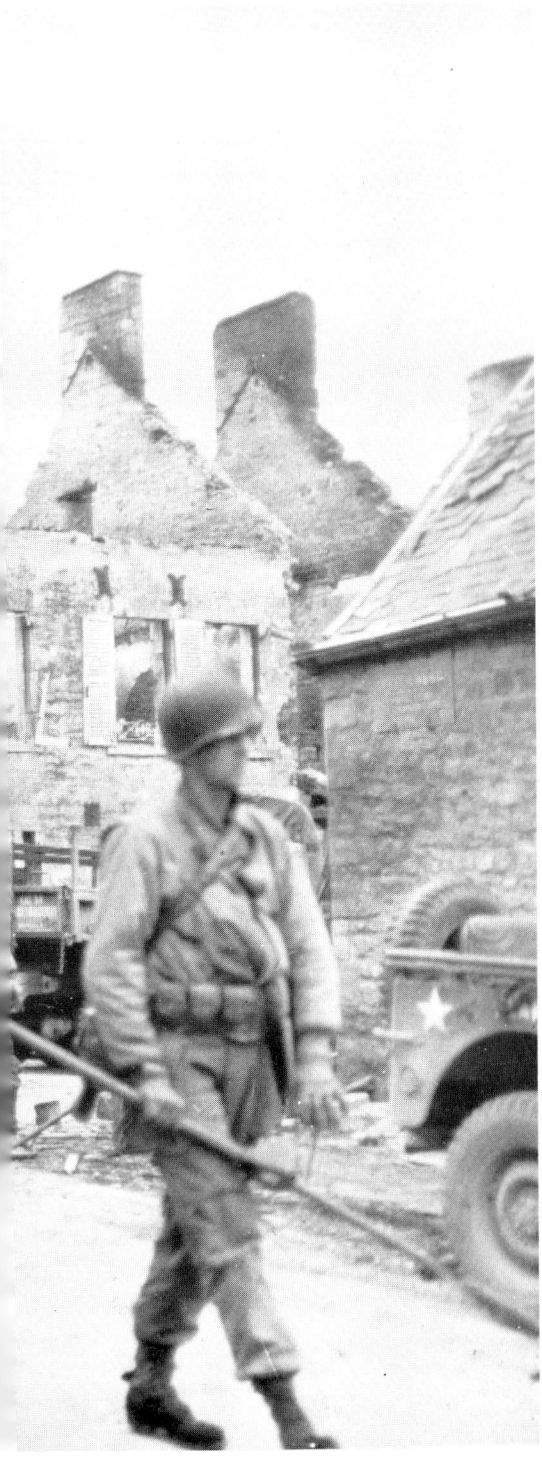

the "V" sign and there are bewildered men and women walking in the ghostly ruins of their towns and villages. Some of them wave and some of them don't. Most of them just return your wave.

There are planes in the skies—Thunderbolts and Mustangs and Lightnings. The trucks and jeeps and tanks rumble constantly along the road. There are tent hospitals where huge red crosses plead to be let alone and there are ambulances bringing the wounded away from the battle.

There are soldiers stringing shining copper wire along the ditches and there are new bridges thrown across creeks by the engineers.

There are M.P.'s waving the rolling convoys on or stopping them so others can pass and there is dust.

There are soldiers marching slowly with weary tread, single file on each side of the roadway and their faces as always have no real expression.

They just move on and on and on, and they have been doing that since D-day, always leaving some behind.

This is war behind the front lines. It is always the same.

Death.

A mile outside of Cherbourg there was a dead American soldier lying by the road.

He hadn't been dead long because no one had had time to cover his face. The G.I. leggins on his legs which lay on the edge of the road told the story that another American would not come home.

This was a sniper's lair. In a moment eight cringing Nazis came out of the bushes. Doughboys surrounded them, and their tommy guns were poised.

The Nazis were kids in their teens but they looked hard and tough.

Even so, they hunched their shoulders and arched their necks in fear.

And then along came a jeep with a Nazi in the front seat and a doughboy right behind him with his finger on the trigger of his carbine and the barrel a foot from the German's neck.

Before this I had seen a dozen trucks jampacked with Nazis. There may have been as many as a hundred in each truck and they all were standing with the wind whipping into their faces as the trucks speeded by.

On many of the trucks only one Negro soldier stood guard. The colored boys enjoyed this. One grinned from ear to ear as he held his gun in readiness.

Marcel Wallenstein of the Kansas City Star was with me as we watched the trucks go by with the Negro guards. "Look at it," he said, "a beautiful sight. Isn't it a wonderful sight."

Along the roads, too, there were barbed wire enclosures with hundreds of Nazi prisoners squatting on the grass in groups or walking aimlessly.

Today I saw at least three thousand Germans and it was a lovely picture of the master race.

TRIBUNE, JULY 4, 1944.

Allies Ruling Norman Skies

WITH THE 9TH AIR FORCE IN NORMANDY (FRIDAY)—Evaluation of Allied air supremacy over the Normandy battle zone is a tricky business but there is no argument that it is highly comforting for us and a terrible hell for the Germans.

You could strike off all qualifications about the sweeping domination of air power except the fact that German resistance continues to be fiercely effective in spite of it, and the fact that the enemy can maintain a high degree of efficiency makes one hesitate about spouting superlatives.

Domination.

But I can tell you some of the things that result from Allied domination of skies:

It means that I can ride in a truck or a jeep 50 miles along a Normandy highway to Cherbourg and be infinitely more concerned about crossing a bridge which is occasionally under shellfire than worried about a possible sudden strafing attack.

Our air supremacy is so complete that soldiers traveling the roads don't even worry about air attacks and sometimes become even too brash about stretching their motor convoys for miles bumper to bumper.

Yet a few miles away from here, behind German lines, a Nazi soldier is in mortal fear when he does no more than drive a quarter of a mile to fetch a pail of water or deliver a message.

Lieut. Clarence H. Olson, Minneapolis, Minn., and several other Thunderbolt pilots drove to Cherbourg today, but the German pilots would never risk a trip like that. And if they did, they would not be rewarded as Olson was, because he saw other buddies descend on a Nazi pocket in a Cherbourg peninsular dive-bombing attack. Olson saw Germans come running out from fortifications waving a white flag.

The dive-bombing was so terrific that Germans came out of the fortifications with blood streaming out of their ears, the result of concussion.

Air supremacy means that at a Mustang fighter base within hearing distance of artillery duels, Capt. Lowell Brueland, ace pilot of Callander, Ia., can lie on the grass outside his tent between missions and play cards without a trace of worry as he did this afternoon.

Yet the Germans would love to bomb and strafe this vital air base if they dared.

At the same base, air supremacy means that Sergt. Robert Hough, Council Bluffs, Ia., a Mustang crew chief, and Sergt. Ronald VanCleve, Davenport, Ia., can do their work on the ground from 5 in the morning until midnight without fear of being molested by the luftwaffe, and then catch a few hours of uninterrupted sleep before another day's work.

Air supremacy means that aviation engineers could come in and turn pastures into this Mustang base which pilots consider every bit as good as the flying field they used recently in England.

Just for fun today, I tried to see if there was a single moment when I could not see Allied planes somewhere in the skies. There was not so much as a minute when I could not. That is air supremacy.

Obviously, air supremacy cannot settle a war by itself, and airmen are among the first to admit the actual dirty job of taking ground must be done by ground troops. But infantry commanders themselves are almost tiring themselves out dictating commendations to air support units. Among these commanders is Lieut. Gen. Omar Bradley, commander of American troops in France.

"Intolerable."

A German officer, when captured, said his men could have withstood the infantry and artillery attacks a much longer time but the air bombardments were intolerable.

It is a mistake to jump to over-optimistic conclusions about air domination, yet there are undeniable factual advantages. Two weeks before the invasion I happened to be in the same hotel room with General Bradley and tried to sound him out regarding the value of air power in the invasion.

"Without it, of course, we couldn't attempt it," he said.

If the air situation were reversed, I assure you I would catch the next boat home, by-passing southern England en route, if I may make a passing reference to another form of air power currently being seen there.

As the prospect of Allied victory became more and more certain, the opportunity for reporters and soldiers to talk directly with the enemy became more frequent. Gammack reported conversations with Nazi prisoners and the attitudes they revealed. An interesting contrast to the feelings and ideas expressed by the German prisoners was provided by Gammack's inquiries among Iowa soldiers of their reasons for fighting and their feelings about the war.

REGISTER, JULY 30, 1944.

Hope Fading, Nazis Admit to Gammack

PRISONER OF WAR COLLECTING POINT, NORMANDY—The vast majority of German prisoners on the basis of their voluntary statements are certain of Germany's doom.

At this collecting point to which the Germans in their mouse-colored uniforms are brought from the front lines, prisoners' predictions see Germany out of the war in from three weeks to two months.

Officers generally cling to the two-month deadline while many enlisted men say three weeks.

German-speaking American soldiers on duty at this barbed wire enclosure say that fully 98 per cent of the prisoners have no belief whatever in German victory.

"The other two per cent consider it their duty as soldiers to believe in victory and to fight as long as they have guns and ammunition," said Sergt. Bernhard Edgar of New York, N.Y.

Of course, it is well to keep in mind that these Germans are the captives of Americans and they always seem anxious to please their jailers. Possibly they are inclined to say things they think we want to hear.

It is difficult to define German prisoners as a group. Heard the conversation of one who was a fanatical Nazi but neither he nor any others I have seen looked arrogant or sullen.

Nor do they look particularly dejected. I think many are happy that fighting is over for them.

Although the physical condition of most of the prisoners seems good they look tired. Certainly they don't look even remotely invincible.

All I have seen are very willing to talk and express their views.

Franz, 37, is an intelligent artillery sergeant who has a good command of the English language. He has been in the army five years and his home is Berlin where his wife, who lost an eye in an Allied air raid, and three children are living.

Franz said he personally was glad to be out of the fighting alive, particularly after the terror of Tuesday's big bombardment, but that if he were free he would gladly do his duty—return to action and take his chances.

"Duty" to Follow Hitler.

He said the revolt of German generals and the attempt to take Adolf Hitler's life were "a great shock." He deplored the fact that these events might have helped the new American offensive.

It was his duty as a good German soldier to follow the leadership of Hitler, he said, while at the same time disclaiming membership in the Nazi party.

Also as a good soldier, Franz said, he had to shut from his mind any prospect of German defeat, but it was obvious he contemplated defeat.

"It's like being sick and dying," Franz said. "One always hopes for a miracle which will save one's life. The soul tries to stop the reasoning of the mind."

Kurt, 33, is an artillery sergeant. He's from Breslau and worked in a distillery before the war. He has a wife and two children. Like so many Germans his blond hair is combed straight back.

When Sergeant Edgar asked him a question, he clicked his heels formally. He stood at attention with his arms rigidly at his side throughout the conversation.

Kurt said he fought for four months in Russia but that his greatest fear has been from the precision and volume of American artillery.

"How does it feel to be a prisoner?" asked Sergeant Edgar.

Kurt smiled just a trifle and said, "Well, at least it is quiet."

"How long will Germany stay in the war?" the sergeant asked.

"I expect the end any day," was the reply.

Kurt told a story of disorganization in the German ranks. German soldiers were told Marigny was in German hands, he said, so they went there, found Americans in charge and were captured.

At 2 a.m. Wednesday, Kurt said, he had a ration of soup, bread and butter—and then nothing for 60 hours until an American sergeant gave him a piece of bread.

Like all German soldiers he had been told that Americans killed all prisoners, and when the Americans laughed at that he laughed too, then stated that he had been treated "very good."

I think Kurt is very pleased about being a prisoner of the Americans.

But Adolf, slight 23-year-old blond paratrooper from Mannheim, is different. He believes implicitly in Nazism and says he believes Germany will win out somehow.

He spoke scornfully of American soldiers and boasted it was easy to infiltrate in American lines. His presence behind American-made barbed wiere made his boast unconvincing.

A soldier asked Adolf if he thought Germany ever could settle down to a peaceful and unwarlike national existence.

"We must win first," he said.

Adolf was unhappy over the realization that as a specimen of the "master race" he submitted himself to capture and offered this explanation, almost tearfully.

"Last night we had orders to pull out. On the road we stopped a jeep with two Americans in it and captured them. I was with a friend in the jeep with the Americans when fire came from somewhere and my friend was shot in the stomach. I tried to get help for him but couldn't.

"We went to a village and went through the houses for something to drink because we were thirsty. When it got light we found the town surrounded by Americans. There were only 20 of us."

Yank Angry.

When Adolf spoke disparagingly of American soldiers, an M.P. sergeant got hopping mad although he said nothing to Adolf. He just kept kicking the dirt angrily and saying over and over, "That's a lot of baloney."

Most prisoners ask for food as soon as they reach

the enclosure and say they have not eaten for three to five days.

"They'll trade you everything they've got for cigarettes," said Pvt. Gordon Carstens of Glencoe, Minn., who knows German because his mother was born in Germany.

Another soldier on duty at the enclosure is Pvt. (f.c.) Max Willardson of Woodbine, Ia.

Among the prisoners are some Russians. Two were shoemakers captured by the Germans at Smolensk and threatened with death if they did not volunteer for service with the German army.

There also are Russian Mongolians who are bewildered by the whole business. But I saw one with a bayonet jab where he sits down grinning at being a prisoner between grimaces of pain during treatment of the wound.

Another Russian Mongolian kept saying, "I'm an American prisoner; that's good."

There are quite a few youngsters as young as 15 among the prisoners although none of their identification cards show them to be less than 17.

Most prisoners wear heavy gray-green uniforms although some have camouflage capes or smocks.

The story they tell is that ammunition supplies up to now have been adequate but that there is a great scarcity of gasoline and food.

Defeat is written in the faces of the German prisoners I have seen.

REGISTER, FEBRUARY 11, 1945.

Iowa Soldiers Tell Reasons for Fighting

WITH U.S. 84TH (RAILSPLITTER) DIVISION (WEDNESDAY)—The fighting soldier's answer when you ask him what he's fighting for is really very simple.

He's fighting to get home, to stay alive from day to day, and to help his buddies stay alive. And he's fighting because he's been ordered to—because he has to, in the misery of mud, rain, snow, ice and cold.

In the terrible anxiety of not knowing what might be his last moment, the average soldier does not think of war in terms of a fight for freedom, democracy or world peace beyond his own freedom to go home to the country and home he loves above all else.

Facts Well Put.

These blunt facts long have been realized by correspondents, but our reactions never have been put so well as by Ralph Harwood in Tuesday's "War Week," which is a STARS AND STRIPES supplement.

"That's the way it is with the American soldier. There is very little girding of loins and pledging to do or die about him. He simply digs in and faces a bad situation and fights. If you ask him why he fights, he will probably tell you that it is largely because there is a war on.

"If you venture something about noble ideas and the larger aims of war like maybe making the world safe for democracy, he says he is primarily interested in killing the Germans for the sake of making the world safer at that particular moment for himself and a few other guys off to the right and left a little ways.

"If democracy cares to ride along on each spot, however, that's all right, too, as long as it doesn't get in the way. This attitude never ceases to be a worrisome thing to the heavy thinkers, in and out of the army. Also, it beats the hell out of the Germans."

Well, I wanted to find out what the Doughboys themselves had to say about this, and at the 84th Division today I found a dozen Iowans who spoke their minds with utmost sincerity.

In fact, they struck me as one of the finest groups of Iowans I've met.

In this group was one outstandingly fine soldier. He talks of other things besides what we're fighting for, but let him tell you. He's Sergt. Carroll Vinzant, 22, Lineville, Ia., and he has been with the division 26 months.

"Our first action was just about our toughest," he started. "It was in the Siegfried line about Aachen. The Germans threw everything they had at us. We were brand new, awfully green. God Almighty! We took an awful pounding that night they cut us off. They brought tanks. Thank God they didn't know exactly where we were, or none of us would have come out.

"But the fellows don't get scared anymore like they did then. They know what it's all about. They know the Germans have to be stopped and, boy, our infantry can do it!

"The Americans have more guts. I've seen Germans come out bawling like babies. Our boys have got what it takes.

"They talk about their discipline. Well, I like our way better. Up front, the officers eat, sleep and fight together. We carry out orders the very best we can.

"An American thinks for himself. If there's a machine gun nest that needs to be taken out, our officers don't have to give orders. They ask for volunteers. The first man up says, 'Let's go,' and he is the leader.

A Private Led.

"A while back, we had orders to take a town. We got into the outskirts just before dark. The Germans held it heavily. It was cold and wet, and we wanted a roof to sleep under. A captain said he didn't think we could take the town.

"There was a private—just a private, mind you—and he thought we could take it. 'Who wants to go

with me and take that town,' said the private, and we all followed."

Little Thought of Politics.

Sergt. Roger Clark, 26, of Nevada, formerly of Cedar Falls, Ia., said, "Don't think there's a man up there who doesn't think about why he's fighting. You've heard it a million times, I suppose, but the main thing is to get it over and go home. The average fellow thinks very little about the political situation and the politics behind it."

Pvt. (f.c.) Clark A. Twobridge of Grand River, Ia., said:

"I'm fighting for what America stands for—for better life for all of us and the kids who'll be coming along. We've got to get rid of every Nazi. That's what it is going to take to end this thing."

Pvt. (f.c.) Bernard Weigert, 28, of Gilmore City, Ia., said, "I guess we've got to get it over so we can get control and stop the Germans from another war. Up there you don't think about politics—I guess you call it politics."

Pvt. (f.c.) Don Frusha, 22, of Walford, Ia., said:

"We've got to do it, and I want to go home. When you get right down to it, that's what most of the boys will say. I know, because we've talked it over in our bull sessions. Fighting for democracy is a reason, all right, but it's not the biggest one. We fellows didn't come over here because we wanted to."

Sergt. Vincent Valentine, 19, of Atlantic, Ia., said:

"I'm fighting for freedom—the freedom to go home and also to give the damn Germans what they deserve. It's a job the fellows don't want to do, but they've got to, and put all they've got in it."

By luck or by instinct or by remarkable planning, Gammack rode in what was believed to be the first American vehicle to enter liberated Paris. In the advance elements of the entering troops, Gammack rode in a jeep with Captain Sach Bollas, a U.S. 9th Air Force public relations officer; Fred Graham of the New York Times; *Charles Haacker of Acme Pictures; and John Groth of Parade Magazine. On August 26, 1944, his report appeared in the Des Moines* Register.

REGISTER, AUGUST 26, 1944.

Tears of Joy as Thousands Cheer Troops

PARIS, FRANCE—The people of Paris went wild with frenzied joy Friday when Allied forces entered the city triumphantly.

I entered Paris about 9:30 a.m. with the leading element of the first troops to reach the heart of the city—an armored column of French forces.

Literally hundreds of thousands of persons jammed the path of the liberators.

They shrieked with joy. Wherever we paused they massed around our jeep, patting our backs and helmets, deluging us with flowers.

Thousands of hands clutched for ours. I was kissed at least a hundred times, although I do not recall that any of the girls who kissed me was a beauty.

The two words I heard most frequently and over and over again were "merci," meaning thank you, and "brave."

One woman said "merci" to me with more fervency than I have ever heard an expression of gratitude.

Tears of joy streamed from the faces of the people. One woman held up her little girl to me and said in English, "May my daughter kiss you?"

First to Enter.

I think it is possible our jeep with Capt. Sach Bollas, 9th Air Force public relations officer who was born in Paris, Fred Graham of New York, N.Y., Charles Haacker of Acme photograph, and John Groth of Parade magazine was the first American vehicle in Paris.

It is also possible that we and a Time magazine reporter were the first correspondents to enter the city.

Near the city limits a beautiful blond jumped suddenly into the jeep and rode to the heart of the city on Graham's lap.

Other girls sat on the hood of the jeep. Two girls climbed to the top of a French tank and rode along, waving their arms wildly and shouting hysterically.

I must report that the people we saw looked in good health and have been having a fairly reasonable amount of food. Several told Captain Bollas they were able to "get by," but said in another two days there would be famine.

Children as well as adults seemed quite robust.

I have had many thrills in a year of covering the war, but they are all trivial compared to the sensation of riding along Boulevard de la Porte d'Orleans through masses of persons enjoying the happiest days of their lives.

There were Germans in Paris, all right, but my personal belief is there will be no very serious resistance.

When we turned left in Boulevard de Montparnasse shots rang through the air, presumably from snipers, and all hell broke loose.

The tanks stopped and shot furiously into suspected buildings.

Parts of buildings fell off, crashing into the street. We squatted by the jeep and hoped for the best.

An atmosphere of anger and fear gripped everyone. Civilians swept like herds to take cover. A

Frenchman yelled at me that some Alsatian women were doing some of the sniping.

Continue Advance.

After about 10 minutes the bedlam subsided, and we continued on along Rue de Severs to Rue du Back to Rue de l'Universite and finally to the Esplanade des Invalides.

The Eiffel tower loomed ahead about four large blocks away. But here we were ahead of the tanks and there was an ominous stillness.

Civilians warned us Germans held all but one bridge across the Seine.

"The Germans are still here," said one Frenchman who was surprised to see us.

We lost no time turning back. Back on Rue de Sevres shooting broke out again and the tanks were firing shell after shell down the side streets.

Of course, during this period the civilian outbursts ceased and many of them came up to warn of the location of snipers.

On the way out of the city we saw long columns of French armor continuing their entry into the city, and except in the very heart of Paris there were repeated the scenes of wild reception.

In late January of 1945, Gammack moved from the 7th Army location near Alsace, France, to join the 9th Army which was in Holland. He was to accompany the 9th Army troops in their major effort to push the Germans back across the Rhine River. In transit to his post, Gammack witnessed the extent of damage done to cities and towns in Luxembourg, Belgium, and Holland. Then he joined the soldiers on their advance into Germany.

REGISTER, JANUARY 28, 1945.

Recaptured Belgian Bulge a Graveyard of Dead Cities

NINTH ARMY, HOLLAND—A move from the 7th Army to the 9th Army involves a trip up the whole length of the American front in four countries.

The most interesting part of the trip north was from Bastogne, Belgium, through what was the German salient, where battles had reduced the towns to rubble and left the roadsides and fields strewn with wrecked tanks, many upside down, and other smashed equipment.

There is ample evidence that we had a rough time of it in that area. But when you see the rugged terrain with deep gorges, rocky slopes and thick forests, it is easier to understand why our commanders did not think the Germans would gamble on an offensive there.

Death to Towns.

The German thrust meant death to many Belgian towns. The driver who took Vic Jones of the Boston Globe and me from Luxembourg to here had been through the territory many times before the offensive, and he kept saying as he was driving through the towns, "Wasn't a building damaged here before the offensive."

Now nothing is left. The people have left and places like Houffalize, the most devastated place I have seen since St. Lo, are truly ghost towns.

Splintered trees in the woods tell another story of the fierce fighting, but for all the ugly sights, winter has turned the entire fringe of the American front into extremely beautiful scenery. The snow is deep and clings to the trees in lovely patterns.

But it is not fun for the men who have to be on the roads.

You see men huddled in the backs of trucks. They look cold and miserable in their thin coats. Snow churned up by the trucks and tanks covers their overcoats.

You see soldiers in halted convoys stamping their feet to get the numbness out.

We stopped by a roadside ordnance outfit to grab a cup of coffee and a bite of chow. The kitchen was set up in a deserted, unheated building and the men slept in icy tents.

"Pretty rugged spot you've got here," I suggested to a sergeant.

"Yeah, but we've got a cinch compared to those poor guys in the infantry," he said in one of those typical tributes to the foxhole doughboys you hear from noncombatant men near the front.

There was an Iowan in this outfit—Corp. Ardel Keefer of Lone Tree—but he was out with the wrecker while I was there.

That morning his tent caught fire and his barracks bag with all his clothes had burned. He had to borrow clothes.

The boys said they kid Keefer all the time about coming from a place called Lone Tree.

Rumors Afloat.

All along the road groups of soldiers are talking about the Russian offensive and many rumors are afloat. Spotting correspondents' insignia, some thought we were experts and asked all sorts of questions.

"Is it true the Russians issued an ultimatum giving the Germans 72 hours to give up?" one corporal asked.

Another said, "We heard Goebbels made a speech

saying it was the finish for Germany." Still another asked, "What will we do if the Germans quit? Take away all their arms?"

Most of the G.I. thinking about dealing with defeated Germany doesn't go much deeper than that.

Our trip took us from Saverne in Alsace through Metz to Luxembourg, then north into Belgium through Liege, and finally into Holland.

On the eve of the "big push" which was to decide the victory over Germany, the might of the Allied forces was, from Gammack's perspective, a collection of frightened but deeply determined Iowa doughboys. Once the battle was on, Gammack accompanied the 9th Army in its sweep to the edge of the Rhine and finally across it.

REGISTER, FEBRUARY 24, 1945.

Gammack Talks to Tense Iowa Doughboys as Big Push Opens

NEAR ROER RIVER IN GERMANY—In the wake of a terrific artillery barrage, Doughboys of Lt. Gen. William H. Simpson's U.S. 9th Army crossed the treacherous Roer river in predawn moonlight Friday and launched a major western front offensive.

Early reports indicated the full-scale attack was progressing well despite extreme difficulties in throwing bridges across the swift, swollen Roer, which had delayed the offensive two weeks.

I went to a command post less than a mile from the Roer to talk to Iowans and Minnesotans as they prepared to attack in the assault wave. I saw and heard the earth-shaking artillery barrage and from an observation post watched the start of the great battle.

Several hundred guns started belching shells at German positions at 2:45 a.m. (in Iowa this was at 8:45 p.m. Thursday), and the "preparation" lasted 45 minutes. Then at 3:30 a.m. Doughboys and engineers started across the river.

The moon was shining brightly Thursday night when I visited "Able" and "Charlie" companies, which were to make the assault for one of the attacking divisions.

There was tension in the air and an eerie stillness.

At a battalion command post the lieutenant-colonel met with his company commanders to discuss for the last time carefully prepared plans. Before the lieutenant-colonel were maps of two towns his battalion was assigned to capture. All the buildings were numbered on the maps, and the commander said each man in the battalion had his assignment.

Streets were named after company commanders. One was called "Pete's Plaza."

German Planes.

In the next room of a battered German home two men slept on the floor and three shot dice on the floor by candlelight. Then came that old familiar uneven hum of a German plane, and the skies became alive with lights. Red tracer bullets flew upward, and white shafts from searchlights tried to spot the Hun.

The night before German planes had been bothersome. When British bombers flew over our positions en route to German targets, the Jerries flew under the British planes and attacked our troops, knowing that with friendly planes above we could not shoot.

We expected to be shelled Thursday night, too. The town where the command post was located had been shelled consistently, and when our group of correspondents arrived high ranking officers said to the public relations officer, "You got cellars for these men?"

"Yes sir," replied the P.R.O.

"Good cellars?"

"Yes sir."

But until our own mighty artillery let loose, it remained pretty quiet. It was very quiet in the "Able" company command post where men waited for the signal to move up.

The Doughboys were scared—scared to death. Their voices trembled when they spoke. They breathed fast. Their mouths were dry. They chewed gum fast, nervously.

Capt. Earl Jackson of Carbondale, Ill., sat at a desk covered with funny papers from the Los Angeles Times.

"Anyone who says he isn't scared tonight is a damn liar," he said.

First Battle.

The captain sent for Iowans in the company. For Lt. James K. Eland of Mediapolis, Ia., it would be his first battle.

"I'm nervous," he said. *"I'm anxious to know how I'll behave under fire. Sure I'm scared. You can say that maybe I'm not as scared as some who've been through it because I don't know enough about what it's like."*

"We're going to make it all right," said Pvt.

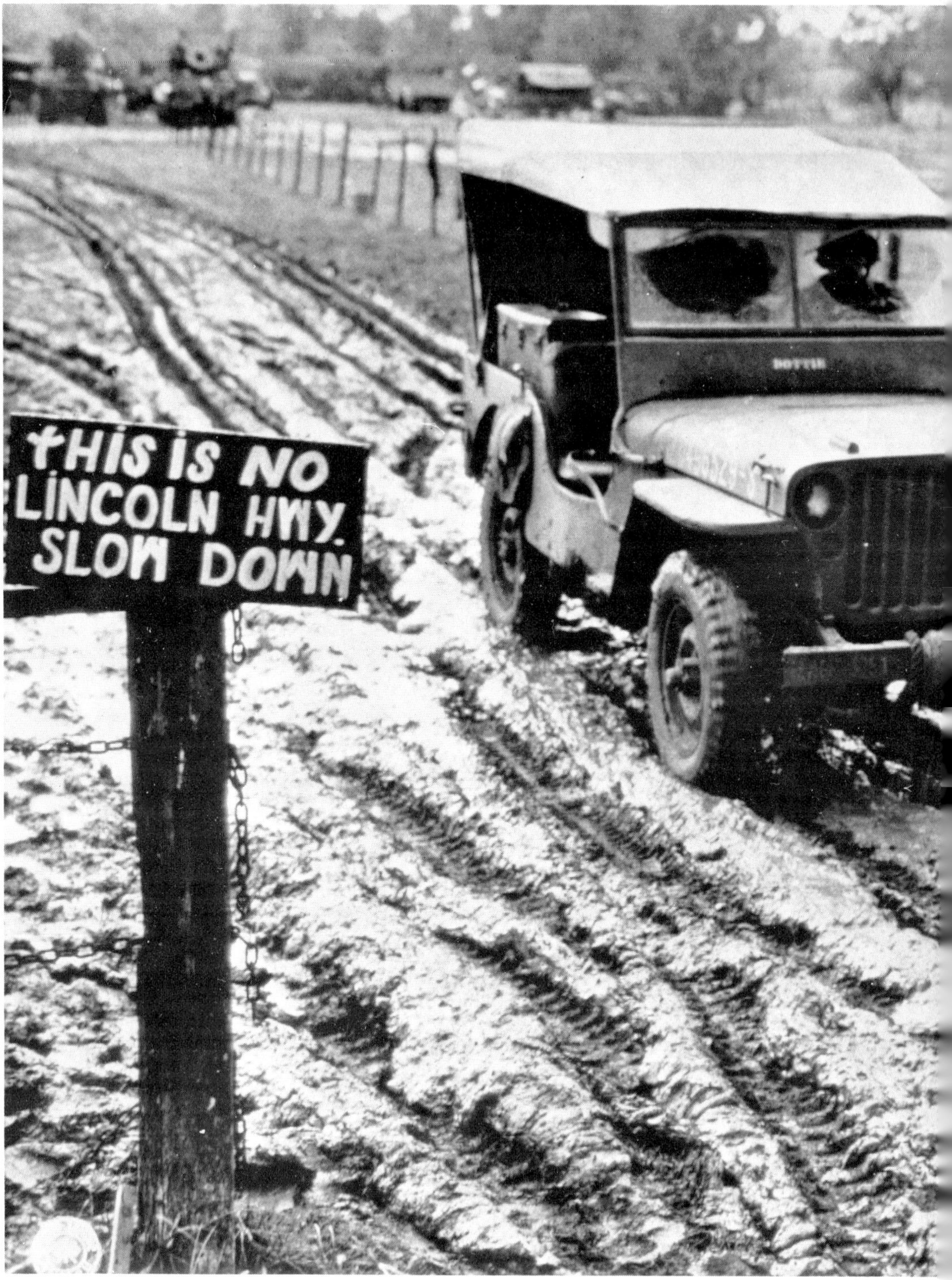

OCTOBER 25, 1944. Mud, caused by fall rains in France, makes the going tough for American troops on the western front, but fails to dim American humor, as evidenced by this traffic sign, referring to the famous American highway. *(AP)*

Theodore Hamann, 35, of Rock Valley, Ia. "I'll be nervous until we get across the river. From then on we're going to give them hell."

Pvt. Jack Myers, 19, of Albia, Ia., said, "I'm glad this damn wating is over. I'm scared a little I guess, but not bad. We've still got to push those Krauts over the Rhine."

"Able" and "Charlie" companies were scheduled to start moving up toward the river at midnight. Shortly before 11 p.m. the men lined up in the street, their silhouettes showing in the moonlight for a chow of pancakes and corn flakes. They didn't talk much. Then they started donning their life belts for the river crossing and stocking up on grenades.

Tries to Sleep.

I left them then and decided to try to get a little sleep. I was tired but couldn't sleep with my boots and all the rest of my clothes on, wrapped well in a blanket on a cot. Sydney Gruson of the New York Times was in the same room and couldn't sleep either.

We'd hear the rapid bursts of a German burp gun down by the river, and one of us would say, "Theirs." And then when slower machine-gun fire was heard, we'd say, "Ours."

Restless, we got up and went out to the street. Now Doughboys were marching up in that awful pattern—two lines, one on each side of the road, with intervals between each man.

It was a grim march. Here were American men unwilling but determined as they walked toward the hell of battle.

They walked silently, some of them heavily laden with machine guns and ammunition. Even the scuffling of feet sounded soft against the hum of a nearby generator. Between the columns of men came a few jeeps with only their pinpoint lights showing.

Every minute or so the columns stopped. Each man halted instantly to preserve the intervals. It was machine-like, but you felt you could hear the hearts of the men pounding. It was a sad sight. Back in our building some one said, "Damn dramatic to see those men marching up isn't it?"

"Yep," said a sergeant, "a lot of those fellows are walking right into death."

Back on the cot I made another attempt to sleep and managed to doze an hour. Then we got up for the barrage. As the time approached, we kept looking at our watches.

Then it happened. The stillness of the night turned into bedlam as guns roared a message to the Germans across the Roer that the time had come.

Our building shook from the blasts. Plaster fell from the ceiling. There were guns all around us, and they fired as fast as gun crews could thrust shells into breeches.

I climbed to an observation post to watch the barrage. Out across the river were great bursts of white fire as our shells landed.

Up ahead we had tanks, antitank guns and antiaircraft guns all shooting direct fire like mad at German positions across the Roer. Tracers arched into the skies like flaming golf balls in flight. Flares lit up the skies. A smoke screen was set up to protect men launching assault boats and crossing the river.

The deafening roar of guns never stopped. The attack was on.

REGISTER, MARCH 4, 1945.

Attic Glimpse of the Rhine for Gammack

NEUSS, GERMANY, AT THE RHINE (FRIDAY)—From an attic window in bomb-shattered Neuss, I saw the Rhine river today a few hours after American Doughboys had reached the city and smashed what little resistance rear-guard German soldiers had to offer.

So we're at the Rhine all right. While elements of the U.S. 2nd Armored (Hell on Wheels) Division, commanded by Brig. Gen. Isaac D. White of Des Moines, plunged forward north and west of the key 9th Army objective of Neuss to reach the Rhine, U.S. 83rd (Ohio) Division Doughboys battled their way into the city.

The German goose west of the Rhine seemed to be cooked for sure.

From 15,000 to 20,000 of the normal Neuss population of 60,000 remained for American occupation and submitted to it meekly. Hundreds of them cowered in bunkers and air raid shelters.

From almost every house hung some sort of a white flag.

All through France, Belgium and The Netherlands national flags were flown as liberation troops entered, but in Neuss the only flag civilians could fly was any strip of white cloth they could find, whether a sheet or towel—the flag of humiliation, defeat, surrender.

I was lucky enough to be with Wes Gallagher of the Associated Press, Sydney Gruson of the New York Times and Vic Jones of the Boston Globe in the first group of American correspondents to reach Neuss on the Rhine.

We entered the city in midmorning and climbed to the sixth floor of a kindergarten school on Koenigstrasse at the edge of the Erft canal to look out and see the Rhine and beyond that the great city of Dusseldorf where shells from American guns were pouring in by the dozens.

It was anything but quiet in Neuss. Seemingly on all sides of the city guns either were firing or shells exploding.

Our divebombers were making a frightful whine as they dived down to hit nearby targets and we were sent sprawling once when German jet planes swooped down 300 feet above the city.

But most Doughboys of the 83rd Division, who had spent much of the night entering and taking Neuss, were so tired they slept. Others patrolled the streets and were rounding up prisoners who still were being flushed out of buildings.

Driving to Neuss, we carefully worked our way along sideroads to avoid possible shellfire. We arrived at the western edge of Neuss and found in a sturdy brick building the battalion command post of Lt. Col. John A. Norris, jr., of Austin, Tex., who told of the city's capture.

"It wasn't too bad," he said, "although one company got into a good fight. To all intents and purposes, we've got the town, and there's no shooting going on (inside the city) now. We've taken 165 prisoners."

"The place is lousy with civilians," he said. "We're concentrating them in bunkers and shelters. We had just one case of civilians shooting at our soldiers, and we took care of that. Actually the civilians have been very co-operative. They've even shown our soldiers where to find beds."

Assigned Guards.

Colonel Norris assigned six riflemen to take us through the city, and we walked through the streets to the tune of battle din on all sides. There seemed to be no remaining resistance in Neuss itself though the riflemen had their guns in a ready position.

Civilians looked out of windows blankly, behaving probably about the same as you would if belligerent foreigners took over your community. Some tried to be friendly, but the tendency of the Doughboys was to take these gestures with a grain of salt.

On Adolf Hitler strasse a little wizened man smiled, nodded and said, "Thank God you've come." But the Doughboys' response was unprintable.

At intersection near Adolf Hitler strasse, Lt. Robert Packer of Brooklyn, N.Y., who led the first company into the city, said he'd try to take us where we could see the Rhine although he said it was difficult because of buildings in the way.

He led us down a street not penetrated before by our troops. We and the riflemen clung to the sides of buildings because at the end of the street was the Erft canal and beyond that possibly enemy pockets.

Hammers on Door.

Packer hammered on the door of the kindergarten school and was about to break in the door when a woman opened it. As we climbed the stairs, the Doughboys with guns at the ready opened all doors.

Then in the attic we saw the Rhine and smoking Dusseldorf. We didn't linger. One look was enough for the time being.

On the way down the riflemen said, "Keep your eye out when we leave. These krauts like to let you get in a place and then let you have it when you come out."

But it was quiet on the street, and the lanky sergeant with us said, "This is the quietest operation we've been on in a long time. It's really quiet here."

"Don't say that," said Gallagher, who had some feeling about stretching our luck.

Few buildings in Neuss were left intact, and inasmuch as the city had not been shelled much before capture virtually all the damage must have been from Allied bombings.

This is the type of Germany we are going to see as we move Berlinward. Smaller communities in the path of our swift advance this week actually benefited from our success because we passed so quickly little or no damage was done.

When we left Neuss, we saw columns of black smoke several miles to the west, and at the command post where we had spent the preceding night we learned the Germans had made a desperate attempt to cut off the 83rd Division's line into Neuss and might have caused lots of trouble if Thunderbolt divebombers hadn't dived down and smashed five of the seven attacking German tanks.

It was one more example of how there are plenty of troubles fighting a war even when winning.

REGISTER, MARCH 25, 1945.

Gammack Watches Tommies and Doughboys Battle over Rhine

ON BANKS OF THE RHINE, GERMANY (SATURDAY)—American Doughboys and British Tommies crossed the Rhine Saturday with a colossal show of devastating power.

This attack had everything. Unlike the Rhine crossings of the U.S. 1st and 3rd Armies, this attack is deliberately aimed to seal the doom of Germany.

With Wes Gallagher of the Associated Press I set out Friday to watch the operation, and first we attended a briefing at the British 2nd Army where a brigadier in typical British fashion predicted a "fine battle."

At dusk British Commandos struck across the Rhine. While the Commandos clung to the east bank at Wesel, the R.A.F. struck at 10:45 p.m. with a view to obliterate the city.

We had a grandstand seat for the bombing and it was a terrific sight. At H-Hour Minus One there followed the greatest artillery preparation I've ever seen or heard.

Terrifying as the sight was, it eventually became monotonous and we returned to the C.P. where someone had fruit cake from home and a radio was playing dance tunes.

When dawn came, the cannon still were barking fiercely and the skies were cloudless again. Reports coming in showed the attack was going "according to plan," or even better.

Smoke hung everywhere, and you couldn't see more than 100 yards. The Germans were still in business, and our flimsy building quivered as enemy shells came whining in.

All indications now are that the entire operation is going smoothly. It's best summed up by the remark I've heard hundreds of times in the last 24 hours:

"This is it."

Gordon Gammack headed for home. He stopped in England and reported the jubilation of victory over Germany. All that remained was to share the thrill of returning to the United States.

REGISTER, MAY 8, 1945.

'Blood, Sweat and Tears' of British Isles Rewarded

LONDON, ENGLAND (TUESDAY)—The awful and the brave years—the struggle from the depths of despair—are over and the joyous relief of the end of the war against Germany spread through the British Isles today.

Almost exactly five years ago, Winston Churchill told his people he could offer them nothing, but "blood, sweat, toil and tears."

Today came the news of Germany's complete finish, the signal for VE-day, the completion of the gigantic struggle in Europe.

Tomorrow is VE-day and Churchill will make the historic announcement at 3 p.m. [London time].

Of course, VE-day was not unexpected. But, anticlimactic as it is, it gave millions of weary Britons the chance to breathe a last sigh of relief.

Before the historic victory news, the possibility that today would be the day was on everyone's tongue, and people were asking "I wonder if the Japs won't quit pretty soon after this?"

I asked a store clerk if she thought the announcement would be made today.

"Oh, I do hope so," she said. "We've waited so long."

"It's going to be great news," said a shabby char-

woman. "But it won't bring my Harry back. That's the worst of it. Nothing can change that."

But, on a subway a beautiful young woman's arms were chuck full of bright gay flowers, and her face was even brighter.

"John will be home tomorrow," she said to a friend. "I thought the day would never come. Four years is a long time."

Not so long ago, London was a very different place. The air was filled with the ghastly throb of buzzbombs and their awful cargoes of death.

Nerves of Londoners neared the breaking point. Fear gripped their souls. Anxiously, they scanned the skies for the monsters.

They dreaded the whining alert siren; longed for the even tones of all clear. And then, came the V-2 rockets which killed without warning.

But, the sounds today are the bells of peace ringing from every church in England and of cheering people in Piccadilly Circus and of clinking glasses in pubs, hotels and clubs as victory toasts are made with the traditional British salute of "cheers."

It is not, of course, entirely a British celebration.

In London and throughout the United Kingdom are thousands of American soldiers joining in the celebration—fighter pilots and bomber crews sensing blessed relief that they have seen their last flak, their last Messerschmitt, their last lost flights in cloud banks over Germany.

Usual London Life Halts.

The usual London has all but stopped. Stores quickly shut their doors. Crowds streamed from theaters on receipt of victory announcement. Hundreds went soberly to churches for prayers of thanksgiving.

But, in all England and throughout the free world, it is a great day.

Full impact of victory came as gradually and as full of suspense as the final unconditional surrender itself.

I had heard the rumor that Churchill would announce it at three in the afternoon.

I thought it would be a dramatic experience to be attending London's gayest musical "Strike It Again," have the performance interrupted with great announcement, then the orchestra breaking into "God Save the King" with the crowd cheering and shedding tears of happiness.

I had seen the show, but I plunked down fourteen and six, which is $2.90 in American money.

I watched my watch as three approached, but it passed and the show went on.

Oh, it will be four or five, then, I thought. After all, one London writer this morning said the official announcement probably ties in with lunch in New York, tea in London, and dinner in Moscow. SUCH A WAY TO END A WAR!

But, four o'clock came and went, and the show was over at five. Everyone stood and sang "God Save the King," but that's just a good old English custom.

I wandered out of the Prince of Wales theater into Piccadilly Circle and a great crowd had gathered.

A newspaper truck drove by with a big sign, "All Over," and newspaper headlines proclaimed the surrender.

Newsreel cameramen focused their cameras from canopies and roof tops.

Peddlers sold flags and lapel colors and noise makers. Said one with a handful of British flags, "Come now, we've been waiting five and a half years for this. Buy a flag."

Yank Can't Believe It.

The crowd swelled and swelled. I walked along with a Doughboy from Kentucky.

"I can't believe it," he said. "I still can't believe it. Maybe there is going to be a future in life for me after all."

Crowds watched the clocks. They'd hear the prime minister's voice come booming over the radio at 5:30. No, well, 6 then. But nothing happened.

More and more flags—American as well as British—were unfurled from window ledges. The war was over, but it wasn't official. The anti-climax grew greater and greater.

London newspapers have been having a field day with the news. The huge Daily Mail headline Saturday proclaims "Germans Capitulate to Montgomery." The Daily Telegraph says, "Surrender: This Is The End." The News Chronicle says, "Monty's Job Done."

It's all over but the shouting, and there won't be much shouting because VE-day will be something like a damp rag—a wonderful, wonderful rag, but damp just the same, from a succession of anti-climaxes.

REGISTER, MAY 22, 1945.

U.S. at Last! Frenzied Joy on Troopship

ABOARD TROOPSHIP IN NEW YORK HARBOR (DELAYED)—That glorious day—the day that every soldier overseas dreams about—had arrived for the 4,000 Doughboys, Gobs and airmen jammed aboard our troopship.

Here was New York. Here was home. Here was safety. Here was the land they had fought to keep free. Excitement aboard was electric.

Somehow, to almost every man aboard, the Statue of Liberty was the symbol of the joy of this day, and the troopship listed sharply to the left as the men crowded the port decks and leaned over the rails to catch the first glimpse of the statue.

"Where's the 'Old Lady?' When do we see her? I won't believe it's true until I see her"—those were the questions and comments that passed from one end of the ship to the other.

But, the ship—the first to leave Europe with homecoming troops since VE-day—was edging its way to pier 16 at Staten Island and would not pass the Statue of Liberty.

Suddenly, the troopship lurched and rolled to the right as if to shed a huge wave, but the wave was of men making a dash to the starboard [right] side and immediately the tunes of a jazz band were drowned in a frenzied cheer.

A few feet from the hull of our ship was an army transportation corps boat festooned with dozens of gay nautical flags and eight American flags waving triumphantly from the top deck.

It was drizzling and the skies were gray, but American girls [Red Cross] lined the railings of the "welcome home" boat, and they waved at the men on the decks of our ship who whistled and yelled and cheered.

A WAC jazz band in rain coats played tune after tune. The girls on the welcoming ship motioned to the G.I.s with a "come on over" gesture which, under the circumstances, was as safe as it was enticing.

300 Wounded Aboard.

We had about 300 wounded aboard. Some were able to come to the decks to share in the celebration.

Others, with arms and legs in casts and some minus an arm or a leg, had to lie in their bunks and just listen to the songs and the cheers.

At the pier, another band played.

The soldiers cheered on the slightest provocation. Even the sight of an M.P. on the dock brought a loud cheer, and the M.P. ducked behind an obstruction in embarrassment.

Ordinarily, M.P.s aren't people soldiers cheer about, but this day was different.

It was early in the evening when we docked and less than 100 men—all naval officers—were permitted off the ship that night.

So, the excitement gradually subsided, and there was a temporary return to the boredom and restlessness which marked the long trip across the Atlantic.

If by nothing else, you could sense the approach to America by the mood of the ship during the last two days.

With two days to go, you could feel a mood of anticipation. Then, on the final day a mood of gayety spread through the ship.

Everyone was singing and whistling and smiling. Indifference among the men changed to friendliness among everyone.

It wasn't only the idea of getting home. Travel on a troopship is a far cry from a pleasure cruise on the Queen Mary.

First class, instead of plushy salons, we went to the decks assigned to us and surveyed the situation to see if there was a vacant space on a hatch big enough to squat on.

Instead of deck chairs, you were lucky to find a hunk of metal to lean back on. Instead of a bar, there were warnings of court martial for taking a drink.

Instead of cabins, all but the wounded and officers of the rank of major and above were in the bowels of the ship, sleeping on racks made by stretching canvas strips across metal pipe frames and in tiers four bunks high.

The food was superb, in keeping with the navy tradition, but the wardroom for officers had limited accommodations, so we had four different "sittings" with half an hour allotted for each sitting and subsequent resetting of the tables.

But, we had steak a half dozen times, turkey twice, fried chicken twice, ice cream about every other day and fresh eggs about every other breakfast.

But, all in all, it was a trip we were glad to have over.

Among the army men aboard were officers and men who had fought in the fiercest battles of the war—Doughboys from the 1st and 9th Infantry Divisions who started fighting in North Africa, battle-weary G.I.s from the 30th, and 83rd, the 84th, the 29th, the 3rd, the 79th, the 35th Infantry and the 2nd, 3rd, 4th and 5th Armored Divisons.

These outfits are among the elect which have seen much of the hardest and longest fighting of the war.

Then, there were pilots and crewmen of the 8th Air Force who had completed their tours of duty and were bound home for furloughs before possible fighting in the Pacific.

And, there were pilots from the troop carrier command who started out in Egypt, the first troop carrier group overseas.

And, naval officers and men from the amphibious craft who had taken part in the North African, Sicilian, Anzio and Normandy Operations.

Excellent Spirit Prevails.

There was an excellent spirit between the men of the various branches of service, and Lt. Col. Thomas Farrish, in charge of all troops, saw to it that all services were treated with equal consideration and that wherever possible, extra niceties went to the enlisted men.

The captain of the ship did an extremely fine thing when he decided to let the whole ship in on a radio conference held every evening among the commanders of all the ships in our convoy and the protecting warships.

The effect of this was to squash about 90 per cent of the rumors that spread like wildfire through a troop ship.

Our ship has just left a British port when over the loudspeaker came this order: "Everyone will wear their lifebelts at all times."

This was a little surprising in that the free world

at that moment was celebrating VE-day, but the order continued:

"In the last 48 hours and since the supposed cessation of hostilities, two ships have been sunk in British waters. There are still many submarines at large."

And, on the second day, our ship shook from the concussion of depth charges dropped by our escorting warships. But, the evening conference informed us just what the situation was.

Several U-Boats Didn't Report.

"We made several contacts today," said the chief of the escort. "A number of U-boats are unaccounted for and have not reported. We think we know about one which will never report.

"We think we got it, at least there was one big explosion that's unaccounted for. Right now, we're looking for more evidence."

But, for us who'd been mixed up in the war quite awhile, submarine reports weren't even disquieting. **We just had infinite confidence in our escort and let it go at that.**

There was one small tragedy during the trip. One evening, this order came out of the loudspeaker:

"The man responsible for bringing a dog aboard this ship contrary to naval regulations will report to the troop office with the dog."

Not one, but five men with five dogs showed up.

There was only one thing to do. If the ship docked and dogs were found, it would be quarantined 72 hours.

One by one, the dogs were taken to the sick bay and chloroformed. Then, they were dropped during the black night into the sea.

One residual effect of Gammack's service at the front was a profound personal sympathy for the fighting men. That sympathy found expression in Gammack's personal campaign for Ralph Neppel, a young man from Iowa who won the Congressional Medal of Honor and lost both his legs in an encounter with a German tank. Gammack inspired a campaign to provide Neppel with needed funds, followed the course of his rehabilitation, and became his personal friend.

REGISTER, NOVEMBER 18, 1945.

Today's column is devoted to the Sgt. Ralph Neppel Fund, which I fervently hope is going to be a tribute to a great and brave soldier from a grateful Iowa.

There are several important things about Sgt. Ralph Neppel, 21, whose home is at Glidden, Ia., in Carroll county. He has been awarded the Congressional Medal of Honor, our nation's highest award. President Truman himself pinned the award on Neppel's breast.

Sergeant Neppel is legless. He left his legs on the shambles of a European battlefield, where, after his legs were sheared off by the shell from a German tank, he somehow grabbed his machine gun, painfully inched himself forward and, single-handed, stopped the enemy attack.

Two weeks ago I made the offhand suggestion that it would be fine if someone started a fund for Sergeant Neppel. Within 24 hours a letter came from Mr. and Mrs. Dick Canfield, who operate Red's Barbecue in Des Moines.

They wrote: "Please let's start a campaign to raise this brave young man a tidy sum. We will start it off with the inclosed check."

And thus, with the Canfields' generous check for $20, the Neppel fund was born.

What better can we Iowans do than to make a great Iowa hero's difficult life ahead a little more comfortable and pleasant? He doesn't need charity. He doesn't want pity. But I do think it would be grand to give him a material expression of appreciation from the people of his state.

In losing his legs, Sergeant Neppel saved many American lives. How many soldiers who returned to their homes and families unharmed would like to contribute to this fund? And how about the Iowa families who were spared the loss of a son or a husband or a brother?

The Victory loan drive—the last of these drives—is in progress. A grand way to help two great causes would be to buy war bonds or stamps in Sergeant Neppel's name and contribute them to the fund. And, of course, checks and cash and money orders will be welcome, too.

It was decided not to start this campaign without Sergeant Neppel's approval. From the McCloskey General hospital in Temple, Tex., where he is starting the ordeal of learning how to walk on artificial legs, he wired: "Am thrilled and overwhelmed."

Then he wrote: "I don't know quite what to write as I am excited. As you know, I am engaged to be married and plan to be married when I leave here with my discharge. (His fiance is Miss Jean Moore.)

"What I do need mostly is a home and car. I am planning on living in Carroll. I don't know what kind of a job I will be capable to handle."

Plans are being formulated to build, with the fund, the kind of a home Sergeant Neppel wants and, with the help of experts in the field, a home which will be ideally suited for a handicapped war hero.

So let's start the ball rolling, Iowans. Make us dizzy here with your contributions. Ralph Neppel did so much. Let's all do at least a little for him.

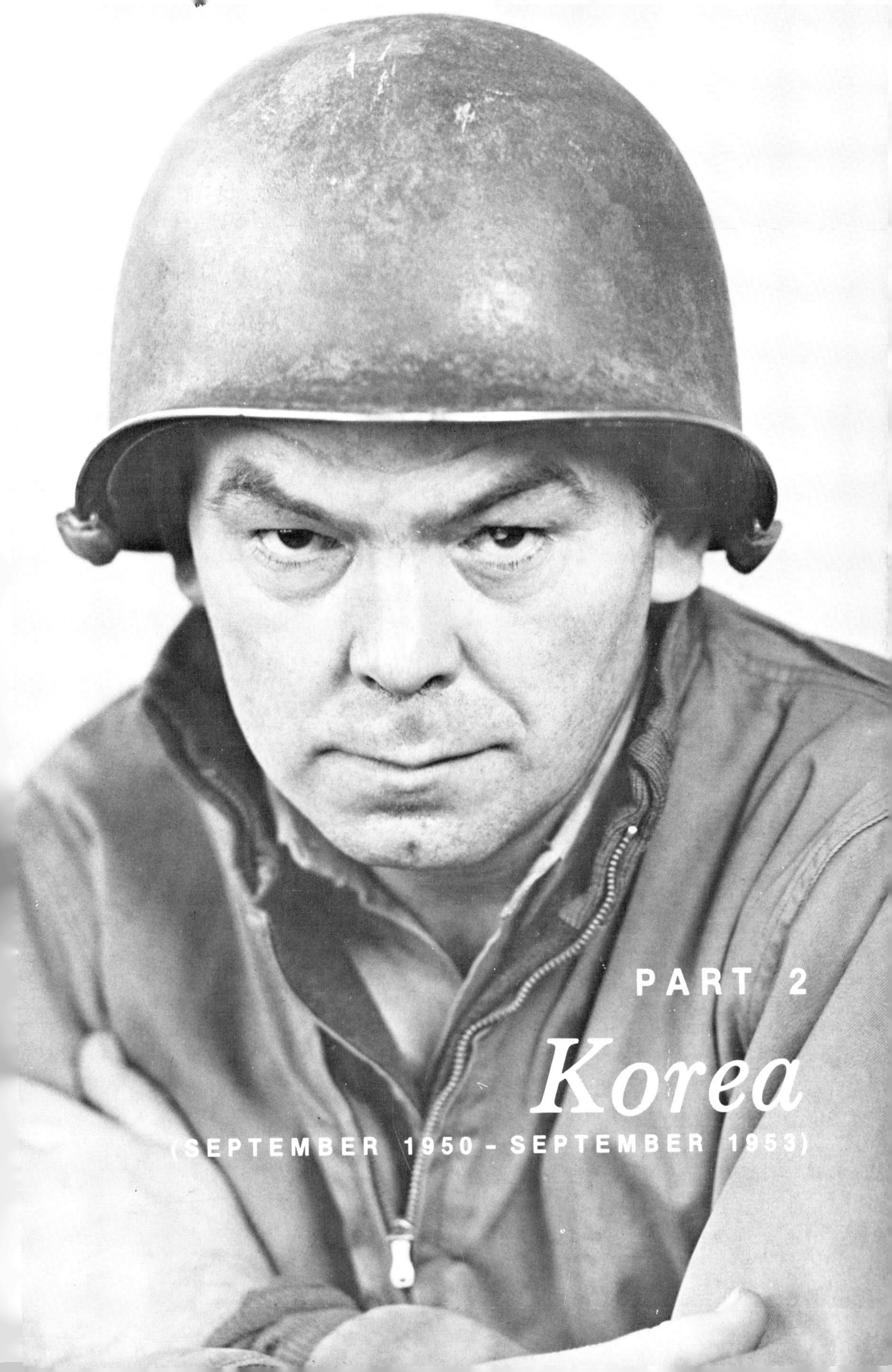

PART 2

Korea

(SEPTEMBER 1950 - SEPTEMBER 1953)

APRIL 10, 1953. On hand at the signing of the prisoner exchange pact at Panmunjom, Korea, Gordon Gammack (circled) listens with other newsmen as Rear Admiral John Daniel tells of agreement. Daniel holds copy of the pact. Negotiation building is in the background. *(AP)*

Introduction

BY Keyes Beech, SOUTHEAST ASIA CORRESPONDENT, LOS ANGELES **TIMES**

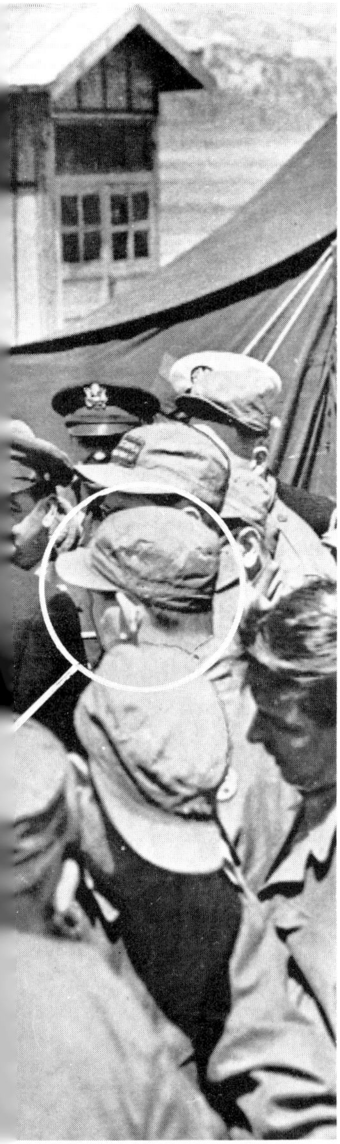

I LAST SAW Gordon Gammack early in 1973 at Clark Air Base in the Philippines. We were drawn there by the release of American prisoners of war from North Vietnam following the Paris ceasefire that sealed the fate of South Vietnam. All we really wanted then was out of Vietnam and our prisoners back. The ceasefire served those ends.

The military, with its usual infuriating efficiency in such matters, had thrown up a protective shield around the returning prisoners. We could see them as they stepped off the planes from Hanoi, but that was it. With rare exceptions, no interviews.

Some members of the press corps, inspired by the "right to know," threw themselves against the military barricades with a storm of protests, to no avail. Gordon Gammack had no time for such foolishness. Days before the first prisoners arrived, Gordon had found an Iowa doctor on the staff of the base hospital where the prisoners were housed.

In no time at all, readers of the Des Moines *Register* and *Tribune* were treated to exclusive and colorful accounts of life among the prisoners inside the hospital. In an equally short time, rockets began to fall on practically the entire press corps.

"Who the hell is this guy Gammack?" some of the disgruntled younger correspondents wanted to know. I didn't need to be told who Gordon Gammack was, for I had known him during another war and another prisoner release 20 years earlier, in Korea.

That prisoner exchange was called Big Switch, and it is worth recalling that, for better or worse, the returning Americans faced the press—yes, and TV too—on the day of their release. Gordon was there to take down what they said, especially the Iowans, although he later had his problems with obstructive army hospital authorities back in Tokyo.

Reading Gordon Gammack's dispatches on the Korean war more than two decades later is a poignant reminder of a time when the world was a simpler place, or our thinking made it so; when there was an "our side" and a "their side" and no treacherous gray area; when you could tell the good guys from the bad guys by whose side they were on; when wars had fronts; when for an American to visit an enemy capital in wartime was equal to treason; when all things were possible; when the dollar was almighty and so was America, which could do no wrong.

It was our time of innocence. Gordon Gammack was a part of that time. Thus he could write unblushingly about how American "prisoners melted toothpaste tubes to make crude crosses and tie them around their necks in defiance of the heathen reds"; or how one is caught "in this fiendish Communist web."

Purple prose? Well, yes, but it was also Gordon Gammack letting you know exactly where he stood, and, by extension, where his readers stood at that point in time.

Yet Gordon was too good a reporter to be blinded to reality. He had sympathy for the Korean refugees, but correctly suspected that their ranks included "some gooks who had been fighting us a few hours before."

(That word "gook" fairly leaps from the page. A term of contempt for anyone "different," it was coined by American G.I.s during the Pacific war and carried over into Korea five years later. My own editors, racially sensitive, objected to my using the word in G.I. quotes from Korea. My reply was that when the G.I.s stopped using it, I would. But the copydesk won. The copydesk always wins.)

Honesty also caused Gordon to note that not all the atrocities in Korea were committed by the Communists. The Korean police, he reported, were a brutal lot who often beat up civilians. The Americans tried to stop this in one village, Gordon reported, with doubtful results. The citizens beat up the police and the policemen quit.

So much for reform, Korean style.

In one paragraph, in a moment of confession, Gordon captured the feeling of every American who knew Korea during that now forgotten war:

"An American in Korea is always depressed and sad that anyone in the world must live such a miserable existence. Squalor and nasty odors are everywhere. There is no joy in life, rarely even a smile. I am writing this on a plane bound from Seoul to Tokyo and I fervently hope I will never have to go back."

He went back though. All of us—well, almost all of us—did.

At another point Gordon wonders why men march

into battle: "They do not do it willingly. What man wants to face death?

"It is as though they were prodded by a bayonet, but actually, instead of physical force it is a general's command, and the consequences of refusal, and the inner compulsion for respect of a soldier's fellowman. And so he plods on to take up man's most awful job."

To me at least, Gordon was as straightforward and uncomplicated as his prose. In this respect Gordon did not change, but the world around him did. Gordon, like so many members of his generation, could not understand the Vietnam war or the forces that shaped it. One thing he could not understand was the adversary role of the press toward the men who were fighting the war.

One night during the sixties Gordon came to dinner at my house in Saigon. It was a pleasant house in a pleasant neighborhood, only half a block from the palace. It was a long war, and I had decided to make myself comfortable.

Gordon asked me to explain the war to him. I tried, going into all the political and cultural complexities, but I could tell from the look on his face that I had lost him. My own doubts were all too apparent.

But if Gordon didn't understand the complexities of the Vietnam war—and perhaps I do him an injustice—there was one thing he understood very well: Never get into a war unless you intend to win it.

GORDON GAMMACK made three separate trips to Korea, just as he was twenty years later to make three separate trips to Vietnam. His initial trip to Korea extended from September 13 to December 8, 1950. Probably the most dramatic episode of that trip was the recapture of Taejon by the 24th Infantry. Grouped with that report of victory are some further observations of Korea and of the American fighting man's experience in what was described as "police action" and perceived as a peculiarly frustrating war.

TRIBUNE, OCTOBER 2, 1950.

TAEJON, KOREA, WITH THE 24TH INFANTRY (DELAYED)—A soldier trudging along the tank-clogged road shouted mockingly, "I shall return."

Another G.I. sang out, "I don't care what the old folks say, I'm going home today. I'm going to Taejon."

That was the mood of the men who had suffered such bloody and terrible defeat at Taejon last July as they neared what was once a city but which now is nothing but a mass of smouldering rubble still named Taejon.

With Hal Boyle and Associated Press Photographer Jim Pringle I entered Taejon with a column of rumbling tanks. We had edged our way along the last eight miles to Taejon while fighter-bombers—F-51s and jets—dropped down from the skies like falling birds and pummeled what was left of the Reds and their guns and tanks.

It was beautiful to see the planes streak in from the south and swoop down with devastating loads of bombs, rockets and the fierce fire bombs called napalm.

This was destined to be sweet revenge for the 24th infantry whose disastrous setbacks had saddened millions of Americans only three months ago.

The conquest of Taejon was executed so carefully that if there were any casualties at all they were negligible.

Iowa Colonel.

I had just entered Taejon when I saw Col. Ned D. Moore of Guthrie Center, who led the 19th Regimental Combat Team in the capture of the city.

There was grim satisfaction in his face when I first saw him, but a few minutes later there was both hatred and sadness in his eyes as he stood in the compound back of the Taejon police station.

Along the wall of this compound was a long slit trench filled with bodies. Colonel Moore walked up to a major standing nearby, and asked, "Are all these dead American boys?"

"No sir," said the major. "From the corner to the

shovel are South Koreans. From the shovel down to here are Americans."

"Good God," said Moore, and then he cursed violently. The major then pieced together the story of how some 30 or 40 G.I.s had been tied together and shot, then covered up with a thick layer of dirt. Two had survived by playing dead.

It was the mood of the day Thursday that transcended the capture of Taejon.

It was near Taejon that the beloved general of the 24th, Maj. Gen. William Dean, became lost while fighting with the desperate front line troops.

His aide, Arthur Clarke of Boone, said, "This is better going this way but I still can't forget that Gen. Dean still isn't with us. I'm going back to that spot near Taejon where I last saw him. He went down a hill to help the boys and just didn't come back."

The night before Taejon fell, I was in a dark tent with Maj. Forres Kleinman of Salt Lake City, and he was talking about General Dean.

"He was so kind," said the major. "Gee, what a kind man he was. He could be tough but he would take time in those awful days to ask me about my wife and whether she was going back to the states. He was so human, so kind."

So it was for General Dean and for the satisfaction of the remaining 24th-ers that the tanks and columns of foot soldiers moved on Taejon Thursday.

At dawn's first full light, as we moved up with the troops past barking artillery, fighter bombers whined overhead in an orbit while waiting for fluttering spotter planes to spot the targets. Then the fighters streaked off for the kill.

In Okchon, civilians said the Reds had taken everything, including wedding rings and watches.

Cheering Civilians.

As we moved closer to Taejon, civilians began lining the roads and raising their arms, allah-like and cheering.

Most of them undoubtedly were sincere, but we felt sure that the civilian clusters included some gooks who had been fighting us only a few hours before and had discarded their uniforms.

The closer we got to Taejon the greater the numbers of cheering South Koreans. They streamed from the hills through rice paddies to the roadside. Many carried South Korean flags.

One teen-ager came over to the jeep I was driving and said, "Thank you very much. I no speak English good, but thank you very much."

One civilian handed a flag to a G.I. atop a tank. The tank crews in a typical burst of American generosity showered down candy, cigarettes, and rations to the cheering groups.

The capture of Taejon was swift and easy, once tanks and troops had entered the city. As we neared the outskirts the men in the tank just in front yelled back, "They're halfway through the city already."

Soon after we entered the city Colonel Moore ordered a swift movement to take the airport about a mile away.

As we approached the airport, our fighter planes still were strafing it, but it was taken easily, and by the time we were driving back from Taejon the roads were clogged with all kinds of trucks, guns, and vehicles moving up in a blackout to consolidate the conquest in force.

REGISTER, SEPTEMBER 24, 1950.

Food Taken, Men Forced into Service

AT THE SEOUL FRONT—The story of the vicious ravages of Communist occupation of South Korea is now beginning to unfold—the story told by those who suffered through it at home and those forced into the Red army.

It is a story I can report thanks to traveling with Bill Hosokawa, former Des Moines Register copy editor, who converses in Japanese and is now a war correspondent for The Denver Post.

At Kimpo airfield we talked with An An Kei Shuka, former houseboy for the United States counter-intelligence chief, and an older man, Shin Yu Li, former chief of the airport messhall.

An told us, "When the Reds came I threatened death. The Communists demanded details on my boss, his work. I expected to be killed.

"The Communists took almost everything we had—food, clothing, household goods, even glass from the windows. In my small village a hundred men were conscripted for either the army or labor battalions.

"Many young men fled to the hills and are now coming back. The farmers were given rice quotas to meet. Our rice reserves were taken away.

"The Communists told us we could keep fruits growing inside our fences but they took everything else."

Hosokawa asked An what he thought of the Americans coming.

"My heart is so grateful I don't know how to say it." An replied.

People Happy.

"Even when your homes have been destroyed by American bombs and shells?" Hosokawa asked.

"That is so," An said. "Farmers, city people, all of us were happy to see the Americans come."

Shin, the older man, chimed in. "If you had delayed your invasion one month we would all be dead. There was nothing to eat. We waited patiently for your return. Now I am sure we will win."

An said Communists ordered the people to stay close to the villages but some slipped into friends' homes in Seoul and listened to radios hidden in dresser drawers.

"They were turned low and covered with quilts. That way they got news from Tokyo Radio that the Red drive was stopped."

Leaving An and Shin we started frontwards and soon saw a truck filled with Red prisoners. We climbed aboard. They squatted, hands clasped behind their heads, looking mostly expressionless.

Many looked extraordinarily young and some actually were as young as 14. Those with cropped hair were enlisted men. Those with longer hair were officers.

The marine M.P. standing guard said, "We shake 'em down, but them South Koreans really shake 'em down. They really give them a going over."

At the compound were many more prisoners, several of them badly wounded. One was barely able to walk because of a large wound in the buttocks.

The prisoners' clothing was fantastically ragged. Many were wearing what appeared to be dirty winter underwear.

Would Be Shot.

The team of Nisei interrogators said 80 per cent of the prisoners had not wanted to fight but would be shot if they failed to move forward.

Hosokawa talked with Um Guon Chin, who said, "I am a 33-year-old farmer and never fired a gun in my life. I was forced into the army. As soon as the Americans came I threw down my gun and surrendered. Not one in a hundred wants to fight."

Later while waiting to cross the Han river we saw two white-garbed Communists being led away. "They are political commisars," said Lt. Jim Costigan of East Paterson, N.J.

"A local South Korean cop here told me one of them killed his brother but told me 'I am a Christian man and can't kill him so I will turn him over to you.' "

REGISTER, SEPTEMBER 27, 1950.

D.M. Chaplain Finds Close Bond among G.I.s in Korea

WITH UNITED NATIONS FORCES AT TAEGU—The one light that shines through the sickening sordidness of the death and suffering of war is the kindliness of one man to another in the field of battle.

It is always thus—there is nothing one man won't do for another in an atmosphere where every moment may be their last.

I was riding in the back of a truck with a G.I. We were complete strangers, yet suddenly he asked, "You got plenty of cigarettes?"

A month from now, if the war is over then and that G.I. is returned to civilian life, he probably won't give a second's thought as to whether anyone is out of cigarettes, but in the zone where the Golden Rule dominates, he did.

I asked Maj. Stephen Kane of Des Moines, a frontline chaplain here, about this. A veteran of the 34th Infantry who was captured at Kasserine in World War II, he said:

"There is a bond among men who face hardship together that transcends anything I know. It is like the bonds of a family, and there will be a closeness among men who have fought together that will last as long as they live."

Father Kane says the men have fought well in Korea. He has seen men shaking with fright in battle, but he says the issue of cowardice has not been raised.

"It's a little different with this kind of army," he said. "Most of these men went into the army realizing there would be tough discipline, and they've followed orders without griping."

Kane reiterated the chief gripes I've heard among G.I.'s about relatively incidental items in the war—the shortage of writing paper, and official reference to the Korean war as "police action."

Talk Sarcastically.

When they are talking sarcastically about "police action," the boys often say things chaplains shouldn't hear.

REGISTER, OCTOBER 1, 1950.

Sweat, Toil for Soldiers Never Ended

FRONT LINES, KOREA—The instant I stepped from a plane at Seoul's Kimpo airfield I felt again that indescribable atmosphere that adds up to war.

There was the crack of our artillery belching out destruction; the sound of machine guns faintly in the distance; the sight of hills and plains, looking so quiet, and the wondering about who holds them, friend or foe.

And the soldiers—marines, in this case—weary from sweat and toil that seems never to end.

And the roar of trucks and armored cars and the great billows of dust they churn up. Everything moving with a grim purpose.

The men are caked with dust, and they do not look like men you have known in ordinary life.

Then, unexpectedly, comes that moment when you sense danger, killers nearby, and an awful feeling claws at your innards. There's the sweet relief when it passes.

And now your attention turns to the miserable innocents of war—the civilians who are tossed about like driftwood in a raging sea.

Looks of Hate.

Some of them stare at you as if they hated your guts—and well they may, because destroyers are never friends of the destroyed.

There was special pity aroused by the sight of Koreans standing in burned-out rubble that was once their homes, humble and drab as those hovels may have been.

In every war, little children are the same. They don't comprehend it and when the fury of it has passed them by they wave and smile and they want to be your friends.

They do it even before they learn that G.I.s love them, too, and will toss them gum and candy.

At home, on a rural road, you are annoyed when the car in front of you kicks up dust, but get yourself in a truck convoy along one of these Korean roads and you'll long for the Iowa country road.

The dust gets in your eyes and they smart and you can't open them. It drifts into your nose and throat, and it's hard to breathe. And if you're riding in the back of a truck there are bounces and bumps that seem to dislodge your insides.

But who can complain. On all sides are men putting up with the same guff.

And in this scene of war is the sad sight of men marching into battle. They do not do it willingly. What man wants to face death?

It is as though they were prodded by a bayonet, but actually, instead of physical force it is a general's command, and the consequences of refusal, and the inner compulsion for respect of a soldier's fellow man.

And so he plods on to take up man's most awful job. On each side of the road he slogs along, laden with his gear. Sometimes a weapons carrier comes honking down the road toward him, and in it is a man on a litter with a bloody leg sticking out.

Sometimes Choke Up.

These doughboys walk silently. When they do talk, they speak in simple, short sentences and if you talk to one and ask him about his folks back home, he sometimes chokes up and tears come to his eyes and he can't talk. So he walks on, hoping a forlorn hope.

In this atmosphere, it is only relatively better when you are winning. At its very best, it is a very, very sad and dirty story.

REGISTER, OCTOBER 21, 1950.

Gammack Tells of Paratroop Landing

ABOVE THE AIRBORNE OPERATION NORTH OF PYONGYANG—War can be beautiful, and I saw that beauty in the North Korean skies Friday. The operation was a two-pronged paratroop attack on Sukchon and Sunchon, roughly 25 miles north of the fallen Red capital of Pyongyang.

The purposes of the attack were to cut off escape roads north and a road linking the two towns and also possibly to liberate American prisoners reported in the area.

It may well have been ugly on the ground, but in the C-47 in which I was riding above the operation for more than an hour, the sight was one of the most beautiful and spectacular anyone's imagination can conceive.

It probably also was one of the most perfectly executed airborne operations in combat history.

The drop, involving 120 C-119 Flying Boxcars and C-47's, originally was scheduled for 7:15 Friday morning, but foul weather over the target necessitated postponements, first to 10:35 a.m. and finally to 2 p.m. sharp.

Circle over Pyongyang.

In order not to arrive too soon over the target, we circled over smashed and battered Pyongyang for about ten minutes. Then we headed for the first zone in the rice paddies one mile southeast of Sukchon.

Hal Boyle, Associated Press correspondent, suddenly yelled, "They're on the ground," and seconds later the ground below was dotted with parachutes—mostly khaki ones the brave paratroopers jumped with, but there was also a pretty pattern of yellow and blue and red ones that eased supplies down, and the big multiple white ones that held the big equipment like trucks and 105 millimeter guns.

Obviously the drop had been perfect. The chutes landed just where they were supposed to. Then we veered eastward and, lo, below us was a flight of 22 "Flying Boxcars," their silver glittering above the ground below.

And suddenly, as if by magic, there was a crescendo of opening chutes.

They looked like pretty, gay balloons floating daintily in the air.

I could see men dangling from the khaki chutes as they descended. Chutes by the score opened and filled the air.

Truck Breaks Loose.

I saw one weapons carrier truck break loose from its chute and plunge to the ground below. Then there was a fiercely bright flash on the ground, indicating the possible explosion of an ammunition drop. It looked so peaceful below for a moment, although it undoubtedly was not.

This drop zone was one mile due south of Sunchon. Soon then our eyes were filled with a scene of fire and death.

Fifty-one F-51 Mustangs came bursting down from the skies to smash the enemies of our paratroopers. First they caught columns of Gooks running north in clusters like mad near Sunchon.

[Gammack and his party then flew from the jump site to Pyongyang. Gen. Douglas MacArthur, after directing the paratroop operation from his plane "Scap" for an hour, also had flown to the air strip in the Red capital.]

As we reached the scene, General MacArthur was walking toward his plane with his arm around the shoulders of Lt. Gen. Walton H. Walker, 8th Army commander.

Both generals were smiling with deep satisfaction and gratification. MacArthur stopped to speak to Maj. Gen. William Tunner, commander of the combat cargo command that executed the operation.

"Magnificent performance you put on today," MacArthur said.

"My men were the ones who did it," replied Tunner.

"We know, but they had a fine leader, and I am recommending you for the D.S.C."

REGISTER, OCTOBER 22, 1950.

Combat Jump Is Goal of All U.S. Chutists

SOMEWHERE IN KOREA—When the average person rides in an airplane the only thing he fears more than death is the possible necessity of having to parachute to safety.

Yet most airborne troops in Korea will be disappointed and bitter if the Korean war ends without a combat jumping assignment.

What manner of young man is this who has such an unnatural feeling? In the first place, they are akin to the marines. Unlike the vast majority of army soldiers, they entered the service with the idea that their primary mission is to fight and maybe die. So they are tough not only physically but mentally.

This slant on the attitude of paratroopers comes from Maj. Francis L. Sampson, 37-year-old Catholic chaplain from Des Moines who was an airborne skypilot in Europe during World War II and who taught at Dowling in 1945 and 1946.

"Most of these boys are high school athletes who feel they must prove to themselves or someone else that they are above average. There is nothing more unnatural in the world than jumping out into space but it's what they want.

"They are extroverts in the extreme. They are very conscious of the special training they've had, and they'd hate to go home and admit they didn't get in on this war."

I asked Father Sampson if all this applied to him, too, and he said, "Yep, I'm afraid it does."

Too Much Time.

Chaplain Sampson said the only time there is any trouble with paratroopers is when they have too much time on their hands. "Then they start getting into trouble. But they're easier to work with than other soldiers. They're even easier to bawl out and so they are easier to control. Every one of these boys volunteered for this assignment. They knew they were going overseas and probably would make combat jumps."

I saw paratroopers toughening up in a field, and they slammed each other around viciously, yet they were laughing and clowning all the time.

Every move of their bodies bespeaks ruggedness, and they are utterly frank. I asked one boy what he would like to do first when he gets home, and he said simply, "Get drunk."

REGISTER, OCTOBER 25, 1950.

Misery Plays Major Role in Korean Life

SEOUL, KOREA—It was a Catholic airborne chaplain from Des Moines—Maj. Francis Sampson—who gave this description of Koreans:

"They are beasts of burden and their burden is life."

I have repeated this quotation to American correspondents who have been in Korea from one to five years and they all applaud it as extremely apt.

Koreans are a difficult lot to figure out but their life seemingly is based on a bitterly intense struggle for mere survival or, put another way, "for that bowl of rice." They seem to be people of few emotions and, unhappily, one of those emotions is cruelty.

The atrocities of the Korean war were not all committed by the Communists. The South Koreans have lots of blood on their hands, too. Again, Father Sampson:

"In a village near Seoul I came across a group of South Koreans murdering suspected Communists. I stopped them but I'm sure they kept right on after I left. Then I found a woman writhing on the ground. She had been shot through both feet. She carried a baby on her back and the baby was shot through both feet, too."

In Korea, policemen are generally a brutal group. Where an American policeman would tell a crowd to move away, the Korean policeman just slugs them back. And Dick Johnston of the New York Times told me that the following example is not at all uncommon. . . .

A citizen is stopped by a policeman and asked what is in his bundle. "Vegetables," says the civilian. "My vegetables."

"You're a liar," says the policeman and proceeds to beat the civilian. Through with the beating, he opens the sack and finds that it does, indeed, contain vegetables and so the officer demands half "for the trouble you've caused me."

Attempts have been made through American leadership to convince the Koreans they do not have to suffer such abuse from the police and a determined experiment was attempted along this line in a South Korean village. But then the civilians beat up the police and the police quit their jobs.

U.S. Interests.

Some American observers feel the Koreans will never accept democracy and they say that while Syngman Rhee has fascist tendencies he is actually very popular with the South Koreans. These observers, including the Times' Richard J. H. Johnston, insist the notion that Rhee is not popular has been fostered by American interests seeking to impose democracy.

Rhee, these observers say, is only typical of the "boss system" that is deeply imbedded in the Korean way of life. The boss of a Korean village, for instance, is the man who has reached the age of 65 and is the man in the community of greatest wealth. He is helped in this attainment by a long line of sons—sons who automatically assume the obligation of caring for their father.

And this demand for sons has made Korea a strangely moral nation. Because sons are so important there is a special sanctity to marriage, a marriage that will produce sons. Daughters are merely tolerated.

Koreans follow their "bosses" blindly, whether in a village, province or any other segment of society. Attempts have been made to eliminate this idea of blind obedience, too, but they have failed. When a democratic system has been imposed in a community the people merely go to their boss and ask, "What shall we do now?"

Probably because Koreans consider life such a dreary and unhappy business, they also are uncomplaining. I have seen hundreds of North Korean wounded and even those with the worst wounds offered no complaint or gave any sign of pain. They apparently just assume that pain is a part of life that's no good anyway.

An American in Korea is always depressed and sad that anyone in the world must live such a miserable existence. Squalor and nasty odors are everywhere. There is no joy in life, rarely even a smile. I am writing this on a plane bound from Seoul to Tokyo and I fervently hope I will never have to go back.

One significant fact about the war between South Korea and the Communists is that it is not entirely a civil war—South versus North—but actually a war between the Republic of Korea and the Communists. Thousands of the R.O.K. forces are actually North Koreans and when our forces advanced on Pyongyang, the Red capital, there were many R.O.K. soldiers who were marching home.

When Gammack returned to Korea in April of 1953, he focused primarily on the exchange of prisoners. But that did not preclude his continued interest in the war as it was being experienced day by day or night by night. In his sojourn with the 40th Division at the front lines he shared with the public an experience that was representative of the fighting man's frustrations and fears in the tedious stalemate of the Korean conflict.

REGISTER, MAY 14, 1953.

Story of Men Holding Line against Reds

WITH THE 40TH DIVISION, KOREAN FRONT LINES—This war is being fought at night.

In the daytime it doesn't stop entirely but it almost does. We throw some artillery at the Reds. They throw a little back at us.

But it's when night drops its blanket of darkness to deny observation of movement that each side moves cautiously against the other.

For a first-hand look at the night war, I spent a night on the front lines, with Charlie company. The San Francisco (Cal.) Chronicle's Jack Foisie was with me.

Late in the afternoon, in a steady not light rain, we started up the mountain toward razorback ridges of the northern rim of the fabulous Punch Bowl on the eastern front. On the steep banks by the roadside were flowering bushes, white and purple and lavender.

And then some 1,000 feet up we came to what they call the "Shooting Gallery." For about a half mile the road runs behind a camouflage net which, alone, denies the enemy observation of movement across it.

Now we were directly behind the MLR—the main line of resistance and to be able to visualize and understand the MLR is to understand, in large measure, the war that has been fought in Korea for many, many months.

Basically, the MLR is a trench that stretches along hill and mountain ridges across the entire 155-mile Korean front. There are a few breaks in that trench, but only a few.

Hold Line.

The bulk of the United Nations combat forces mans that line. And each soldier on it is responsible for one small section of it.

Right now our whole military purpose in Korea is to prevent the enemy from penetrating that strong line. In addition to the soldiers on the line are dug-in tanks and machinegun positions.

Running in front of the MLR are "fingers," trenched spurs or ridges in the rugged terrain and, down the slope toward the enemy, are outposts manned by soldiers whose mission is to intercept and fight off any enemy movements toward the MLR.

Just in back of the MLR are the sturdy bunkers, dug into the steep slopes, and it is here that command posts are located, supplies are kept and weary men sleep.

As we moved toward the battalion command post a heavy fog had dropped on the ridge and the rain had made the road muddy. We eased down a finger on the reverse slope and entered the battalion C.P.

We were greeted by Lt. Col. Robert B. Spilman, the battalion commander, a 1942 graduate of West Point and the son of Dr. and Mrs. H. A. Spilman of Ottumwa.

He was cordial and smiling but his thoughts were on the Charlie company patrol that soon was to go out.

We sat on boxes and ate with him—liverwurst, canned ham, toasted cheese sandwiches, rolls, raisin cobbler. They get good food to the men at the front in this war.

The phone rang and the captain answered and relayed a message to the colonel.

Good Start.

"That patrol wants to start out two hours early—with the fog they can get a good start before it gets dark—and they won't be seen," he said.

"That's O.K.," said Spilman, "But tell 'em that doesn't mean they can come in two hours early."

When chow was over we put our armored vests and helmets back on and Colonel Spilman said he'd show us the MLR. His primary purpose, though, was to check the patrol. Now the road was treacherously muddy and when we started up a short, steep hill we were blocked by a jeep coming down.

Mostly, before, there had been a quiet, reassuring smile on the colonel's face but now it disappeared and he stopped the oncoming jeep.

"Don't you know that vehicles coming up a hill in weather like this have the right of way?" he demanded sternly of the driver.

"You should have pulled off as soon as you saw us. Now do you understand the reason for it?"

"Yes, sir," said the driver.

"You see, if you force someone into the ditch and block the road you might hold up someone carrying something that's badly needed. O.K.? Do you get it? Then be about your business!"

Friendly, Precise.

As we passed G.I.s, the colonel called out, "Good evening," and "How are ya?" Here was the friendly, yet precise professional soldier demanding that things be done as they should.

The colonel led us up steep steps made of sandbags to the MLR trenches, the sides of which were lined with telephone wires. At one strong bunker built into the trench he explained, "This is where they bring the generals to have a look at the war."

He showed us an indenture in the trench that was an observation post. In front of us there was little to see but the fog.

"If the weather were clear," he explained, "it wouldn't be too healthy here. Those North Koreans have damn good snipers. They can shoot right between your flak vest and helmet and get you between the eyes. We've been losing some men that way."

In a platoon bunker, last-minute preparations were being made for the patrol. A Sergeant McCaskey was calling for a M-1 grenade launcher.

And he was testing the telphone connection to the mortar outfits. He kept whistling into the phone, three short whistles and a long one. If the patrol was going to need help from the mortars, by God, they were going to have it.

Checks Map.

Colonel Spilman checked the patrol route map with the leader, Lieutenant Robes. It was to be the lieutenant's first patrol and the colonel wanted to be sure.

"What checkpoints you got?" asked the colonel.

The lieutenant pointed to his map. "There's a mound there, sir. And a big black stone there."

"O.K. Good," said Spilman.

And then we went back to the road where the patrol was gathering. The patrol would be out more than six hours but it was going forward only a half mile.

The object of the mission was to try to make contact with the enemy North Koreans and also to spot paths that Red patrols might use against us. The patrol would go one-half mile into no man's land to a little knoll within hearing distance of the enemy.

The main patrol of nine men—Lieutenant Robes . . . a corporal named Red, the pointman who would lead the way . . . Red's pal, a Pfc. named Ralph, a 21-year-old with a drowsy face and a limp, blond mustache . . . a corporal named Bobby . . . a corporal named Pete, a small guy with a pock-marked face and heavy eyebrows, with a walkie-talkie strapped to his back and a submachinegun slung under his right arm . . . and four KATOUSAS.

A KATOUSA is a Korean attached to the United States army. On patrols the "buddy system" is used. One KATOUSA with each G.I. The G.I. can indicate orders to the KATOUSA and the ROK is vital for anything heard in the Korean language.

Obviously, Red was the take-charge guy. Even the young lieutenant would depend on his skill. If there was any fear in Red's soul, there was not the slightest sign of it. Even in the thickening fog, the red of his hair and mustache showed clear. His foxlike features stood out.

Marine Veteran.

He'd been a marine paratrooper for three years and now had finished three years in the army, much of it as a paratrooper. In action, he was terrific, a terror. Back in the rear (a sergeant confided) he wasn't worth a damn.

Which are the best soldiers—the North Koreans or the Chinese?

"The North Koreans are more fanatic, more vicious," said Red. "But the Chinese are smarter. They're better soldiers. Those North Koreans are --------s. I'll always remember one American officer I saw. The North Koreans cut his head off and then in his own blood, they put on a sign beside him, 'This can happen to you.'

"Then there was a G.I. the North Koreans caught. They slashed him across the legs with a bayonet, trying to make him talk. Then they had to take off in a hurry and they stabbed him to death in the stomach."

Red quit talking and checked his men's equipment. He opened ammunition pouches of the KATOUSAS to see that they had enough; sent two men back for grenades. Each man had two grenades clipped to his chest pocket. Red pointed to one expressionless ROK: "Here's a good man," he said. "He's kill crazy."

Except for Pete with his machine gun, each man carried a carbine, muzzles down to keep out the rain. And Red had a bayonet on his. Each man also had his pants legs bound with thin telephone wire.

"In weather like this," explained Red, "you do it so it won't make any noise when your pants get wet and brush against each other."

Now the fog was so thick you couldn't see more than 50 yards.

Just up the road from the main patrol was the support element—another group of nine men. The leader was another lieutenant on his first patrol. And again there were four G.I.s and four KATOUSAS.

Patrol's Function.

The support element would start out on a different route; would be in constant radio contact with the main patrol; would move to within 300 yards of the objective; would be ready to spring into action if the patrol ran into trouble, and would join up with the main patrol on its way back.

At 7:15 p.m., Red called to the patrol to form up. The time had come.

Colonel Spilman led us up to the MLR again and to an observation post. Dusk now was falling.

With Red in front, the patrol moved down the trench leading to the open. For a moment they were out of sight.

Then we saw them emerge beyond the barbed wire barrier and start down the steep hill toward the enemy. Against the fog only the men and barkless, lifeless scrub trees could be seen.

There was five yards between the men. Their gait was determined. There was no sound.

And then, one by one, the men disappeared into the swirling mist—and the deathly unknown.

REGISTER, MAY 15, 1953.

Tense Waiting as Men Go Out to Meet Reds

WITH THE 40TH DIVISION, KOREAN FRONT LINES—As soon as the night patrol started down the steep hill, toward the enemy, the Charlie company command post became, through radio and telephone, its guiding hand.

For all the skill and daring of the nine men in that patrol, their fate depended on the support and protection they would get from just behind the MLR—main line of resistance.

The Charlie company C.P. is a bunker, about 12 feet by 12. Its supports are thick, heavy timbers. Its walls consist of more logs and it is encased in sandbags. Probably, it could withstand almost any enemy shell.

(The saying at the front is that the more stuff the enemy throws at an area, the better the bunkers become.)

There are five bunks in the C.P., made of steel supports and rods and wire strung between them. Shelves and cupboards made from ration boxes, are against one of the walls.

In the middle of the bunker is a pot-belly stove. It is filled with burning wood and it is very hot.

Just to the right of the door leading into the bunker is the company commander's desk and beside it is his bunk. On a small shelf at the head of the bunk is a colored photograph of a pretty brunette and beside it is a colored newspaper reproduction of a painting of Jesus Christ.

A crude wooden table is the commander's desk.

Above it is a month-by-month calendar and the May sheet is decorated with a shapely girl in a very sexy pose.

"May's pretty good but June may be even better," quips the company commander.

He is 1st Lt. Charlie Dougherty—he pronounces it "Doggerty"—of Philadelphia, Penn. He has a pleasant Irish face, a little boyish, a jaw that juts out slightly and a closely-cropped crew haircut.

Right-Hand Man.

Dougherty's right-hand man and executive officer is Sgt. Jim Dunn, a soft-spoken army veteran from Columbus, Ga. His job usually is held by an officer.

Other men come and go and an armed guard stands always just outside the C.P. but tonight's work here will revolve around Dougherty and Dunn.

Dougherty's working tools are simple but vital. He has a basic map of the area and then a set of acetate overlays that pinpoint coded spots for artillery, mortar and other tactics in support of the patrol.

At easy reach are three telephones. On one he can reach, through his own switchboard—Charlie Switch—all the companies in the area, the battalion command post and regiment.

On another he can reach by telephone the support element of the patrol because it is trailing wire as it moves forward.

And on the third he can reach by radio the support element and, at least until it gets too far out, Corporal Pete and his walkie-talkie with the main patrol.

Dog Nan.

For this operation, the code name for Charlie company command is Dog Nan. It's Dog Nan Able for the patrol. And Dog Nan Baker for the support element.

The code for the battalion command post is blue and Lt. Col. Robert B. Spilman, of Ottumwa, Ia., the battalion commander, is Blue Six.

After we had seen the patrol start off on its mission, Jack Foisie of the San Francisco, (Cal.) Chronicle and I went to the Charlie company C.P.

About 8 p.m., 45 minutes after the patrol had started, Spilman telephones Dougherty, suggesting an artillery shoot on the patrol's objective—to shake up any enemy in the area.

"You don't think it will tip off what we're up to, sir?" inquired Dougherty, and then, after a pause, he says, "O.K. sir. Will do."

Dougherty picks up the radio phone and calls, "Dog Nan to Dog Nan Able. I want to fire ahead of you on your path. I want to warn you."

Dougherty presses the phone hard to his ear, trying to catch the reply.

"Dog Nan to Dog Nan Able," he says finally. I read (hear) you low and distorted. Call Dog Nan Baker and have them relay the message."

In a moment the reply comes back from the patrol: "Fire at will."

Fire on Position.

Sergeant Dunn is on the other phone to the artillery, "I think I'll have a mission for you," he says.

And in a moment Dougherty grabs the phone from Dunn and orders to the artillery, "Fire on position Savory Item . . . And give us an 'on the way', will you?"

Dougherty says to Dunn, "Pass the word he's going to fire two batteries."

The phone rings, Dougherty listens a second and then grabs the radio phone and calls, "Dog Nan to Dog Nan Able. Artillery on the way."

We can hear the distant crack of our guns from down the hill. The shells are whistling overhead, rifling toward their target.

Up to now Dougherty has been working without letup. But now the patrol must proceed on its own for a while and the company commander relaxes momentarily.

"How about a beer?" he asks—and Sergeant Dunn opens a trap door in a corner of the bunker—into a cool underground earthen compartment they call their "icebox" and brings out several cans of American beer.

Dougherty strips to his T-shirt. He takes small sips from his can of beer, handles some incoming calls and reports intermittently to Spilman's C.P.

He calls to the support element, "Did you people pick up a flare out there? . . . Left rear, eh? Well, keep your eyes open. It may be the gooks but it's probably a searchlight bouncing down from the low clouds . . . Hear anything from Able? . . . How long since you heard from them? . . . Well, maybe they can't talk."

Alert Area.

Dougherty is on one phone after another. He gets a call from Colonel Spilman and then reports to the company on his right: "The colonel tells me Easy company heard some noises and threw up some flares. Someone threw in some grenades. We threw in some mortars. Heard nothing since."

The whole area is intensely alert. Any noise, any light must be tracked down and explained.

The stakes tonight—and every night—are as high as life itself. Every enemy move must be stopped cold.

Dougherty takes another call and then he chuckles and says, "Well, the juke box is on again." That's the Reds' loudspeaker, playing music, popping off with propaganda and telling our G.I.'s to surrender and get good food and treatment.

Fifteen minutes later Dougherty gets another report on the "juke box."

"Yeh, we knew it," he says, "but we would have known it sooner if you'd called soon as you heard it."

A report on the patrol's position comes to Dougherty from the support element and he passes it along to Spilman.

"I'm just as satisfied he's moving that slow, sir," he concludes.

Red Fire.

About 9 p.m. we hear a metallic whine and a swish. It's gone in the tiniest fraction of a second and in the same breath then there's a shaking cr-r-rump not far away.

"That's incoming," says Dunn.

Twice more there's the whine, the swish and the whack.

"Jeez," says Dunn, "I hope they don't lower the range a bit. They're aiming at the line and goin' over. Thank God for that."

A moment later we hear two more explosions, not so loud as the others. Dougherty calls for reports on the enemy shells and then reports to battalion.

"Three down the hill behind our mortars and two to our left on Easy company . . . No, sir. No damage."

A G.I. messenger comes in with a report for Dougherty.

"Rough out there, eh?" inquires Dougherty.

"You said it, sir. Can't see a thing. Damn near went off the cliff three times."

"Good thing you didn't," says Dougherty.

"Yeh," says the G.I., "the jeep would cost me money.

On Position.

At 9:45 Dougherty gets a report from his patrol relayed from the support element.

"They're on position," he says. "We'll let them stay there an hour, then start back."

More reports come in. Dougherty calls to another outfit, "Tell the quad-50's to watch it. Our outposts are feeling the impact. Tell them to add five-zero." (Increase the range 50 yards.)

All the while the machine guns on our line are rattling a tattoo of fire into the mist, toward enemy positions—just harassing fire to keep the enemy nervous.

At 10:45 Dougherty calls Spilman.

"I think it's about time to call them back, don't you, sir?" he asks—and, with his superior's approval he picks up the radio phone.

"Dog Nan to Dog Nan Baker," he orders. "Tell him to come back and tell him for God's sake to come back slow. Move 10 yards. Stop. Check in every direction. Move 10 yards. Stop. Check in every direction. Tell him he's still got to get 36 points before he goes home."

Apparently, the patrol had no contacts with the enemy.

Now time drags. . . . Reports come in intermittently from the incoming patrol. . . . When they reach George Three, an inner outpost, they'll be safe. They'll go the rest of the way in a trench.

Finally, Sergeant Dunn puts down a phone and smiles.

"Five minutes more and they'll be in."

And then Dunn gets the word that they are in and he reports to Dougherty, "That lieutenant sounded so darn relieved he could hardly talk over that phone. And he was sure puffin', too, from comin' up that hill."

It is 1:30 a.m. when the patrol reaches the outpost.

Soon, Dougherty calls to have his jeep driver awakened. The patrol would come to an "eating bunker" a half mile down the road for the de-briefing. Foisie and I elect to go with him.

We wait in the wet blackness of the night for the driver. The rain is harder. The fog is so thick you can't see 10 feet.

We start on the treacherous ride. The jeep slithers and balks in the heavy mud. As we move along, never more than two or three miles an hour, Dougherty holds his flashlight down and spots it along the right side of the road.

We flirt with disaster. Inches away is the precipice and a straight drop of 1,000 feet.

On the left is a ditch that would trap the jeep.

Turns Edgy.

All night Dougherty has been utterly calm. Now he's edgy.

"Left!" he yells at the driver. "Left, dammit. Left! God, I don't want to get it THIS way!"

"I know, sir," pleads the driver. "If I got to do anything, I'd rather go in the ditch."

The trip seems endless. And along this road nothing is taken for granted.

Out of this mist comes the stern cry from a guard. "Halt!"

"It's Lieutenant Dougherty."

"Go ahead, sir," a voice replies and we see the vague form of a man on our left.

Then Dougherty sees two men slogging along the road toward us and their bunkers.

"Who are you?" he demands.

Part of Patrol.

"We're part of the patrol, sir," says one of them.

"Go to the eating bunker," says Dougherty. "You were told to do that."

Finally, Dougherty spots a familiar mark on the road and tells the driver to stop. "Here we are," he says.

We slip and slide down a bank and into the eating bunker. There's another pot-belly stove and around it, on benches are the men of the patrol. Through the weariness and grime etched in their faces, the relief that the nasty job is over shows faintly.

They bend over, their elbows on their knees and their chins cupped in their hands.

All except Red.

He's casually reading a magazine. He's scanning a cartoon strip showing a bear chasing a man and it's titled, "Bear With a Grudge."

Red closes the magazine. It's "Outdoor Life." And that makes him laugh.

"Hah!" he says.

"Cripes, it was dark out there," says Red's buddy, Ralph. "You couldn't see your hand in front of your face. We could have been five feet from the gooks and we wouldn't have known it and they wouldn't have neither."

Coffee and Cakes.

Coffee and cakes are handed out to the men. All of them take it eagerly but the KATOUSAS in two files wolf down the cake.

The two lieutenants of the patrol don't share in the coffee but stand to one side and report to Dougherty.

The tall lieutenant who led the support element tells Dougherty, "I didn't hear a thing but after two hours it seemed like every tree was moving in on us."

The men of the patrol seem eager to get to their bunks, but also their souls protested against slogging that last half mile to their bunkers.

Gradually, though, they pull themselves up from the benches and file out, into the night again.

To them, that night, the war that is idly called a "stalemate" was very real.

The truce talks in Korea and the subsequent exchange of prisoners of war were, as Gammack's editors were quick to point out, the "No. 1 world story." From Wilfred Burchett, an Australian Communist, Gammack learned that an Iowan was to be included in the first group of prisoners exchanged.

Gammack was perplexed by Burchett, who, according to Gammack's perspective on Communists, ought to have been untrustworthy and reprehensible but who proved himself a completely reliable source of information and an ingratiating colleague. The acquaintance and tentative friendship between the two journalists was to continue through their coverage of the war in Vietnam.

REGISTER, APRIL 14, 1953.

A Desolate Dot Circled by the War

PANMUNJOM, KOREA—The scene was incredible, fantastic.

Four miserable little straw-roofed huts on one side of a dusty road—on the other, a critical conference that could shape the course of world history.

I could look across the road at this dreary Korean landmark and see into the windows of an ordinary structure with fading yellow sides.

I could see the representatives of the United Nations and the Communists stand up in turn to state their views on the exchange of wounded and sick prisoners.

In front of this scene were the North Koreans with their expressionless faces and their rifles with fixed, thin bayonets—and the American military police with their shiny boots and glossy helmets.

And to the east and to the west were the sights and sounds of bombs and shells, the swoosh of diving jet planes and the rat-a-tat of machinegun fire, the crump and the bark of explosions.

This is Panmunjom—a tiny, protected finger that intrudes on a battlefield—a confused vista of peace talks surrounded by war.

My visit to Panmunjom Wednesday started really at the railroad station at Munsan, 13 miles away.

There is a parked train where correspondents sleep in triple-decked bunks. They rush through breakfast and climb into two trim army busses for the convoy trek to Panmunjom.

Ahead are jeeps with administrative staffers for the prisoner-exchange talks.

"Little Switch."

In clouds of choking dust, the convoy wends slowly around the endless bends—past crews working hurriedly to build compounds and hospital units for the sick and wounded if the exchange of prisoners comes true.

There is talk of "Little Switch," and "Big Switch," referring to the possibilities of first exchanging sick and wounded and then of freedom for all prisoners—and truce.

Even if all this ends in failure, we are preparing for the best—soldier carpenters are swinging their hammers.

Our convoy moves along the inviolate road beyond the front. On both sides are endless bands of barbed wire, part of our massive defense fortifications.

We see enemy fortifications, too—wide and deep trenches winding through the hillsides, and we know that Red troops are there.

And atop one rocky hill no more than 500 yards to our right is an Allied outpost from which the enemy can be spied upon. The convoy moves quietly but the sounds of shellfire roll in from both sides.

Panmunjom—a desolate dot in the landscape with a civilian population of zero—comes into view. Floating lazily above it are three barrage balloons, marking the one-mile-radius sanctuary of the truce-talk zone.

Our pilots call it "Holy Land."

Our group is carefree compared to the deadpan Red writers and observers. One American writer says, "I will say this is a great place to write a comic opera."

In the Red group is a slight man wearing a red and gray sweater and a red tie with white collar tabs awry. He is Wilfred Burchett, an Australian Communist foreign correspondent.

It seemed incredible to hear this man speaking refined English referring to the Red Chinese and North Koreans as "our side."

Helicopter.

He chats with surface friendliness with our correspondents, predicting a truce period.

Our top negotiators arrive by helicopter and go to the dark green tent to await the exact meeting time. The Chinese in long, mustard-colored coats and the North Koreans in heavy, dull green coats arrive by jeep and go to a light gray windowed tent with a light green door.

Precisely at 11 a.m. the negotiators file into the conference building from opposite doors, and the talks begin.

Some correspondents click stop watches to time the session. When recess comes, writers flock to get a statement from Admiral Daniel. There is a murmur of disappointment at his report. The Reds offer to return only 150 non-Korean sick and wounded prisoners.

And thus this day of prisoner-exchange talks proceeds. Finally the talking is finished until tomorrow, and we go our way and the Reds go theirs, clouds marking the divergent courses to the north and south.

But all around the rumble and roar of war go on and into another night of hope and fear.

REGISTER, APRIL 16, 1953.

No Warmth at Signing, Gammack Says

PANMUNJOM, KOREA—Signing of the agreement for exchange of sick and wounded prisoners was a cold, hard thing.

There was not the slightest trace of friendliness or even informality. Both sides dealt as fixed enemies.

From watching through the windows of the conference building and talking later with United Nations staff officers who were inside, I learned what happened at the historic signing.

At the precise meeting time Communist negotiators entered from the north, and Allied representatives from the south. Neither side recognized the other. There was no word of greeting, no nod, no smile. It has been that way for a long time.

When the truce talks started long ago, meetings started more informally. Greetings were exchanged. Then as the heat of the discussions mounted, cold formality increased. Greetings were replaced by polite nods. But even that ended, and the atmosphere has been steely cold ever since.

In the middle of the room is a long table with a baize green top (like that of a pool table). On it are small Communist and United Nations flags on standards. There also are ashtrays, pads and pencils, and that is all.

Saturday, as he had all week, Rear Admiral John C. Daniel, chief Allied liaison officer, sat in the center on the south side of the table, with Maj. Gen. Lee Sang Cho, chief Communist liaison officer, directly in front of him. Intepreters stood directly behind Daniel and Lee, who are the only persons to speak.

Speak Impersonally.

The negotiators speak most impersonally, speaking always of "your side" and "our side."

After a discussion of resumption of plenary sessions and a recess while the final drafts were checked, Lee said, "I propose to begin to sign."

Daniel replied, "I agree."

Then signing started, each signing six times, three copies for each side in English, Korean and Chinese.

Meantime there was a great clamoring outside by United Nations photographers. None were admitted to photograph the signing while the Reds admitted photographers with several cameras each. The United Nations admitted only two military cameramen.

It seemed strange that the Reds were willing to admit all correspondents, and our newsmen scoffed, "Fine thing, having the Communists as defenders of the free press."

Word of the signing flashed quickly down the line to the high command. In a tent near the conference room, a junior officer shouted into a phone, "Daniel signed at twelve oh eight, they signed at twelve oh nine, Daniel signed again at twelve oh nine and a half," and so forth.

Less Stubborn Haggling.

Staff officers who have been inside for the negotiations this last week say there is no perceptible change in the personal behavior of the Communists despite less stubborn haggling on terms. The Communist negotiators act as if they are only following closely the orders from above with no individual discretion.

I asked Admiral Daniel if they had been in any way difficult to deal with during the week. He replied, "No—there have been no real disagreements."

Certainly this is far different from the past. The exchange agreement was reached on the sixth day of negotiations whereas previously there had been 21 months of talks without achieving a cease fire.

Another sign of the relaxed Communist attitude is shown in the almost steady flow of mail being permitted to come from Panmunjom from Red prison camps. Capt. Albert Jones of Watertown, N.Y., Saturday picked up 1,774 letters from imprisoned

Americans. The letters soon were going statesward.

He estimates that about 10,000 letters from American prisoners have been released in the last three weeks compared to virtually none for the preceding 2 months.

Every day Jones hands the Communists more than 500 letters to American prisoners from home. He does not know whether they are delivered.

REGISTER, APRIL 17, 1953.

Gammack Gets Tip from the Reds

FREEDOM VILLAGE, KOREA—There is excellent reason to believe that at least one Iowan is among the sick and wounded prisoners of war to be exchanged by opposing forces here.

My information comes from Wilfred Burchett, Communist correspondent who has given newsmen at Panmunjom many advance tips and who has not been wrong on any factual information.

I am unable so far to determine the Iowan's name, home town, or the nature of his disability.

One day last week, on an outside chance, I asked Burchett, correspondent for the French paper "Humanite," to find out if any Iowans were in the group of prisoners to be exchanged. He chuckled and said he would find out what he could.

Saturday morning at Panmunjom I asked him, "Got my list?" He laughed, slapped his pants pocket and replied, "Right here." Then he added, seriously, "I can tell you this much. There is an Iowan."

A little later I took a private walk up the road with Burchett while other correspondents questioned Alan Winnington, another Red correspondent. Winnington, who represents the London Daily Worker, has come from the Red prisoner camp, talking with our ill and wounded prisoners as they make the trip south.

"A Fluke that I Found Out."

When I was alone with Burchett, I asked him for more information. He replied, "Actually, that's all I know and it's sort of a fluke that I found out that much.

"I was chatting with Winnington and I thought about you and asked if there were any Iowans. He told me, 'Why, yes, I chatted with an Iowa man on the trip down.' "

Later I asked Winnington for more information, but he declined further information on the grounds that, according to the Communist-United Nations agreement, no names would be released until Monday.

But I do trust Burchett's information. Last week he told an Associated Press reporter the breakdown by nationalities of the United Nations ill and wounded. Two hours later the figures were announced officially and he had hit it right on the nose.

If Burchett and Winnington should be wrong about the Iowan, it probably would be because of foreigners' confusion about our states, and maybe they thought that instead of Iowa I actually said Ohio or Idaho.

Winnington told a dramatic story about our ill and wounded coming from the prisoner camps. Their sendoff was celebrated by drinking Chinese wine. "I won't say it was champagne," he said with a grin. "There was lots of singing."

Winnington continued, "The fellows staying behind brought out banjos, guitars, mouth organs and other handmade instruments. The attitude of those staying was very good. Their morale went soaring because they felt that the departure of the sick and wounded is the first step toward their own liberation."

Many were so excited that they couldn't sleep at night, Winnington said, and some were slightly hysterical.

"There was lots of caution, too, because they had had false hopes before. Some of those leaving were sad to leave their buddies behind, and some cried."

If Winnington is right, the prisoners to be released are in pretty good shape. He said there were a large number of ailments, "really quite minor." He said there were very few litter cases and no psychos.

Most Can Be Interviewed.

His idea is that at least 99 per cent are fit to talk to the press. Among the ailments he mentioned were deafness, ulcers, high blood pressure and faulty vision. None is too ill for repatriation, he said. "All are anxious to get home."

Winnington hedged when asked about the breakdown of new and old prisoners. He said, "Quite a number were captured a long time ago and a good number were captured recently."

He also used this expression: "Many are well on the way to recovery." Winnington said the trip to the Kaesong area involved two overnight stops. The first night was spent in barracks-type buildings with wooden bunks, fresh mattresses and clean blankets. The second night was spent in heated tents.

In telling how the men are fed, Winnington hinted that the Reds are treating the men more generously in order to turn them over in the best possible condition for propaganda effect. He said they were fed mostly canned stuff, bread, hardtack, fruit and sausage. He added, "And I believe they were issued beer and port wine."

The walking wounded traveled in open trucks with the prisoners sitting on quilts. Litter cases traveled in trucks with canvas tops.

Winnington told us of another Red gesture. The sick and wounded G.I.'s who had had watches and other personal items stolen had them replaced just before leaving.

The Communists' receiving center, just north of Panmunjom, is fancier than the tent center where our men will be received. While ours is austere and utilitarian, theirs is marked with paths of white crushed rock. On the ground is a big star fashioned from red bricks and in the center a small fir tree has been planted.

Chinese laborers still were busy policing the area Saturday to make it spic and span.

Back here at Freedom Village behind our lines the stage is set for the dramatic exchange.

Every imaginable preparation has been made. And now there is tension and excitement in the air as everyone awaits the stroke of 9 a.m. Monday (6 p.m. Sunday, Iowa time) when the Communists are scheduled to open the "Freedom Gate" for sick and wounded prisoners.

Symbolic Name.

Freedom Village is just a symbolic name. Actually it is a tented hospital—the 45th MASH (mobile army surgical hospital).

It is beside a sloping road, and below are banks dotted with freshly blooming yellow forsythia. On the other side of the road are scrubby, dust-coated pine trees.

Inside the large tents where liberated prisoners will be brought immediately are neatly made-up rows of cots. Atop the khaki blankets on each are a maroon robe and white canvas slippers. By each bed a pair of bright blue pajamas, a white towel and a washcloth are stacked.

It is here that the sick and wounded will be examined by the medics. The hope is to rush each man through and have him en route by helicopter to the 121st Evacuation hospital at Yongdongpo near Seoul within a maximum of 20 minutes.

REGISTER, APRIL 20, 1953.

Iowan Tells Gammack of Life in Prison

FREEDOM VILLAGE KOREA (MONDAY)—Flashing as happy a smile as you ever saw, Cpl. Richard O. Morrison, 22, of 1001 S. Fifth st., Burlington, arrived at Freedom Village this morning.

He was in the first ambulance arriving here from Panmunjom after the exchange of ailing prisoners of war. He looked a trifle weary but said he felt fine.

"I am so happy," he said.

Morrison was captured Dec. 1, 1950, while serving with engineers of the 2nd Division.

He said his ailments were nearsightedness, high blood pressure and "I couldn't stand greasy food."

Broke His Glasses.

One of the greatest handicaps for him was that he broke his glasses shortly after his capture and they were never replaced.

I only had time for a brief interview with Morrison, but he indicated there had been some recreation for the prisoners. They had a playground and were able to play baseball with equipment provided by the Reds.

I asked about food. He grinned, "Plenty rice."

He said to tell his folks he is fine and not to worry. But when I asked him if he wanted to write a message, he replied:

"I wouldn't know quite what to say."

He said the Allied prisoners ran their own kitchen, handled sanitation and kept up the playground. He said the prisoners organized religious groups and held meetings.

No Chaplains.

Morrison said there were no chaplains in his prison camp, but "we had church services every Sunday and I think they held Bible classes every day."

He said soldiers who had Bibles were not required to give them up.

Morrison said there was no "forced labor" in his camp.

The P.O.W.s, he said, lived in Korean-style houses heated by wood. He added that he believed letters were censored by the Reds because they "were opened when we received them."

Morrison said that at the time he was captured there was "no medical treatment."

Speaking of his wounds, he said, "I just remember running into a clump of trees and there was a big flash."

Asked if the Communists tried political indoctrinations, he said "yes," but the censors would not let him enlarge upon his comment.

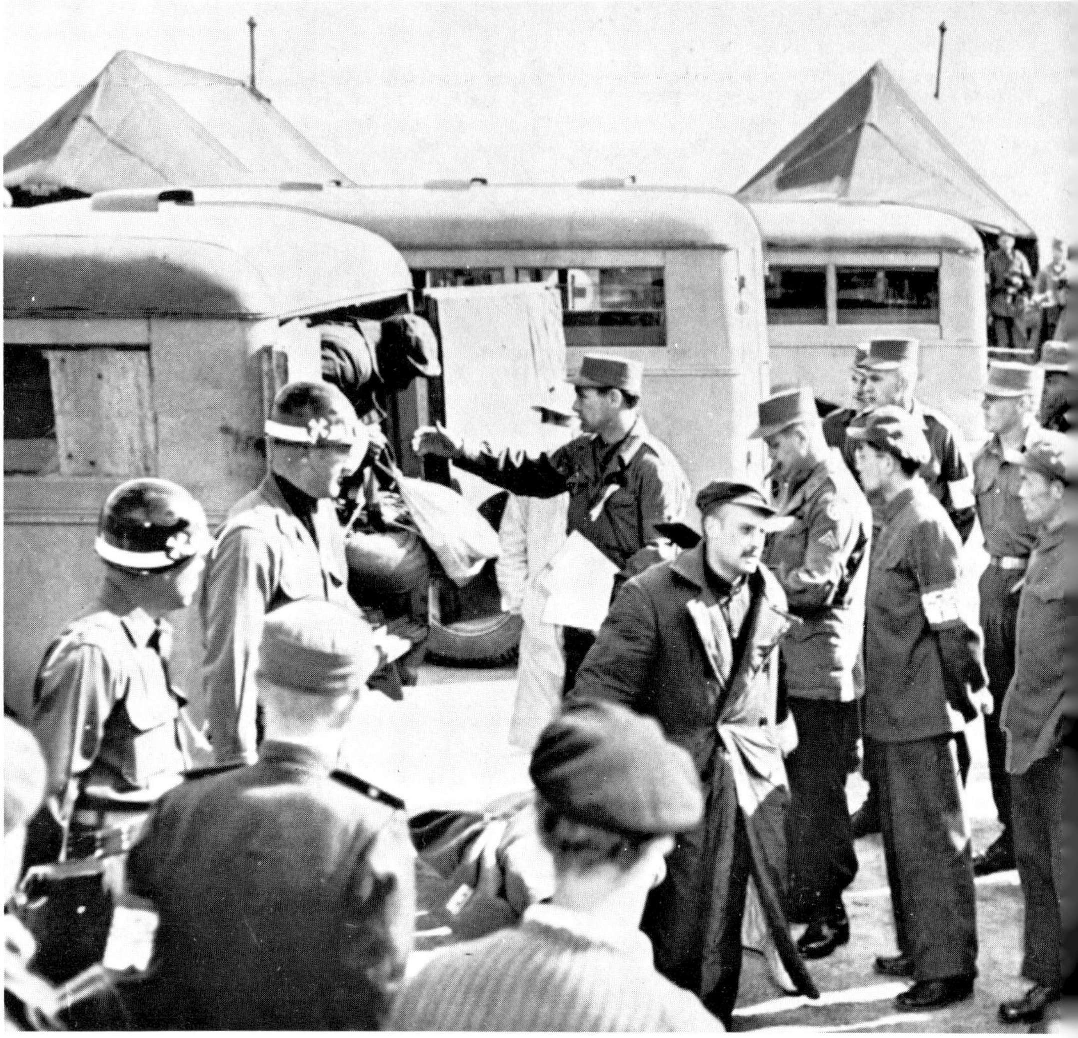

APRIL 22, 1953. Exchange of prisoners at Panmunjom. While U.N. and Communist officers watch, a U.N. soldier is lifted from a Communist ambulance. Another returned prisoner, able to walk, is moving toward the U.N. tent (right) for first step in processing. *(AP)*

In reporting on "Little Switch," the exchange of ill and wounded prisoners of war, Gammack emphasized for the first time in his career a gap between the official information released by military authorities and the information he was able to gather on his own. He saw his responsibilities shift from relating information to investigating independently what was really going on. The disquietude he expressed in Korea prefaced his determination in Vietnam to develop and utilize a private network of information sources.

TRIBUNE, APRIL 23, 1953.

'Much More' to Delay on Interviews

TOKYO, JAPAN—Evidence makes it increasingly clear that there is much more to the delays in interviewing exchanged war prisoners than the official claims that they require further medical processing.

Other correspondents and I, maintaining vigils at two army hospitals here, are satisfied that medical

officers have been told by higher authority to take the responsibility for delays on medical grounds.

From mutterings among enlisted personnel around the hospital, you gather they have heard enough to convince them that this is the true situation.

I heard one non-commissioned officer say to another, "There are more intelligence officers in this hospital than patients."

Change.

This implication was that sick and wounded returnees are spending more time being talked to and questioned by intelligence officers than in medical examinations.

Twenty-four hours ago I was impressed by the convincing statement by Col. James B. Stapleton, 8167th hospital commander, that medical considerations alone were responsible for the delays, but reliable information obtained meantime refutes this.

At Freedom Village only a few returnees were kept away from newsmen, but in Tokyo only four have been available for interviews so far although two more rejected the chance to be interviewed.

The whole situation has resulted in wisecracking comments to the effect that the returnees still are prisoners.

Even so they are being treated as VIP's (very important persons). They get to eat whatever is available at the hospitals.

Most of them are eating steak after steak.

There is much mystery about the delays. Every time I call the hospital to ask about Cpl. Richard Morrison's availability, the answer is, "He is not available yet. We can't tell you anything else. We have no idea when he will be available." Morrison is from Burlington, Ia.

Wednesday night one officer said, "A friend of his is also waiting to see him. Chances for tomorrow are good."

But the persistent reply Thursday was, "Still unavailable."

Contrast.

There is a striking contrast between statements made by medical officers at Freedom Village that the men are in surprisingly good condition and the repeated pleadings of army spokesmen here that this is not necessarily true.

Take the case of Morrison. When I saw him at Freedom Village he looked weary but reasonably robust under the circumstances.

His only health complaints were that he had headaches because of his eyes, high blood pressure and that greasy food makes his stomach burn.

Yet he has been incommunicado ever since.

There is speculation that the army brass may be disturbed by the lack of bitterness about prison treatment. There are growing signs that by oriental standards, of the men returned to Japan so far, treatment was not intolerable, at least in many cases and at least in recent months. However, it should be recalled that the Communists released the "most healthy" of the ill and wounded first.

REGISTER, APRIL 26, 1953.

Finds Army Deception on Interviewing P. W.s

TOKYO, JAPAN—Solemn dignity was etched in the scene—a young marine seated in a wheelchair.

Under the glare of floodlights fine beads of sweat made his face moist and glistening. His left pajama leg lay limp against the chair. Below the knee stump the right pajama leg also was limp.

With a soft smile he said, "Yes, I've always had pain—ever since it happened—except since I was freed. Then I was too excited to feel it, I guess."

There was dignity, too, in the quiet calm of Pfc. Raymond Medina, The Bronx, N.Y., as he told how he had long hoped to go to college but his elderly parents now need his support, how prisoners melted toothpaste tubes to make crude crosses and put them around their necks in defiance of the heathen Reds.

And then for emphasis he wagged his finger before the television camera and said, "If any God-fearing Americans are listening, stay away from Communism. It's no good."

There is dignity in every returnee but there is no dignity in anything else in the Tokyo scene of returned sick and wounded prisoners.

It is a bizarre combination of Hollywood settings, comic opera overtones and a labyrinth of official deception.

In the room where returnees are brought for interviews are camera directors crying, "Let'er roll; let's try that again; say that again, Joe; talk louder, will ya?," et cetera.

Scurry Around.

Japanese technicians scurry around with tape measures, extra lights and sound devices. The returned G.I.s fidget nervously with their fingers, glare uncertainly into the strong lights, grope for words that won't offend intelligence officers who apparently have coached them on what to say.

It is production business to the point where one marine was brought to the interview room two hours late while the military interview planners awaited arrival of a one-star general.

Medical and public information officers told so many lies about the delay in permitting interviews—on stern orders from above—that the lack of expression on their faces seemed to say, "This isn't true. I know it and you know it, but that's my story and I'm stuck with it."

One officer told correspondents the absolute direct opposite to what I had chanced to hear him say over the phone 10 minutes before.

Mysterious Trend.

The interviews also are taking a somewhat mysterious trend. Word filtered down from the wards where the returnees are virtually prisoners that one man had a strong anti-Communist story about mistreatment by the Reds when he was badly wounded right after capture—how though his leg was shattered his captors threw him into the street when he refused to give military information or say anything good about Communism.

Instead he told his captors, "I don't believe anything you say—America is my country."

And he told in the ward how he was kept in a tunnel for four days while gangrene ravaged his wounds. Yet when newsmen asked questions directly, opening the way for this story, he said nothing about it.

The same returnee on a mimeographed form answered a question about treatment with, "Awful—worst possible."

When asked the same question during an interview, his reply was, "I would not say it was bad or good—just poor."

Later he said he withheld his story because he thought that if it were used and associated with his name it might result in retaliation on his buddies who still are imprisoned.

He said he was not told by intelligence officers to withhold it. Apparently the returnees' primary thought is not to tell anything which will hurt their friends still imprisoned.

Just what the high brass is up to is the subject of much speculation. While there is obviously a clampdown here, returning correspondents say that returnees talk comparatively freely at Freedom Village.

In the corridors of Tokyo hospitals are streams of officers, captains through colonels, with infantry and artillery insignia. What they are doing in medical installations is obvious—they are members of intelligence teams going over the returnees with fine-tooth combs.

Everyone concedes the whole situation is delicate at this time, but instead of official requests for cooperation with a general explanation of the situation, correspondents have been told a succession of apparent falsehoods.

The clamps are so tight that I was told that two simple notes about returnees not remotely involving security must go "through channels."

Evidence is now growing that some men freed in the first groups Monday may be closed off from the outside world for many days—may even be shipped statesward without notice.

In August 1953, Gammack made his final trip to Korea to cover "Operation Big Switch," the exchange of well prisoners of war. The stories he heard from returned American prisoners and reported to his readers were, in part, the stories of atrocities imposed by the enemy. But they were also, in part, the story of treacheries done to Americans by other Americans and of the occasional erosion of American will.

The contrast between the behaviors of the "good guys" and the "bad guys" was not nearly as clear as it had been at the end of World War II. One indication of that change was in the emotional responses of prisoners to the exchange. Observing the stoicism of Chinese Communist prisoners, Gammack speculated on the "unrestrained joy" that would characterize their American counterparts. But four days later, when liberated U.N. soldiers had begun to arrive at Freedom Village, Gammack reported on the dulled senses and emotions that characterize men who have suffered long captivity, regardless of their political allegiances.

And as he talked with released Americans in the following days and weeks, Gammack observed that, far from uniform, the responses of Americans had run the gamut from heroism to cowardice.

REGISTER, AUGUST 2, 1953.

Hate in Their Faces, Gammack Reports

ON ROAD TO PANMUNJOM, KOREA—Behind barbed wire fences, Chinese Communist prisoners of war squatted on the ground—with knees near their chins, in peculiar Oriental fashion.

There were some 600 of them, and the faces of most were a combination of glumness, hate and disinterest.

Three or four were stripped to their shorts, because they ripped off their outer garments in a defiant propaganda scheme against the United Nations command.

They cut holes in their clothing with sharp rocks, then help each other rip the garments to shreds whenever U.N. guards aren't looking.

These Reds were only days from freedom, yet if there was joy in their hearts, either their deadpan faces or stoical allegiance to the Red propaganda line concealed it.

Some miles to the north are the first of American prisoners to be liberated Wednesday. And you don't have to be with them to know that joy—perhaps unrestrained—is written on their faces and their fervent daydreams of home are uncluttered by political dictates of their government.

As I saw Chinese prisoners in impassive huddles, I wondered if here wasn't unfolded the sinister nature of Communism—these men on the threshold of liberation ripping their clothes in blind obedience to political masters.

TRIBUNE, AUGUST 6, 1953.

Dulled Senses and Emotions

FREEDOM VILLAGE, KOREA—There's a look in the eyes of liberated U.N. soldiers like that of a man who has been in a terrible auto accident and suddenly learns he's the only one who came out alive.

That's the description of Navy Lt. Richard Paul of 7004 Sunset Terrace, Des Moines, medical officer who's checking the health of freed prisoners.

He also says the men have flattened emotions and dulled senses.

"That's why they don't seem more exuberant—why they don't show joy as men their age should under such a situation. They've been so thoroughly shaken that they don't respond to their environment. They've had pretty poor care and they've had to keep their emotions in check for so long."

Paul says he's seen the same type of reaction among casualties after brutal battles.

"Last month, when the marines replaced the 25th, one of our outfits was thrown into a fierce fight at Berlin outpost in pouring rain. They had no sleep for more than 48 hours. The Red artillery was terrible.

"When I saw the wounded from this battle, they had the same flattened emotions. There was no emotional response, not even to pain. It didn't take long for them to get over it but with these liberated men it will take longer."

But Paul thinks that except for the seriously wounded cases the overwhelming majority of freed men will be restored to full physical, mental and emotional health. They'll even be vastly better by the time they get home, and reunions with loved ones will speed their full recovery.

Paul believes the health of all prisoners has suffered, mostly from the effects of malnutrition, including chronic boils and skin rashes. But a good diet will quickly correct that.

"They probably all have worms, too," said Paul. Quite a few cases indicating tuberculosis already have come through, and there'll be more, but Paul believes there'll be complete cures—or "arrested," to use the correct medical term.

When the G.I.'s are first freed there are seemingly restrained smiles on most of their faces.

But except for the emotional Turks, there are no exuberant demonstrations, no kissing the free soil, and virtually no weeping for joy.

By the time they complete the 13-mile trip to Freedom Village, they seem primarily bewildered but pathetically anxious to please.

REGISTER, AUGUST 9, 1953.

G.I. Tells Gammack of Yank 'Informers'

FREEDOM VILLAGE, KOREA—The men who have been left behind—that is one of the big stories that is developing after the first four days of prisoner exchange—Big Switch—in Korea.

They fall into three categories.

There are those who are dead—probably more than 7,000. They died during unbearable death marches after capture under the North Koreans or they died of disease, wounds or starvation in the first year of the Korean war. Or they died in battle and their bodies have never been recovered.

There are those who, according to reports from first repatriates, are being held in far North Korea on trumped up charges of "instigating against peace."

Finally, there are those who reportedly have elected to reject their natural heritage and stay behind Iron and Bamboo Curtains.

Men Without a Country.

First reports from liberated men indicate there are at least seven Americans who have elected to cast their lot with the Communists.

And implications are they are cowards about to find themselves men without a country.

I heard about three of them Saturday—mainly from a baldish G.I. who talks with a northern accent yet lists his address as Columbus, Ga., because his wife now lives there. He is Pfc. Louie Leach.

Determined fury started building in the eyes of Leach as he talked about the informers.

"They did everything they could to hurt us," he said bitterly. "They were stool pigeons. They would run to the Communists with every bit of information against us they could get. We hated their guts."

Then I asked Leach, "Do you think that these informers are staying behind because they are afraid of retaliation from the loyal men?"

"You're damned right I do," snapped Leach. "I know men who'd give their lives to get them and they won't rest until they do. Our men told 'em if they ever got on the same ship with them they'd dump 'em overboard."

This was the judgment of a man who had been in misery against weak men who had made his misery worse.

Undoubtedly some of the "informers" have been among those who have been liberated or will be freed soon. Undoubtedly they will be marked for life in the eyes of the men who risked and got punished for standing firm.

Steadfast Men.

I'm curious, for instance, about one of the obviously steadfast men—Cpl. Donald Sherrick of Sioux City.

I learned from a thoroughly reliable source that as soon as Sherrick arrived at Freedom Village he said, "I want to talk to an intelligence officer. I've got something important to tell him."

Correspondents are agreed that many of the liberated men have stories in their hearts that they are not telling publicly for the moment. They may be biding their time.

By and large, the nobility of the great majority of liberated Americans is shining through in these first days of the exchange.

I think, for instance, of the savage-like Communist prisoners who have hurled away their clothes, beat their fists against the ground, thrown crutches and canteens at United Nations officials.

And then I think of Lt. Col. Tom Harrison, a jet pilot who lost his leg when he was downed by enemy fire, and the touching story he told how friends made an artifical leg from pieces of wood, leather and metal and even a hinge from a North Korean door.

And how the Communists tried to make him talk—by the medieval water treatment—clamping his head back and putting a wet towel over his face and nose and adding water to it until he couldn't breathe and passed out.

And how then his North Korean captors revived him by thrusting lighted cigarettes onto his body.

Ask yourselves, in the quiet of your homes that remain peaceful, thanks to such men, whether you would have the determination to deny the enemy information under such torture. I asked myself—and the answer was no.

Connived Charges.

Another group apparently being punished for their persistent loyalty comprises those who are reported to have been tried and jailed on connived charges of instigating against the peace.

In their mystifying way, the Reds have plucked them from hundreds of other loyal prisoners and framed charges against them. But strong hopes persist they will be freed before the exchange is completed.

We have now heard that some of the men given jail terms have arrived at Kaesong, seven miles north of Panmunjom, and may be liberated soon.

For the loved ones of the several thousand who are listed as "missing in action" but who long have been dead there will be no joy, no solace, from this unique truce and prisoner exchange.

TRIBUNE, AUGUST 10, 1953.

Freed, Iowa Men Tell of Mass Death

FREEDOM VILLAGE, KOREA—The tragic story of mass death in a Communist prison camp by the banks of the Yalu river was told Monday by three Iowans.

They are Sgt. Kenneth R. Darrow, 23, Charles City; Sgt. Gordon Schmitz, 22, Le Mars; and Cpl. Dale L. Reeder, 25, Waukon. They said between 1,600 and 2,200 G.I.'s died in the bitter winter of 1951.

"I know there are two hillsides filled with our boys," said Reeder. And no matter what access the United Nations may have to those hillsides in the future, there is little likelihood that there will be recovery of identifiable bodies.

Fear.

"Bodies were just dumped in big holes, three to six bodies in a hole," said Reeder.

"Most of them didn't even have dogtags. They just covered 'em with dirt."

Schmitz told of the terrible fear every man had that he would be next.

"Every night you wondered whether you'd be alive by morning," he said. "Many times I'd wake up to find a buddy beside me dead."

Another Iowan with whom I talked Monday, Lewis Gordon, 24, of Webster City, said his best buddy died because the Reds refused to give him medical care.

"They tried to get him to sign a propaganda peace petition," said Gordon. "He refused, so they wouldn't give him medical treatment. If they had, he'd be alive."

Stool Pigeons.

The Iowans are bitterly angry toward the prisoners known as "progressives," who played ball with the Communists.

Schmitz, Darrow and Reeder all said the "progressives" they knew were among the first men liberated, although emphasizing that the majority of the first repatriates were loyal.

It is likely that these "progressives" have been pinpointed by army officials.

This raises the possibility that this is the reason so many have been unavailable for interviews at Inchon.

It also raises the possibility that hostility will flare openly on the ship that is to return the P.O.W.'s to the states.

In prison the loyal men were known as "reactionaries." They didn't dare retaliate against the "progressives." The result would have been dire punishment. They could only shun the "pros" and, as Darrow put it, "We just didn't have a damn thing to do with them."

But now these men are free and at least can get off their chests the hate that has been in their hearts these many long months.

"Those 'pros' better not say anything to me," said Darrow. "They did everything they could to hurt us.

"The Chinese found out things about us they couldn't have learned from anyone else. The 'pros' were dirty lousy stool pigeons."

"There'll sure be some retaliation," said Gordon.

REGISTER, AUGUST 17, 1953.

Survival of P.W.s Called a 'Miracle'

FREEDOM VILLAGE, KOREA—It is almost a miracle that so many American prisoners of war survived the ordeal of Communist barbarism, cruelty and inhumanity.

Take the case of Pfc. Robert T. Kohl, 24, of Lisbon, Ia. He was captured Feb. 13, 1951, in "Massacre valley."

He was in a convoy blocked on a road when a tank ahead of him was knocked out.

"It was at night," Kohl said, "when we went into the mountains. We walked all night trying to go south. But next morning at 10 o'clock the Chinese spotted us.

"They moved in from all directions. There were too many of them. We could do nothing but surrender."

Four-hundred G.I.s in Kohl's group who started the march didn't make it.

"They were just too weak to keep going," said Kohl, who was released by the Reds Sunday. "Chinese guards kept making us go faster. They beat us when we couldn't, jabbering in Chinese at us all the time.

"They beat me with a club three times. Three guys tried to escape. The Chinese tied their hands together and hung them from a log so they had to stand on their toes.

"They kept them that way all day. When it was over those poor guys were almost dead.

"They accused us of all kinds of crazy things, like signaling our planes. They made us hold our hands out, palms up. Then they beat our hands with heavy boards."

Kohl said if he had known that the worst was yet to come he wouldn't have had the will to keep on.

He was in a group of 700 G.I.s who started the march Apr. 25 from Bean Camp 7 to Camp One at Chongson. Only 300 were left when the march was finished on May 17, and many of those 300 died later in camp.

Kohl said, "We just trudged along, always wondering who would be next to die.

"I kept praying I'd live to see my wife and kid again. One night I tried to escape. I never should have tried it.

"But I tried—God, how I tried. I had no socks and got terrible blisters from rubber shoepacks. Every step was torture.

"Dark Cave."

"I only got 3 miles. The North Koreans spotted me. They threw me in a dark cave. Once in a while they threw me a ball of rice.

"Sometimes Koreans came by and stared at me kinda' like a monkey looks at you. They saw me tied with my arms behind me and they took me away."

I asked Kohl what he thought about while miserably alone in the cave.

"Nothing—nothing at all," he said. "I was too low. I didn't care. I thought sure I was going to die."

Kohl's misery continued at Camp One. He had dysentery and "fever in my feet—don't know what it was. But the pain was awful."

He weighed 209 pounds when he came to Korea. He got down to 135.

"We were all skin and bones," Kohl said. "They gave me size 32 shorts and they wouldn't stay up. They slid down my thighs. The Chinese treated us like dogs. They called us warmongers, rapists and all that stuff.

"Then when the truce talks started, things got better. They made us go to lectures but we just sat there. Everything went in one ear and out the other. Most of us, that is.

"Some guys fell for their line."

Grew Stronger.

Gradually Kohl grew stronger in body and spirit. And he longed for freedom. Rumors constantly swept through the camp raising false hopes.

"We heard Americans had started a push and thought they might liberate us. When one of our planes would fly over, for a few days afterwards we'd try to make ourselves think it meant the truce was signed."

As Kohl became a free man he appeared surprisingly strong, bronzed from the sun, clear-eyed and steady. Now he's longing to see his wife, Eloise, and his 3-year-old boy, who was only 3 months old when Kohl last saw him.

Another Iowan who endured unbelievable hardships was Pfc. Glenn Carico, 28, of Route 5, Des Moines. He somehow lived through another cruel Communist march.

Two months after his capture he was in "mining camp" when he became dreadfully sick. "I was so weak I couldn't even stand up," Carico said. "For 10 days I just lay in the hut. I couldn't eat. My appetite was gone.

"Buddies would bring me food and try to get me to eat, but I couldn't. Two other guys in the hut with me were sick and too weak to get up.

" *One night one of them died. The next night the other one died. But friends always stayed with me, trying to lift my spirits.*

"I just lay there all the time thinking about my wife and boy and my folks. I thought sure I'd never see them again.

"I prayed, but I thought sure I'd die. It was just a matter of time. Then all of a sudden I started feeling better, but the Communists never gave me one bit of medical care."

Carico will never forgive the "stool pigeons" in his camp.

I asked him if he planned revenge.

"If I ever run into one of those squealers I don't know what I might do," he said.

REGISTER, SEPTEMBER 3, 1953.

P.W.s Lost Will to Live, Simply Let Themselves Die

FREEDOM VILLAGE, KOREA—Americans in Communist prison camps who lost the will to live often perished according to their own timetables of death.

This is the story told Wednesday by the first two American medical officers liberated—Capt. Clarence L. Anderson, 30, of Creston, Ia., and Capt. Sidney Esensten of Minneapolis, Minn.

The doctors told how hundreds of men, weak from lack of food and cruel treatment, had accurate premonitions of their deaths.

They told how time after time men would say, "Don't bother to wake me in the morning. I won't be able to get up anyway. I'm going to die."

"The strange thing is," said Anderson, "in the morning they would be dead."

No Organic Cause.

Said Esensten, "When men talked like that I'd listen to their heartbeat with my ear and use a spoon for a tongue depressor to look in their mouths.

"There was no organic reason why they should have died. But for many months now I've been wondering how much the mind has to do with life or death of a human being."

Esensten recalled caring for a 19-year-old G.I. with dysentery.

"He refused to get up," said the doctor. "He wouldn't take care of himself. He just lay in his own filth and wouldn't do anything about it. I couldn't persuade him to try to live, and God knows I tried. Finally I got exasperated and told him he had to fight for life. He said to me, 'Doc, you can't make me live.'

"I left this boy to look after another sick man. Two minutes later I turned around, and the boy was dead. He shouldn't have died."

Anderson and Esensten told of the Communist attitude toward them as doctors. One time the two doctors professed interest in a Russian operation and requested information about it.

The Communist leader told them, *"It's not important for you to learn medicine here. The important thing for you to learn here is about Communism.*

"When you go home and your country is finally liberated you will go to school again and learn who to save and who not to save, who to treat and who to cure—not what to treat or cure."

Accused Doctors.

Anderson and Esensten said the Communists used the offer of medical care to woo American prisoners.

"If a man refused to play ball he got no medical care," they said. "They'd win some over with medical care, then conspire to make them work to the detriment of fellow prisoners."

The Communists accused Anderson and Esensten of deliberately letting G.I.s die so the Chinese would appear to be responsible and make them look bad.

PART 3

Vietnam

(FEBRUARY 1970-1973)

JULY 12, 1968. U.S. Marines walk toward pickup point for last convoy out of the deactivated combat base at Khe San, South Vietnam. *(AP)*

Introduction

BY Peter Arnett, AP SPECIAL CORRESPONDENT

THE OLD MAN limped into the Saigon AP office breathing heavily because the power was off again and he had had to haul his portable typewriter up four flights of dark stairs. He was wearing baggy khaki trousers and a faded brown shirt. He was squinting under a cloth cap from what I later learned was his one good eye, and when he saw our wondering stares his impish face split into a grin of comraderie. Gordon Gammack had arrived to cover his third war.

Many other reporters had struggled up those same stairs because this was 1970 and the war had been going on officially since 1961 as far as Americans were concerned, two decades longer if you were Vietnamese and had survived the Japanese and French conflicts. The AP office in the center of Saigon was a sort of clearing house for arriving reporters seeking their bearings or wanting to file copy over our teleprinters to their hometown papers. But Gammack was special because he had been preceded by a personal letter from the AP president, Wes Gallagher, with the instructions, "Take care of Gammack, my World War Two buddy." And that constituted an order.

For most of us covering Vietnam, World War II was personally just a vaguely remembered shadow on our childhood. We met military men who often recalled that war, but only rarely did reporting veterans of the Normandy Beachhead or the Liberation of Paris arrive upon the Vietnam scene. Generally, they were senior executives over for a quick, puzzled peek. With the impatient arrogance of youth, we tended to look upon most of them as survivors of an earlier age with little capacity for understanding the subtleties of our war. When Gordon Gammack walked into our office I was placing him in that category. I was wrong.

Several hundred reporters were covering Vietnam when Gammack arrived, working mainly for the wire services, news magazines, TV networks, and a few major newspapers. He characterized himself deprecatively as "one of the little people from the sticks" because his reports served just one newspaper. After I came to know Gammack well it amused me to watch him act out his protective charade, that of the intimidated newcomer adrift in the confusing environment of the war. In reality he knew more about the combat condition than most, and he was as competitive as a hunting hawk. When he pounced on an occasional news scoop he carried it aloft in triumph.

Not that there were many scoops left in the war when Gammack arrived. By then American troops were starting to trail back home, and even the most detached newsmen were pulling back to peacetime assignments at home or opting for wars of likelier finality in Africa and the Middle East. Newcomers complained that while stories were just as dangerous to find, usage was much less spectacular than in the days when editors were still unsure about the eventual outcome of the war. But such sentiments were not for Gammack.

From our first lunch in a favorite Saigon bistro where he politely declined to tell us any World War II stories, thereby proving his modesty but also depriving us of anticipated gossip about our AP president's war correspondent days, Gammack impressed me as a reporter deadly serious about his business. Here he was going on 60, in questionable health, and at the wrong end of a war. Yet his professional interest seemed as enthusiastic as a cub reporter's, and he jotted down in a dog-eared notebook scraps of information on unit locations, contacts, and story ideas. I marvelled at the pure journalistic force that propelled this old man and I wondered if it would survive within myself when in some distant conflict I might be confronted by similarly disrespecting youth and feel required to prove myself yet again.

That Gammack succeeded in superbly covering his third war is evident in the articles that follow. He was equal to the punishing physical requirements of the job, never letting his colleagues in the field know what he was sometimes hinting in letters home: that his health wasn't holding up too well toward the end. Gammack's unerring reporting instincts quickly led him to the real stories of the war, that the U.S. Army was disintegrating from within because of plunging morale, and that there was a persistent attempt by the authorities to paint a much rosier picture than the reality. Because he made his own discoveries of what we had long regarded as the central dynamics of the war, Gammack became a favorite of the Vietnam press regulars. I hoped that he numbered us alongside his colleagues from earlier wars.

The beneficiaries of Gammack's doggedly persistent

reporting and skill were the loyal readers in what he called his "*Tribune* territory area," those thousands of people next door whom he had captured years earlier and kept because they must have sensed in him an honest purveyor of the news. As a wire service reporter writing for a national audience, I had often struggled with the difficulty of communicating successfully with the editors and readers of the hundreds of newspapers scattered across the land who depend on us for much of the news. I envied Gammack his direct pipeline to his people, his hometown connections, the support and trust. But most of all I envied his shining sense of journalistic mission that carried through one generation and into another without loosening a principle.

AUGUST 19, 1965. On the Van Tuong Peninsula. *(AP)*

GAMMACK'S introductory article about Vietnam was particularly important to him. It provided him with his first insight into the prevailing attitudes toward the press among the military authorities and he was initially impressed. He wrote back: "The cooperation is terrific, excessive perhaps because you're escorted wherever you go. I suppose you could argue that it is a curb of some sort but I don't think so; more for safety. My escort winced when that boy talked of how many prisoners were handled on recon but he didn't ask me to forget it. . . . Aside from everything else, I thought the piece indicated how war can brutalize nice guys and how the marines can make kids actually like that kind of duty."

Dennis Smith of Fonda, one of the marines interviewed and photographed for the reconnaissance article, ultimately became the subject of a series of two articles Gammack wrote in November of 1970 on the difficult process of returning to civilian life (see page 95).

TRIBUNE, FEBRUARY 16, 1970.

How Iowans Capture Viet Reds

DA NANG, SOUTH VIETNAM—The toughest, guttiest men in any war are the ones dropped by helicopter behind the enemy lines—in this case the "eyes and ears" of the 1st Marine Division near here.

They are members of the division's reconnaissance battalion.

Being surrounded, then reaching safety on chain ladders dangling from helicopters is almost standard procedure. Their comings and goings in the jungles and forests are known rather academically as "inserts and extracts."

Want an idea about how hard-nosed these Marine characters are?

Then listen to Lance Cpl. Dennis Smith, 19, son of Mr. and Mrs. Albert M. Smith of Fonda, describe a "prisoner snatch" mission—capturing a prisoner for interrogation:

"You go out and you hope you don't run into a whole battalion, just a small group, and you can ambush them and catch one alive and keep him alive.

"You catch him physically, tie him up and bring him back. Our men are pretty good at that. They can rough a guy up if they want to. They've had lots of practice at it. And you take his shoes and blindfold him and stuff something in his mouth and thump him on the head a couple of times just to talk him into going our way."

What if a recon patrol captures, say, a dozen North Vietnamese (N.V.A.'s) or Viet Cong (V.C.'s)?

"Kill most of them," Smith replied. "You couldn't hardly take them all back. Six men can't control 12. You just keep the one that looks the most important."

Hard . . . and Articulate

What impressed me particularly about Smith and five other Iowans I found in the battalion was that in addition to their physical hardness—the average man would only hurt his hand if he hit one of these guys on the jaw—was their ability to express themselves forcefully, clearly and even brashly on their role in the war.

I had finished talking (I thought) with Lance Cpl. Ted Godlove, 19, son of Mr. and Mrs. Max Godlove of Milo, and stuffed my notebook in a pocket when suddenly he inquired about the address of U.S. Senator Harold Hughes (Dem., Ia.). At first I thought he wanted to berate the dovish senator, but he explained:

"There are some things going on over here that I think are tactically unsound," he said, "and I think he ought to know about them. And I want to tell him about a buddy of mine who died unnecessarily, all because a lieutenant lost his guts."

Again, I thought I had finished a chat with Lance Cpl. William Johnson, 21, son of Mrs. Levi Miles of Waterloo, when he said, "Sir, would you put something in the paper for me. It doesn't matter to me personally because I'm 21. But tell them that all the men under 21 feel they ought to be able to have the right to vote when they get home.

"They're out here in the jungles, leading patrols and they're responsible for carrying out dangerous missions and they're responsible for the lives of the other recon men and, by God, when they get home, they ought to be able to vote—and have a drink if they want one, too."

Johnson is black and I asked him if he had experienced discrimination.

"Not in the Marines, no, sir," he replied . . . "In the Marines, we are all one color—green." (Green is the Marine Corps color.)

Proud of Medal

Godlove is especially proud of his Navy Commendation Medal, awarded for his action in what was known as Sherwood Forest.

He and seven other marines on recon found a North Vietnamese base camp.

"Once inside, it was much bigger than we thought and it had a big tunnel complex. We destroyed five bunkers, but then they started to overpower us and we were surrounded.

"They sent a rescue mission but we had to wait two hours. Helicopter gunships gave us fire support and hit so close that dirt flew in my face. They dropped napalm so close I could see the N.V.A.'s between us and the napalm. Finally, the helicopter dropped a ladder in a haze of smoke and I got out."

Of the eight-man mission, two were killed, three wounded and only three got out unscathed.

Yet these men seem to relish their grim work.

"I kind of like it," said Godlove. "It's a job to do. The experienced people are the ones winning this war and I'm glad to be doing my share."

"Any place in Vietnam is dangerous," said Johnson. "Any place in the world is dangerous. We're all born to die. It's going to happen some day."

"I wouldn't swap for a job behind a desk," said Lance Cpl. Kelly Ford, 20, of Sioux City, who lit a cigarette with a $7 lighter that carried the inscription, "We fight for the protesters so they can be free to protest."

Ford talked of the high priority on a "prisoner snatch," especially when intelligence information is crucial, and how what amounted to bounties once were offered recon men.

"We used to get five days R and R for bringing in a prisoner," he said, "but they're not doing it any more. There is one incentive, though. Once you've got a prisoner, out of the jungle you come"

Taking prisoners isn't always practical, though.

"Come face to face with one of their recon patrols, we kill 'em," Ford said.

"Say," Ford added as an afterthought, "I hear zero is considered a heat wave in Iowa this winter."

The recon men encounter all sorts of animals in the jungles, monkeys and rock apes and occasionally there are tigers in the areas. The Iowans I talked to hadn't seen any tigers and were thankful for it, too, mainly because they might be faced with the choice of being mauled or shooting and giving away their position to the enemy.

Recalls Ambush

The day I visited the recon battalion, Lance Cpl. Brad Brown, 19, son of Mr. and Mrs. Thomas F. Brown of 1092 Forty-fifth st., had been assigned to a mission. He had daubed his face with black and green paint, but the mission was scrubbed because helicopters were grounded by fog.

"The patrol I remember best was on Charlie Ridge. We found lots of footprints," he recalled. "We set up an ambush and then another guy and I spotted two gooks.

"We yelled 'Chieu Hoi' (the word for "surrender"). One of them dropped to his knees but the other started to run and we shot him up pretty good. I hear he lived but lost an arm."

Enemy wounded are removed by helicopter and, by the book, are supposed to have priority over wounded marines on the theory that information obtained from the enemy may save many marines' lives.

But when the marines of the recon patrols have the decision to make themselves, it doesn't usually work out that way.

Occasionally Gammack sensed a conflict between his instincts as a seasoned reporter and his commitment to providing news of central Iowans, but his instincts typically prevailed. He wrote a veiled apology to his editor, Drake Mabry, with the following article.

"Neither of us is going to be completely happy with the volume of Tribune *territory names, one reason being that when I asked information types to line up Iowans, I can't rattle off the 17 counties and say those are the ones I want. Today was a disappointment in that respect. I went up with the 7th Regiment Marines; they are almost completely isolated and are supplied only by helicopter and one daily convoy, out in the real boondocks where the fighting occurs (but mostly at night) and had been led to believe there were plenty of Iowans. There turned out to be just three and not one in our* Tribune *range. Yet I think it's a good story*

on the gut business of pacifying a hostile area. The trouble is that in peaceful areas where men are congregated, we'll have much better luck with the central Iowans and less guts in the copy."

TRIBUNE, FEBRUARY 22, 1970.

Pacifying Vietnam

WITH THE SEVENTH MARINE REGIMENT AT XUAN PHUOC, VIETNAM—It is out in the bush country where the "grunts" of the Marine Corps prowl and the enemy lurks behind the ridges that the guts of the Vietnamese pacification program has been taking hold.

In the area of the 7th Regiment of the 1st Marine Division some 25 miles south of Da Nang, villages and hamlets once considered in enemy control have been pacified through a program that has Marine sloggers working in unison with young men of the Popular Forces (P.F.s) and Regional Forces (R.F.s), which correspond roughly to our National Guard.

Militarily, the program keeps Viet Cong and North Vietnamese at bay but meantime the Marines work also to keep the people of the hamlets content by tending to their minor ailments, furnishing lumber to rebuild destroyed homes, sharing meals in bare hootches and even showing the villagers such American ways as wiener roasts with potato chips.

In substance, the Marines are both fighters and good guys who are kind to women and children.

I had been in the Xuan Phuoc area only a few minutes when I met Corpsman Ralph Sawyer, son of Mrs. Pauline Vanscoy of Carroll, who had just treated a village girl for a skin disease akin to "jungle rot."

"I just cleaned her up and put on some ointment," said Sawyer.

"I think the stuff will clear up but if it doesn't we'll med-evac her to a hospital. This program is paying off. The people appreciate what we're doing and they've become real friendly. They call me Boxi or something like that—for 'doctor.' "

Moments later, Sawyer was busy helping put two village children, a boy and girl, (squatting in baskets) into a truck for evacuation to a hospital.

During the night South Vietnamese troops had fired at a band of Viet Cong. The bullets didn't hit the enemy but did penetrate a hootch, killing one child and wounding these two.

The marines engaged in the pacification program—mostly they set ambushes and patrol at night and sleep and rest in the daytime—are detached and remote from the world as we know it.

In fact, as I climbed into a truck at Alpha Company headquarters to go to the village, the grimy-faced driver grinned and said, "Welcome aboard," and I asked him where he was from.

"In the world, Oklahoma," he replied.

The business of getting to the 7th Regiment, at a desolate wasteland area code-named Baldy, emphasized the isolation of the men who long for home and work hard at the pacification program because they think it may speed the day when they can board a "Freedom Bird," a plane bound for the U.S.

Twice a day helicopters that can carry 33 passengers each make a run to Baldy, and to an even more remote outpost tabbed Ross, from 1st Marine Division headquarters with stops at other Marine posts on Hill 55, Hill 65 and Hill 37.

During the runs, machine gunners stand watch, peering intently at the ground below from positions just behind the cockpit. But mostly the choppers soar above the range of possible fire.

At Baldy, Capt. James Van Riper of Pittsburgh, Pa., 31-year-old career Marine, describes the pacification program. He holds a map to show the hamlets that have been involved, starting last December.

"Teams of 14 men and a corpsman are assigned to each hamlet," he says. "They live with the people, help and protect them. At night they set up ambushes. Anything that moves after dark is fair game.

"Just last night a North Vietnamese Army captain chieu-hoied (defected) and he told us the Marines and the P.F.'s had been working the area so well there was no sense keeping up the fight."

But conversation among the Marines at Alpha Company indicated that the enemy remains pesky.

I was taken in tow by Lt. Michael Starick, Orchard Lake, Mich., a soft-spoken platoon leader, who explained the procedure of getting to Xuan Phuoc.

"We can go part way in my truck," he says, "after that we have to travel in convoy. Colonel's orders. There's a place along there that Charlie's been mining regularly and we've got to have armored vehicles go first.

"You know, this pacification program is working two ways. We're making the hamlet people like us. But the average grunt hates all Vietnamese at first because they're responsible for us being here. But then they get to know the people in the hamlets and they like them."

We came to a clearing by the road where a half dozen Marines were stationed and with them were a dozen or so teen-age boys and girls. But although the boys appeared to be just that, some comparable to our junior high youngsters, they actually were P.F.s. Some of the girls sat on the ground and were playing gin rummy, with apparent competence.

I started to take a picture of three of the P.F.s who chanced to be standing together and one of them moved impulsively out of range.

"Don't do that, sir," says Starick. "To them it's bad to take a picture of three. They are very suspicious. It means one of them will die."

And after that none of them would let me photograph them. But a bright lad who has learned quite a bit of English and who serves as interpreter was anxious to have his picture taken. They call him Bill, he's 15 years old, and Sgt. Danny Walker of Anaheim, Calif., says "he's bright as hell."

Walker, the Marine in charge of this unit, explains the pacification program as he sees it.

"We're trying to show the P.F.s a few things so we can go home faster. And we learn a lot from them, too—like how to tell when the V.C. are in front of us when you can't hear or see them.

"But the P.F.s can tell—from a dog's barking or birds suddenly flying away. In some ways they're better than the ARVN (Army of the Republic of Vietnam) because they know the area and who the V.C. are and where their booby traps are."

With Lieutenant Starick, I continue south and he points to Vietnamese on motor bikes ahead of us and tells his truck driver, "Let them be point for us—if there are mines, they'll hit 'em."

Along the road we meet Staff Sgt. Norbert Fliss, son of Mr. and Mrs. C. W. Fliss of Waterloo, who explains the fire fight of the night before in which the Vietnamese child was killed.

He got on the subject of student war protesters.

"Let 'em walk up and down this road for a while and do their protesting," he said. "The other night we killed a V.C. and you know what? He was wearing a University of California sweatshirt. That ticks me off."

(Fliss' attitude about student protesters is by no means general. One G.I., caught in a fire fight during a patrol and scared, told Mike Putzel of the Associated Press, "You tell those student protesters we're with 'em all the way.")

Lance Cpl. Gary Lee Dundee, 18, son of the Curtis Dundees of Postville, has been in Vietnam less than two weeks but he's sick of it already.

"I'd just as soon go out and shoot them all, blow them out of the place and get out," he says. "Except the kids. They're great, even friendlier than American kids."

Gammack maintained in Vietnam the special concern he had always felt for medics and for the wounded. The unique depth of Gammack's historical perspective was suggested in his article on the tribulations of a medic: the soldier with whom he spoke remembered Gammack's having interviewed his father during World War II.

The report on Leon Smith's grave injuries was followed up, four months later, with a report on Smith's rehabilitation, just as Gammack had followed up on Ralph Neppel's injuries and rehabilitation during World War II.

TRIBUNE, FEBRUARY 27, 1970.

Iowa Medic Sick of Battle

CHU LAI, SOUTH VIETNAM—After going into a clearing as an infantry medic to pick up eight dead buddies, five of them "shot to pieces," Pfc. Jimmy Ogden of Perry decided he couldn't stand the sight of another corpse.

So he became a truck driver in the rear area.

A guy can do that in today's American army. After he has served eight months, he can re-enlist—and, as a plum, pick his job, or come pretty close to it.

When you see reports of soaring re-enlistments, especially from Vietnam, this is one main reason

Tells of Incident

"I decided I just couldn't pick up another dead buddy," said Ogden, whose father is Larry Ogden, a Perry packing plant worker whom I interviewed in France during World War II.

"It was on New Year's Eve," Jimmy Ogden recalled. "We knew the V.C. were around but we were under a cease-fire and couldn't get permission to fire. Then they opened on us—and that's when I had to go after those eight guys.

"I came right to the rear, you have the right to do that, and re-enlisted. Of course, that meant starting my Army stint all over again, three years of it, but part of the deal is that I get an automatic 30-day home leave. In fact, I can go anywhere in the free world at government expense. You get that every time you extend.

"Now I'll have to come back here again after my leave and stay until Nov. 30, but it will be as a truck driver, same as I am now."

(Of my interview with Ogden's father, Jimmy recalls: "You made a recording of an interview with my Dad in France and I remember him playing it for me first when I was eight years old. He kept playing it now and then until it got scratchy but I think he lost it when we were moving a while back.")

Ottumwan

An Iowan who works in the office that handles re-enlistments for the Americal Division is Spec. 5 James Hasley, son of the O. J. Hasleys of Ottumwa.

He says that while some soldiers are using the re-enlistment route when they simply cannot stomach any more combat and the sight of death and suffering, many others sign up for new hitches because of career opportunities.

"There's computer training, for instance," says Hasley, "and when a guy finishes service, he's in line for a good job."

Hasley, like most G.I.'s in Vietnam, knows precisely how much longer he has to serve here.

"How much more time do you have," I asked.

"Exactly 208 days," he replied.

The military offers incentives galore for men to remain in service, including cash bonuses.

A lieutenant told me of a teletype operator who was given a $6,000 cash bonus for signing up for a six-year hitch. A specialist in repairing fork lift trucks got a $10,000 bonus for signing up for six years.

The Army also is paying for acceptable proposals from "suggestion boxes."

If an idea is adopted, someone figures out how much saving it will mean in dollars and cents and the man making the suggestion gets a percentage of that.

Get Out Sooner

Just as some servicemen are electing to stay in service longer by re-enlisting, others are agreeing to stay in Vietnam a little longer to complete their service sooner.

Take Hospital Corpsman 2nd Class Donald G. Kinney, son of Mr. and Mrs. Emmett Kinney of 936 Boulder, Des Moines. He could have been eligible to go home early in April but he extended for three months and will stay on at the big Navy hospital in Da Nang. His reward for that will be an early termination of his Navy enlistment and he will be able to enter Drake University next fall.

"I figure I have a good safe job here in Da Nang and three more months over here won't hurt me," he explained.

TRIBUNE, FEBRUARY 24, 1970.

'I Have Seen My Friends Die . . .'

CHU LAI, SOUTH VIETNAM—It was only a matter of time before the war in Vietnam would give me an emotional jolt.

It came at the bedside of Pfc. Leon Smith, 20, son of Mrs. Sarah Dodge of 3128 Sixth ave. He is recovering from severe wounds at the 27th Surgical Hospital here.

Most of his body quivered convulsively and I wondered whether I should leave. But doctors said the boy's trembling was caused by the emotion of seeing someone from his home town—and a determination to be at his best.

His legs didn't tremble though. They couldn't.

The right one, fractured by a bullet, was in a cast. The left one was in traction, red from wounds that severed three arteries and exposed raw nerves.

Leon's other wounds seemed minor by comparison—a lost thumb covered by a cast. A six-inch scar with stitch marks in the left shoulder. Eight wounds,

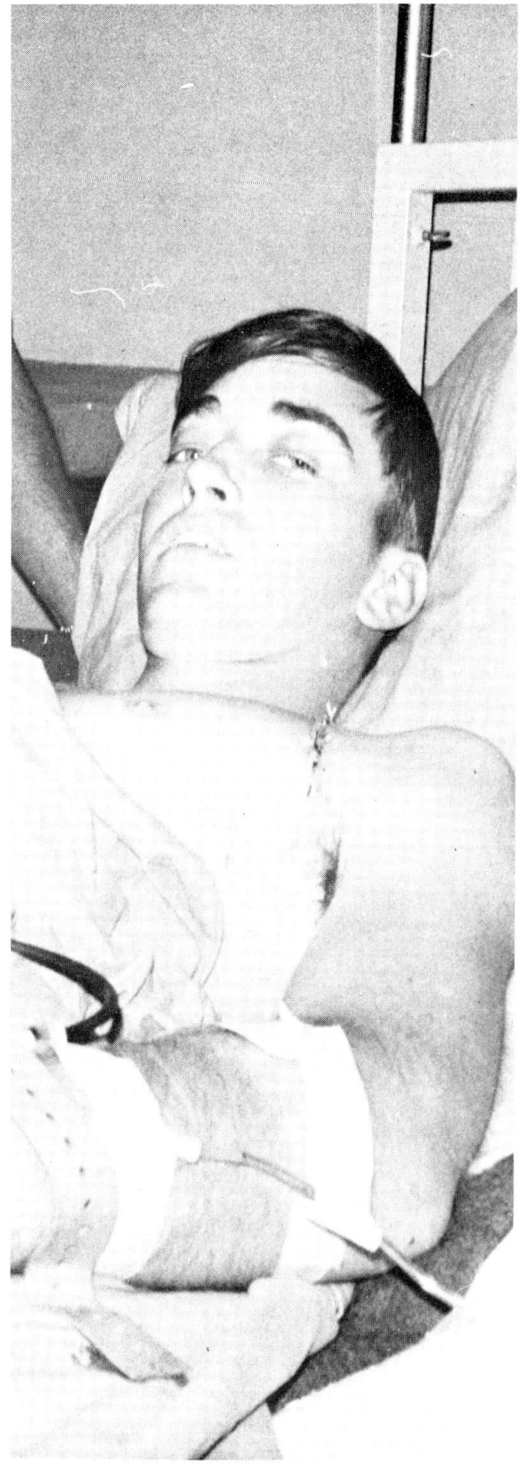

FEBRUARY 24, 1970. Wounded Leon Smith of Des Moines in hospital in Vietnam. *(Gordon Gammack)*

in all. The boy's eyes were a bit glassy, but he managed to smile now and then.

At times the pain is awful but Leon doesn't complain and he told me, "I'm getting kind of used to it now."

His reaction to his combat ordeal: "I feel lucky. I've seen a lot of my friends die.

"And I've got a philosophy—there isn't anything over here that's worth the life of one G.I."

Leon, a Des Moines Tech High graduate, tells how it happened. . . .

Hit 8 Times

"Our perimeter (with an Americal Division unit) was overrun. I was asleep inside my bunker when grenades started exploding. My buddy and I started scrambling for weapons, and I was just outside the bunker with my rifle and there was a dink—you know, Charlie.

"And he opened up on me from three feet away. He hit me eight times and knocked me back inside the bunker. I think he thought I was dead and I just lay there and didn't dare call for help 'cause I thought the dink would come back with a grenade and blow me up.

"So I waited and waited and then I saw some silhouettes and one of them was Doc, our medic, and I called to him and he carried me to a helo (helicopter) pad and they brought me back here."

It was two weeks after Leon was hit that I saw him and while doctors were confident of his recovery they continued to watch him closely.

Lt. Col. James E. Shaw of Boone, Americal Division chaplain, was also at the bedside and he told Leon, "Your country is proud of you and I'm sure you are proud of your country."

The boy smiled wanly and replied, "I think I've done my part, sir."

[Later, Leon was transferred to a hospital in Tokyo. His left leg had been amputated above the knee.]

Eventually, Leon will be sent to a hospital in the United States.

He is longing for the day when he can see two women—his mother, a nurse's aid at Mercy Hospital, and Jan Humphrey of Oskaloosa.

"I hear you and Jan are going to get married," I said to Leon.

"Sure hope so," he said. "I sure love her an awful lot."

There are many emotions in a battle zone hospital. The quality of our mercy and the mandates of medicine are such that enemy soldiers also are receiving the best of care.

Spunk

And always there is the American spunk.

In the bed beside Leon was a red-haired kid who had lost both his legs—and as we were leaving, he called out to Chaplain Shaw, "When you go out in the bush, tell 'em to take care."

And in the corridor, the chaplain shook his head and said, "You know what that boy said when he stepped on the mine that took his legs off.

"He yelled back to his buddies: 'Watch that first step, guys—it's a kicker.' "

TRIBUNE, MAY 4, 1970.

D.M. Amputee: Pain, Laughter after Fall

DENVER, COLO.—From childhood, it was Leon Smith's habit to get out of bed left foot first—and he moved that way instinctively when he was awakened from an afternoon nap to take a phone call.

He was only half awake and his thinking was fuzzy or he never would have done it that way.

Because Leon, a 20-year-old Des Moines youth, doesn't have a left leg any more. It was amputated, above the knee, last February after Viet Cong bullets severed three main arteries.

Leon tumbled out of bed and landed square on the stump and then sprawled crazily, helplessly on the floor at Fitzsimmons Army General Hospital here. There was sharp pain for a moment. But then it passed and Leon laughed about doing such a silly thing.

Other amputees in Ward 512 helped him up and some of them kidded him for sleeping all the time. But they understood, really, because they know he is down to about 105 pounds from the 155 pounds he weighed when the enemy pumped him full of lead in Vietnam. They know his lost leg accounts for only seven of those lost pounds.

The amputees know, too, that ridiculous accidents occur in their closely knit fraternity. They have nightmares—of being back in combat and of enemy artillery or mortars suddenly coming at them.

They fling themselves out of bed, too, subconsciously diving for cover and, like Leon, they land on their stumps.

But they are a stoic clan, the amputees. Few of them complain or feel sorry for themselves and those who do get no sympathy from the others.

The loss of a leg or an arm, or multiple amputations, is a challenge to these gutty guys who are determined to be self-reliant citizens and who like to think the worst is behind them.

'I've Got Bad News'

Leon Smith is an example. He was a forlorn lad when I saw him in the 27th Evacuation Hospital at Chu Lai, Vietnam, last Feb. 14. His left leg, a mass of raw flesh, was in traction. Surgeons had all but concluded they had lost their fight to save the shattered limb.

Shortly after I left the hospital, one surgeon came to Leon's bedside and, as Leon recalls, he said, "I've got bad news for you. I've done everything I can but that main artery is just too badly damaged. I've got to take your leg off, Leon."

Leon cried.

"I didn't cry when I got hit and I didn't cry when they did things to my leg, things that hurt real bad," he recalls. "But I cried when the doctor told me that and then I told him I wouldn't let him do it. I said I'd rather die.

"After that, they put me to sleep because I made such a fuss about not going along with them. Next thing I knew, they'd done it."

The decision to amputate was especially traumatic for Leon, because, as he puts it: "When they were trying to save my leg, you know, they told me I'd lose my little toe, but hoped to save the rest of the leg. I was really happy, you know, and the doctor would come in, all smiles, good reports. I thought everything was going to be fine."

Several days after the amputation, a doctor examined Leon's stump.

"He gave me some morphine and said it wouldn't hurt very much, but then he stuck his hand in—and he must have touched every nerve in there because I never remember screaming so loud in all my life.

"And after that, any time a doctor came to look at my stump, I just about went into a state of shock I was so terrified."

As soon as Leon's condition was stabilized, as the medics put it, he was flown to Japan for additional treatment and then was evacuated to Fitzsimmons—one of the centers for amputees—and he has been here since about Mar. 1.

At first he got around in a wheelchair. Then he progressed to crutches. Now, with the stump ready for it, he has been fitted for an artificial leg.

I chatted with Leon as we rode in an Army bus from the hospital to the Arapahoe Basin on the western slopes of the Continental Divide—a 2½ hour trip—where he and other amputees have been learning to ski.

Between runs, Leon and his mates gathered around a wood fire in a shelter house and sometimes the fire would crackle and pop. The noise caused some of the amputees to tense and jump back from the fire instinctively. Even those noises reminded them of enemy fire.

The men started talking about medals—profanely—and the awarding of Bronze Stars especially and Silver Stars occasionally to men who, in their opinion, didn't deserve them.

"A Bronze Star and 15 cents will get you a cup of coffee," one crippled G.I. remarked.

"And the Purple Heart is for the birds," said one guy with a leg off. "You don't have to do nothing to get that."

"Less than that," said Leon. "I was sleepin'."

"The only thing that matters is payday," said another.

"I'd Never Trust 'Em"

Leon Smith isn't bitter about his handicap. But he is bitter about the war in Vietnam. Lying on his hospital bed at Chu Lai, he said, "There isn't a dink that's worth the life of one G.I."

And by "dink" he meant the South Vietnamese as well as the enemy.

On the ski bus I told him that some G.I.'s who had worked closely with the South Vietnamese had become quite fond of them.

"Well, I might get to like them, but I'd never trust them," he replied.

"I remember this kid who used to ride through a town where our outfit was. He was on a motor scooter and on the back he had styrofoam buckets filled with ice and Cokes and he'd sell 'em for 50 cents a bottle. And we'd buy 'em because in our outfit we were issued about two a day and they weren't cold.

"That kid must have made a barrel of dough out of us G.I.'s.

"And the night I was hit I caught a P.F. (South Vietnamese Popular Forces soldier) trying to steal my flak jacket and I gave him a rough time taking it back.

"You know, he might have been the dink that hit me because some were P.F.'s in the daytime and Viet Cong at night. No, sir, I'll never trust any of them."

Leon retains some bitterness for a few of the officers known to draftees as "lifers," or career officers.

"We had one platoon leader who was gung-ho for rank and he volunteered for a mission," Leon recalls. "Now, you just don't do that unless you're buckin' for something. And so he got the mission and one of our guys was killed on it. You don't forget that kind of thing."

Leon showed me a letter he'd just received from the medic who had taken care of him after he had been hit. (The Des Moines boy had lain in a bunker, in awful pain, for 20 minutes before he called for help because he thought the Viet Cong would finish him off with a grenade if he showed signs of being alive.)

And the medic wrote Leon: "We're back now and the lifers are a pain in the ____; Flak jackets and steel pots wherever we go and Article 15 if you don't get a haircut or have a dirty weapon.

"Not much more to say, Leon. I only wish I could have done more for you."

Now, Leon Smith's morale is high. Pain remains commonplace, an everyday thing. But he pops pain-killing pills into his mouth, grits his teeth and keeps on with what he is doing. Twice a day he goes to the physical therapy department and exercises to gain strength.

And he does odd, little things, such as take arithmetic classes because it may help him in whatever he elects to do as a civilian and resumes his education in some way, as yet undetermined.

He and other amputees are free to leave the hospital most evenings and weekends and they go to taverns to drink beer and talk.

They go to the movies a lot, too. The other night Leon saw M-A-S-H, the bloody satire about a field hospital near the front during the Korean War. In one scene a surgeon saws off a G.I.'s leg and the sound of the sawing is heard.

"That took me back for just a second," says Leon. "But it was a hell of a funny picture."

Given the freedom to follow up whatever leads seemed most interesting, Gammack took advantage of tips and acquaintances, even if they placed him in some jeopardy. Of his junket on a helicopter spy mission, he wrote: "That Loche ride was a trifle risky perhaps, but I was sort of caught in not wanting to turn the guy down. He was obviously anxious to take me. And naturally I was tickled to death that I did once it worked out well. I did turn down a hunter-killer mission, on which the little chopper tries to draw fire so that a lurking Cobra gunship can pounce."

TRIBUNE, MARCH 2, 1970.

Iowan Prowls Skies over Viet

ALONG THE CAMBODIAN BORDER—As dusk approaches in Vietnam, helicopter observation pilots prowl the skies to keep an eye on what Charlie, the enemy, is up to.

They spy on the enemy not only in South Vietnam but also in Cambodia, where North Vietnamese forces often seek sanctuary.

These missions, called "last light" flights, are flown over rice paddies, fields and hillsides where legitimate Vietnamese workers are supposed to be in their homes for the night.

Thus, anybody out in the open is immediately suspect. When the enemy is spotted, potent flying gunships (Cobra helicopters) are called in.

One of the pilots of these LOCH's (light observation choppers) is Warrant Officer Terri Bachi (pronounced "Becky"). His chopper is named "Sweet Pea"—the nickname of his wife, Carol, who is waiting out Terri's Vietnam tour in Batavia, Ia., with her parents, Mr. and Mrs. Russell Taylor, and her 5-month-old daughter, Gwen, whom Terri has never seen.

Bachi took me on a "last light" flight that took us directly above the imaginary line separating Cambodia and Vietnam—"On your left is Cambodia, on your right, Vietnam," he said as he made a slow turn at the border.

And from this vantage point we could clearly see a North Vietnamese Army (N.V.A.) base camp, secure from U.S. attack because of its Cambodian position.

Before the flight, Bachi, a graduate of Parsons College at Fairfield, talked about flying the small, effective choppers nicknamed "flying football" or "electric olive."

"The way to stay alive on this job is to fly high, at least 1,500 feet, above small arms fire, or low, below treetop level, where you're a damn tough target at 90 to 100 knots an hour," he said.

"Everything between those altitudes we call 'dead man's level'."

Bachi says his helicopter section, part of the artillery of the 25th Infantry Division stationed at Cu Chi, has been mighty lucky, with very few casualties. He points to the flight helmets he and his mates wear, with the double inscription, "Jesus' Children," and "God Is Our Co-pilot."

Talking with Bachi, then flying with him, brought home what may well be the telling factor in the Vietnamese war at this stage—the ability to spot the North Vietnamese and Viet Cong (V.C.) wherever they are and wherever they move.

He talked of the refinements of the miracle gadget, a black box called the "people sniffer," carried aboard some helicopters.

"The sniffers used to pick up Charlie by detecting human odor," he explained, "but the chemicals used were hard on the machine. So now they are concentrating on dust readings with the gadget. The strength of the dust indicates the number of people—Charlies in most cases—in an area. An 'A' reading is heavy; 'B,' small and 'C,' not strong enough to be a reliable indicator, could be animals.

"When we spot Charlie we call in the Cobras," he continued, referring to the helicopter gunships that spit rockets and can fire 4,000 bullets a minute.

"At night the artillery ruins Charlie's sleep, if nothing else. One V.C. told us he surrendered because he couldn't sleep at night with our artillery, and because every time his unit moved he got socked with artillery."

"First Light"

Bachi said that at dawn his outfit flies "first light" missions to survey the effectiveness of artillery fire during the night.

"That's the time for flying below the treetops," he said. "First I go fast, then if it seems safe, I slow down and take a careful look. Sometimes the civilians are scared and pull yellow Vietnamese flags from their pockets and wave them to show they are loyal, and aren't V.C.

"One morning a V.C. came out of the bushes, waving his arms and indicating he wanted to surrender. I had a rifleman with me so we went down and took him in."

Surrenders sometimes follow the dropping of "Chieu Hoi" leaflets promising good treatment, even cash bonuses, to defectors, and Bachi and his fellow pilots from time to time dump the leaflets.

2 Near Misses with Death

Bachi winces when he recalls what happened two days before he joined his wife in Hawaii for a "rest and recuperation" leave.

First, he was slated to fly a special mission but was replaced at the last minute by another pilot.

On that mission the chopper was hit by ground fire, exploding tear gas grenades the craft was carrying. The pilot was blinded by the gas, flew into a hillside and he and six other persons aboard were killed.

The next day Bachi lost his bearings in bad weather while flying and suddenly found himself the target of intense enemy fire. He then realized he was directly over a North Vietnamese outpost in Cambodia. He departed in a hurry.

Mostly, the Vietnamese countryside looks peaceful from 1,500 feet, although craters from shells and bombs are scattered as far as the eye can see.

"Have a good flight," the radio controller told us as we were cleared for take-off. Because Bachi knew he was going to fly over U.S. artillery positions, he obtained a precise check on targets and fire direction, lest he be hit by one of our own shells.

"I'd sure hate to get it from friendly fire," he said through the intercom in our flight helmets. Soon we stopped briefly at Firebase Jackson to drop off a radar operator, then headed over swamps and rice paddies toward the border.

Ahead and to the left of us was a series of brush fires Bachi said we had set with gasoline to deny hiding places to Charlie.

When Bachi told me we were in an area dubbed "Angel's Wing" at the Cambodian border—the fields and foliage did look somewhat greener on the Cambodian side—it was an eerie feeling to see what Bachi pointed out as a heavily armed North Vietnamese Army base camp.

Not far from it were two hamlets, one a neat diamond-shaped one and a smaller one, with a border check point, above it.

"The first one's in Vietnam; the other in Cambodia," Bachi said.

Roller Coaster Ride in the Sky

As we headed back, the Iowan said, "I want to show you something—a real good job that Charlie got away with," and he flew over Go Dan Ha, a village where a major bridge had been effectively dynamited, and now was being repaired.

As we left the village, Bachi said, "Now let's go down. We do it fast, 3,500-feet-a-minute rate, you'd call it a nose dive, I guess."

And down we went, first following Highway 1, after he leveled off. Frightened civilians on motor bikes ducked their heads, thinking we were low enough to lop them off.

Then Bachi flew over the fields and paddies and tree lines and all of a sudden it was like a lifetime of roller coaster rides rolled into one. Time after time I thought nothing in this world was going to stop us from hitting a tree. But Bachi is skilled at his trade.

He roared over fields, skimming the rice growths, then rose just enough to miss the tops of trees by a foot or two. He admitted he sometimes brushes a tree top with the chopper's belly "for good luck."

He dipsy-doodled all over the place and once or twice, to get through trees, he tilted his craft on its side and slipped between them.

"This makes a pretty tough target for anyone to shoot at," he said, "but it's no time for an engine failure. Then you're in kinda bad shape."

The Vietnam war, like every other, had its swingers and in Gammack's estimation they were principally quartered in the Air Force. "The fly boys really have the perfect war—air-conditioning, wall-to-wall carpeting, excellent food and, as guys who love to fly, they've got the going after the enemy with bombs which involves almost no risk whatever to themselves." He later added: "I have a ball with these crazy glamour boys of this war—purple scarves, nutty rituals and all that jazz."

TRIBUNE, MARCH 4, 1970.

'Time of My Life' for Some Pilots

BIEN HOA, SOUTH VIETNAM—American fighter-bomber pilots here are jaunty and gung-ho.

Their workshops on the ground—operations headquarters—are air-conditioned with wall-to-wall carpeting. Their living quarters are roomy and air-conditioned. They whisk back and forth on motorbikes they got from Japan for about $250 each.

They eat and drink well, at modest prices.

But above all, they are doing what they like best, under conditions they consider just dandy—they swoop down on enemy positions, impersonal-

ly dropping their bombs and rockets, but run very little risk of death, wounds or capture.

"I hope my wife will understand when I say it, but I'm just having the time of my life," said Maj. James Keating, 34-year-old son of Mr. and Mrs. Stanley Keating of Charles City.

Actually, Keating, a 13-year Air Force veteran, came close to disaster recently—and that's rarity in a war in which our fighters have virtually complete freedom and domination of the skies.

Normally, the fighters do not invade Cambodian territory, but on one mission Keating and his wing man got permission from high authority to go in for a retaliatory strike.

As they came in, a rain of 50-caliber bullets tore up at them from a North Vietnamese Army (N.V.A.) position. Keating recalls saying to himself: "You guys shouldn't be doing that to me—because now I know where you are."

Keating then went into a dive and dropped two 500-pound bombs on the position.

The Best Two

"They were the best two I ever dropped in my life—right square on the nose," he said. "And all of a sudden that gun position was real gone. I can only guess what happened to the machine gun crew.

"War is impersonal to us—we don't see what we do to people. Our forward air controllers, sitting up there in small planes, can see individuals—and they tell us things like, 'there's a man hiding under that tree,'—but we're going too fast."

Anyway, the A-37 jets of both Keating and his wing mate were hit by ground fire—and Keating has one of the bullets, plucked from his fuselage, as a souvenir.

Because of the almost complete safety of the fighter-bomber operations, there is gay camaraderie among the pilots. It's not, however, to the detriment of serious and precise attention to business on the ground and in the air. And it's a sort of carefree existence because it is very rare that they have to pause in sadness for a friend who doesn't return.

The one thing the Air Force is absolutely determined to avoid is the capture of a U.S. pilot. The precautions are extraordinary, starting with a survival training course in the Philippines, a must for all Vietnam-bound pilots.

The parachute, rescue and survival gear carried in flight by each pilot weighs more than 100 pounds. Should a pilot be forced to bail out, the opening of the parachute automatically triggers a beep-beep-beep alert to a wide variety of rescue elements.

The pilot's survival jacket includes two radio transmitter and receiver sets, all designed to bring rescue helicopters and protective gunships to the scene on the double.

Earlier in the war, Carl Fye of Denison, now a Trans World Airlines pilot, was forced to bail out and was on the ground only 40 seconds before a helicopter pulled him to safety.

The survival gear also includes an intricate microphone that allows communication by barely audible whispers, a compass, tourniquets, bandages, a first aid kit, extra rounds of ammunition, a fire starting kit, small gun flares that can penetrate a jungle and "blood chits" that guarantee cash rewards to natives who assist downed pilots.

Keating says the helicopter pilots are the ones he admires.

Bows, Arrows

"You have no idea what they have to contend with," he said. "Why, do you know the bad guys have even shot down choppers with big bows and arrows? And they put mines in the trees that are set off when the breeze from the rotor blades make the branches sway."

Another pilot in Keating's outfit is Capt. Larry Livingston, son of Mr. and Mrs. Ralph Livingston of Davenport. He is a veteran of 160 missions in Vietnam and remembers especially one when "we scambled at 4 o'clock in the morning to help infantry troops who were in bloody contact with the N.V.A."

"Friendly artillery lighted the area with flares and we came in level at 500 feet and dropped our bombs. I think we did the ground guys some good."

That mission of Livingston's was right against the Cambodian border.

Livingston recalls that a forward air controller spotted a North Vietnamese who was wounded and, limping, was trying to enter the sanctuary in Cambodia across the border.

The controller told Livingston to fly down and knock the guy off before he could get to the border.

Livingston did.

Winding up his first trip to Vietnam, Gammack could not resist speculating on the future course of the war, although he bemoaned sounding like "an insufferable expert."

"My estimate of the war is that it has ground to something approaching a stalemate. It's an awful thing to say when 100 or so U.S. kids are getting knocked off every week. It could continue for a long time at this level, with our casualties declining more and more as the Viets take over. The bad guys simply can't wiggle their toes without our knowing it and then our artillery planes kick the stuffing out of them. And any full scale offensive by them would mean a slaughterhouse. One of my chums confided, by the way, that we have advised any and all would-be coup plotters that if they get away with anything, we will pack up and go home right now—and that's why Thieu is relatively secure. He says the Army has done

magnificently with the most difficult military assignment in U.S. history and that is marred only by the disgusting use of the war to wrangle promotions and rotate commands to get the job done at the highest levels."

Only one assignment remained for Gammack's 1970 Vietnam tour and that was to pursue the question of how American soldiers were adapting to civilian life after service. He chose as his subject Dennis Smith, whose experiences as a reconnaissance patrolman had structured Gammack's first Vietnam article.

TRIBUNE, NOVEMBER 19, 1970.

In Vietnam, 'Kill' Was a Small Word; Back in the World, 'It Gets to You'

MARYVILLE, MO.—It has been a torturous conversion for Denny Smith—from conditioned behavior of part man, part animal, from killing as a way of life to "The World," as soldiers in Vietnam refer to the civilized way of life.

The road back has been from the bush and jungles of Vietnam and the miserable, fearful existence of a marine behind enemy lines to his home in Fonda and then to the campus of Northwest Missouri State College at Maryville.

The character of a boy with a man's job changes radically when he knows that any minute he may be killed. Fear of the enemy, and thus hatred, is the one overwhelming emotion, and leeches sucking on his body and mosquitoes swarming and whining in 130-degree heat become tolerable trifles.

And so at the time, Lance Cpl. Dennis Smith was not ashamed when he got the skull of a Viet Cong, had his buddies autograph it, and then shipped it home to Fonda. Air mail. Parcel post. But now, in retrospect, a sense of shame is visible.

He now attempts to analyze his motivations as a member of a Marine Corps reconnaissance outfit dropped by helicopter behind enemy lines for four to 14 days to capture—and kill—the enemy.

"Kill becomes a small word," he says. "In the jungles, it's a fast-moving game of kill or be killed. It gets into your system as it does with an animal. It's just a part of you.

"It was fun then. You're psyched up. You're there to kill; that's your job, and if you're not doing your job, why are you even there?

"It's after you get home and you have time to think about killing other human beings that it gets to you."

But memories of killing are only a part of the adjustment to civilian life that a jungle fighter must make.

Intense Jumpiness

In Smith's case, there were weeks of intense jumpiness. Raw nerves. Once he awoke with such a start when his mother awakened him suddenly that he flailed away, unthinking, and struck her in the jaw. And the first time he got in a car, all of a sudden he was racing 100 miles an hour, oblivious to the danger.

Faith and trust in other members of his five-man Marine patrol team were everything, all that counted, really, to Denny Smith in Vietnam, and so, back home, he became afraid of crowds and distrustful of strangers.

There were times, too, when he became overcome with rage—when civilians looked at his Marine jacket with disdain, and when he went from Minneapolis to Omaha to Sioux City and any number of smaller towns, looking for a job, and always was turned away.

He was half angry, half amused, he recalls, when a meat inspector at the Maryville Packing Co., where he now works part time, became hostile about his hair, which he had let grow long, and had told fellow employes, "Someone ought to tell that kid to get a haircut. He looks like a hippie."

Some folks in Fonda were concerned about Denny when he first came home last June.

"One night he came to my house and we talked until 3 in the morning," recalls Wally Parman, Denny's football coach at Fonda High School. "He needed help, someone to talk to.

"He told me that whenever he was on patrol the thought came to him that it was the same as a football game, that if every man does his job, you'll get along fine unless you meet someone too strong. But if one guy doesn't do his part, it doesn't take much to overcome you.

"That's the way he was as a football player. More than winning, he wanted to be part of a team, make a contribution. He was rough on kids who didn't do their part. In fact, there were some fights after games . . ."

"Hard-nosed" is the adjective you hear in Fonda when Denny's name is mentioned.

His mother, Mrs. Albert (Rose Marie) Smith, recalls the time he smashed the windshield of her car, simply by smacking it with his fist to emphasize a point in an argument.

It was 2 o'clock in the morning when Denny came home, awakened his mother and told her he had enlisted, at age 18, in the United States Marines.

"It was the right branch of the service," recalls Mrs. Smith, with a knowing smile.

At the end of basic training, Denny volunteered for reconnaissance, perhaps the most hazardous of all Marine duty in Vietnam, because his buddies were doing it and because it promised excitement.

Denny was a veteran of the jungle patrols when I had a memorable interview with him near Da Nang in Vietnam last February and he described a recent "prisoner snatch," capturing a prisoner for interrogation.

It was last Christmas that Denny got his skull. For a while, before that, the ears of enemy soldiers were trophies, but commanders ordered an end to that. Then gold teeth became war prizes but, Denny recalls, "they were pretty hard to come by."

Denny told the story about acquiring the skull with a faltering that betrayed embarrassment. He seemed sorry that he had discussed it at all.

His patrol had come across a large patch of freshly dug dirt. A command post, contacted by radio, gave instructions to dig—and several caskets holding Viet Cong dead were bared. That's where the skull came from. And Denny's patrol had matched competing U.S. patrol teams that had brought back skulls from the bush.

Denny recalls the night before he left base camp for home. He was taking a shower when he heard gunfire.

"I thought, 'Oh, Jeez, here it comes. After all I've been through they're attacking the base and I'm going to get it here before I get to go home.' "

He ran from the shower, naked, and found a bunker. But he knew that even with this protection his white skin made a prime target and so he scooped up mud and furiously lathered his clean body with it.

Dreams, Guilt Ahead

Then the shooting stopped, as suddenly as it started, and he found out what had happened.

Two of his closest buddies, guys he'd trained with, had gotten into an argument with another marine and one of them had slugged him and knocked him cold.

The felled marine was in a blind rage when he came to and went after his attackers with his automatic weapon.

"He shot off my buddy's right foot," Denny recalls. "And on the night before we were going home."

When Denny boarded a "freedom bird," a U.S.-bound jetliner, the next day, he felt as though he could lick the world.

"I was confident, 100 per cent sure, when we landed in California," he recalls.

But disillusionment, troublesome dreams, occasional spasms of guilt, frustration, loneliness and anger lay ahead.

TRIBUNE, NOVEMBER 20, 1970.

'Normal Life' Doesn't Return Easily for GI

MARYVILLE, MO.—Dennis Smith didn't realize how completely the other four Marines in his Vietnam jungle patrol had become a part of him and how he depended on them until he was back in "The World" on his own.

He analyzed this dependence and other adjustment problems at Maryville, where he is a freshman at Northwest Missouri State College.

"I had a locked-in feeling when I got home and I was with people I didn't know, didn't know whether I could trust. I still have that feeling," said Smith, now 20.

"I was used to being one of five guys. We knew each other like the backs of our hands. We lived together, slept together, ate together, fought together. A man becomes a machine, more than an individual. We were not five individuals, we were one five-man whole.

"So when I got home, as time went on, I knew that something was missing. Then it came to me that it's the other four guys, that's what's missing. I would wake up in the middle of the night and all of a sudden I'd be yelling out loud, 'Hey, where's everybody at?' "

This led Denny to the conviction that the Marines and other branches of the military must help men bridge the gap from jungle living to civilization, from the unnatural, unholy atmosphere of war to the conditions of peace and civil law.

"You have to break yourself down after a life of combat," he says. "And they (the military) should do some work on that, help these guys get back to a normal life gradually before they are discharged. A fella is not prepared to just take off."

He's Calmed Down

Denny's mother, Mrs. Rose Marie Smith, and other adults in Fonda who have long admired and respected the boy, agree.

In fact, they're almost frightened when they recall the first days home last June of the hard-nosed marine.

"It's just in the last couple of weeks that Denny seems to have calmed down," says Mrs. Smith. "He was so jumpy. I hardly dared talk to him. He wanted to be by himself a lot of the time. We had a place out in the country and he stayed there by himself with his TV and hi-fi."

Utter boredom, lack of action, also bugged Denny, whose marine rank was lance corporal.

"There was nothing going on in Fonda, nothing to do," Denny recalls. "I'd go watch a movie. After a while, I'd just do anything—run, for instance. Or I'd go fishing. But fishing was kind of a drag, too,

NOVEMBER 1970. The two worlds of Fonda's (Iowa) Dennis Smith—as combat Marine in Vietnam (left) and as student on Missouri campus. *(Gordon Gammack)*

because fish never bite for me. Made for a dull afternoon."

Then Denny Smith became angry.

He didn't feel like a hero but he did think he had served his country with enough distinction (he got the Navy Commendation Medal for carrying three wounded buddies to safety from a hail of enemy fire) to merit a civilian job.

"At first, I thought I'd aim for something that wasn't too hard physically but would keep me busy, but pretty soon I was willing to accept anything," he recalls.

"I covered half the state, and I went to Minneapolis and Omaha and Sioux City, looking for work. I'd hit at least two places a day, sometimes three or four, and some places they wouldn't even talk to me. At others they'd say 'I doubt it,' 'Not now,' 'I don't think so,' 'Maybe in the fall.'

"One man really tried to help. Carl Mauer in Sac City. He runs a construction company and I'd worked for him when I was in school. First time I talked to him he didn't have any jobs, but he scouted around and found a spot for me. By then I was off somewhere else, looking for work, and by the time he found me the job wasn't open any more.

"I did have one temporary job, pouring concrete all night long, 7 at night until 7 in the morning, but it only lasted a few days and that was a lousy way to live anyhow.

"Finally, I just gave up. It was getting close to the time to start school and I just said the hell with it."

Even now, Denny keeps having dreams that disturb him.

"There's one especially that stays with me," he says. "There's this hill in Vietnam. We got hit there bad in August of 1969, and in this dream I was the only one there. I was attacked, not by the Viet Cong but by American (war) protesters.

"They weren't shooting back at me but I had a machine gun that didn't work too good and I was only getting five or six rounds off at a time. I was killing these guys and I figured as soon as they got me they were going to do me in.

"I knew I couldn't shoot 'em all, the way the gun was working. But I kept at it until they were just all over me, on top of me, and they took the gun away from me and they said, 'The war is over and we're stopping it our way now.'

"And that's all they ever said to me. They didn't tie me up or chain me or put me into anything and all the time I tried to put my gun together again so I could make a getaway. But every time I tried to leave, they stopped me."

Denny doesn't like to talk about it, but memories of killing other human beings haunt him from time to time. (He estimates he personally killed 10 enemy soldiers in close-in fighting.)

"The feeling comes and goes," he says. "It gets to you if you let it. Sometimes you overcome it. Other times you think you're going to forget it, but you don't—and then all the problems come down on you at once and get you down. It works on you until you can bust out of it again."

Denny seems to be following a reasonably calm and conventional course now. He is quite serious about doing well in college, though he still hasn't decided on a career. He doubts that he is "shrewd" enough to compete successfully in business.

He gets $175 a month under the GI Bill of Rights and earns about the same amount working as a meat trimmer at Maryville Packing Co., weekdays from 7 a.m. to 11 a.m. and extra on Saturdays.

Usually his classes are from noon until 3 p.m. and the rest of the day is devoted to study, either in the college library or at the attractive $140-a-month apartment he shares with a Navy veteran, John Michael Steele, son of Mr. and Mrs. John G. Steele; 7609 Horton St. in Urbandale. (Denny prepares the meals, Mike does the dishes.)

Denny is a Roman Cathlic and in Fonda he went to church regularly. But his religious philosophy has changed since Vietnam.

"I didn't go to mass much over there," he says. "You couldn't when you were out in the bush so much. I guess I made it about four times the year I was in Vietnam.

"Now, to me, it's the priest, how he goes about it. If I didn't like the priest, I wouldn't go to church. I try to go Sunday afternoon here. We've got a younger priest with new ideas; he's not so locked up in the old church. Take abortion, who's to say whether it's right or wrong?

"I believe in God, but I can't see that they can say you've got to go to church when you don't want to. That's your business. Why make it so strict? The older priests make it an order, you have to do this, you have to do that. That's not right."

On Vietnam, Denny is not an extreme hawk despite his gung-ho war actions. In fact, he respects those who sincerely oppose the war. He does not believe, however, that a cut-and-run policy is practical. And he suspects he would be willing to spend 30 days in jail for personal vengeance against anyone he encountered carrying a North Vietnamese flag.

Why Is Hair a Big Thing?

Some Vietnam veterans at Northwest Missouri State are wearing their hair long as a protest against the war, and Denny had his hair rather long until recently.

"I didn't have long hair as a protest against anything," he says. "I just like long hair. It's a fashion, just like bright colors in clothes. I wish older people would quit making a big thing out of long hair. What the hell's wrong with it?"

"I get so mad at the people in the downtown stores here in Maryville. You walk in and you're wearing an Army or Marine jacket and because your hair's longer than theirs their eyes just burn holes through your back. Sure, they'll take your money, fine and dandy, but they'll curse you for the way you do things.

"What we've got to do is all get together and go in the same direction and appreciate the things we have. I've learned how much things mean to me that I used to take for granted—a refrigerator, a stove, food, sleep, a house, a car. Things like that."

And he says the good things in life are to be cherished, because he remembers:

"Walking in two, three inches of water with leeches crawling over you and after a while you get so disgusted trying to keep them off, you just quit trying. Let 'em eat and fall off. You ask yourself how can any man put up with the heat, the mosquitoes, the bugs, the disease, the water and the enemy, too.

"One at a time, you forget these things. . . . And so the only thing you really feared was the enemy."

The future for Dennis Smith?

"I'm going to keep fit physically; that's important. I'm going to study hard, get a college degree. Then I hope to do something worthwhile, contribute something."

Gammack's second trip to Vietnam, early in 1971, began with a very big story. He was one of the first American correspondents into Khe Sanh, which was the hub of the Allied buildup along the Laotian border. Written before the news embargo that accompanied the invasion of Laos, Gammack's stories and pictures were released and printed as soon as the embargo was lifted, providing the Des Moines Register *and* Tribune *with a bona fide scoop.*

Gammack was modest about his coverage of the buildup at the Laotian border. "This has been wild," he wrote to his editor from Quang Tri immediately after visiting Khe Sanh. "It would be fun to say that I had the right tip at the right time but the fact is that I headed for the Fifth (Mechanized Infantry Division) at Quang Tri almost as soon as I reached Da Nang because I heard they had a good, cooperative setup. And it wasn't until I arrived that I found that I'd landed in a hornet's nest."

TRIBUNE, FEBRUARY 4, 1971.

Now Near Laos, Iowans 'Scared'

KHE SANH, SOUTH VIETNAM—Utter desolation was the scene as United States GIs and engineers moved into Khe Sanh, scene of the historic siege of U.S. marines in 1968 and now in Viet Cong territory, without a fight.

Arriving by helicopter last Sunday morning, scattered groups of engineers were in sight, starting repairs on the shell-pocked old metal runway and blowing up shells, mostly duds, left behind by the marines.

Helicopters came in swarms, landing at the rate of at least one a minute, bringing in supplies. Heavy vehicles and other large equipment were brought in by giant helicopters, the loads in slings suspended from the bottoms of the choppers.

A major danger was minefields sowed by the marines before they pulled out and GIs, infantrymen of the 1st Brigade of the 5th Division (Mechanized), moved through the brush and tall elephant grass cautiously.

Earlier, en route to the Laotian border staging area, Iowa GIs, including James Harrington of Des Moines, told of their concern and worry—mainly because they didn't know what faced them.

Pfc. Larry Schwennen, 21, son of Mr. and Mrs. Jake Schwennen of Nashua, Ia., a machine-gunner who was on the third helicopter to land at Khe Sanh told his reactions:

"I didn't know exactly what was up here. We were all pretty scared, I guess. But we just got out and took it from there. I figured we'd take some mortar fire last night but it was all quiet.

"We sent out a long-range patrol, found Viet Cong hootches (house) and old marine communication wire—evidence that the enemy is out here. Just haven't seen 'em yet," he said.

"Man, I'm seeing an awful lot. It's hard to believe we can move all this machinery in on such short notice. They told us the engineers were going to work 24 hours a day. It was kind of hard to believe, lights on, the whole ball of wax, but by God they're doing it. They're good those engineers, damn good.

"You can't believe the support we've got up here," he added. "We've got everybody."

Montagnards Praised

Spec. 4 Jim McGough, 19-year-old son of Mr. and Mrs. Paul McGough of Fort Dodge, was talking with two Montagnard (Vietnamese) scouts. He explained:

"I walk point and these scouts walk with me. They spot a lot of things I miss. They're really good."

Regarding his reaction to the Khe Sanh mission, McGough said, "They briefed us before we came in, told us they don't know whether any hostile forces were in the area. I was in the thirteenth bird so I felt pretty good that there were twelve in before us."

One of the most popular GI's at Khe Sanh is Spec. 5 Ralph (Doc) Mertz, 22, son of Mr. and Mrs. Donald Mertz of Sioux City.

His buddies reported that on another mission Mertz applied tourniquets within 30 seconds on a man who had both legs blown off by a mine, and saved his life.

"They tell you to go and you go, do what you have to," Mertz said of the present mission. "I don't know really what to expect. Don't think anybody did. I thought they might rocket and mortar us. Nothing's happened yet and I hope it stays that way."

One of the men with 27th Engineers is Spec. 5 Stephen Wingert, son of Mr. and Mrs. Clare Wingert of Wesley. His father works as a mechanic in Algona.

Wingert said he enlisted in the Army because "I wanted to do something different and it's sure as hell different up here. I'm glad to get away from base camp, gives you something to do."

Wingert was waiting for his heavy equipment, a truck loader, to arrive, to start his regular assignment.

Another engineer, Pfc. Ron Edgerly of Cedar Rapids said he was excited about coming to Khe Sanh "after I heard what happened to the marines up here. I hope we can stay out of trouble because that's the surest way of getting home."

Dramatic Episode

The most dramatic episode at Khe Sanh Sunday was the arrival of three choppers carrying seven Vietnamese and two Americans on metal ladders suspended from the helicopters.

One wounded Vietnamese was strapped to the ladder.

Indications were the men had been on a secret reconnaissance mission and one chopper pilot became angry and tried to stop television crews from filming the arrival.

He threatened Steve Bell, formerly of Oskaloosa, and demanded the destruction of Bell's ABC network film. The threat was not carried out.

The protesting pilot's face was frozen in silence when asked if he had been to Laos. A peace symbol was painted on the helmet of the U.S. medic who cared for the wounded Vietnamese.

On the muddy, rutted dirt roads leading to Khe Sanh and the Laotian border, Iowans in the 1st Brigade of the 5th Division (Mechanized) admitted to being worried and apprehensive.

Even though U.S. troops are not scheduled to cross the border into Laos, they were moving into unchartered territory, sometimes occupied by the Viet Cong.

Their mission: Support a planned Allied thrust into Laos, backing up South Vietnamese troops with air support, helicopter gunships, medical evacuations and artillery.

At "Charlie Two" fire support base, self-propelled artillery was being moved out to join the attack and one gunner, James Harrington, 20-year-old son of Mrs. Marie C. Harrington, 3901 Cornell St., Des Moines, said, "You've got to go, that's all there is to it, but I'm scared.

"I've never been in a big operation before. That's life, I guess."

Said Spec. 5 Thomas Roy Engle, son of Mr. and Mrs. Roy Engel of Radcliffe, "This is my first big operation and I'm looking forward to it. I'm in charge of one section and I feel the extra responsibility.

"I'm not real sure of all that's involved but I know I'm going to have to take care of my men and so I'm a little apprehensive. It will be good to get out of here, though. I've been in this area for 3½ months."

A Dismal Life

It's a dismal, dreary life at "Charlie Two" and other fire support bases in the DMZ area. It has been miserably cold and raw and the GI's were reluctant to leave the safety and relative comfort of their underground bunkers to move into the uncertainty and the unknown of the open country to the west—near Laos.

But during the three days while U.S. and South Vietnamese troops moved into position, all sorts of activity mounted.

What had all the earmarks of confusion was delicately timed co-ordination.

All day and all night trucks and other vehicles moved over every road and highway in convoys heading west. Children flashed a peace sign as the troops passed by.

There was no letup in the throb and putt-putt sound of helicopters and other planes with various assignments in the general area.

High-ranking officers arrived by the dozens and hustled into secret conferences at brigade headquarters.

There were many signs that news of the operation would be controlled from Washington. Activities of newsmen were closely restricted during the staging phases of the offensive and an embargo was placed on all news dispatches from this corp area, which includes all of the northern area of South Vietnam.

TRIBUNE, FEBRUARY 6, 1971.

Major's 'Cookout' Wasn't Ordinary Army Picnic

QUANG TRI, SOUTH VIETNAM—The caper actually began last week at the Quang Tri airstrip while I was on my way to talk to Iowans in the 5th Mechanized Infantry Division along the demilitarized zone (DMZ).

Pfc. Randy Hendricks of Dubuque and a sizable Vietnamese dog he called Remf met me, and immediately hustled me off to Maj. Al Lamonica, the information officer in the division's 1st Brigade.

"You came up here to talk with men from Iowa, right?" he asked. "Well, you'd better come out back with me."

He led me to a grassy patch in back of his shack and said, "You walked into something. We're involved in a big operation, really big, so big it will probably be announced by Nixon.

"Can't tell you more right now except it's offensive in nature. But talking to Iowans won't be easy. Some units are on the move already. The others are real up tight, no time to talk. In one way, you came at a bad time.

"But you're in on something very few correspondents know about. I called the bureau chiefs of the television networks and invited them to a party. Told 'em I was having a cookout. Well, no one in his right mind has a cookout at Quang Tri this time of year. They got the message."

Within a few minutes I picked up the basic information about the mission.

The South Vietnamese (ARVN) were going to invade Laos and the 1st Brigade of the 5th Division, plus other U.S. units, were to seize historic Khe Sanh and secure the vital highway for supply points to the Laotian border.

I was a prisoner of the operations. I couldn't have left if I'd wanted to, but I certainly had no wish to be anywhere else. My journalistic companions were two wire service reporters.

The next morning, Friday, I went by helicopter to "Charlie Two" fire support base. There in the monsoon muck and mire, were tanks, which were going to stay to protect the base, and self-propelled 155-mm. howitzer artillery, about to move out to the border area.

"Living in a Dump"

There were several artillerymen from Iowa and we talked about the planned operation and life in the dreary wasteland just south of the DMZ.

"It's awful dull here, except when you get to shoot the guns a lot," said E-3 James K. Harrington, 20, son of Mrs. Marie Harrington, 3901 Cornell St., Des Moines.

"Sometimes we shoot 60 to 80 rounds a night and that's all right. It keeps you busy. Other times, you just sit around and wait—play volleyball, watch TV and listen to the radio. We run out of beer a lot. They let you drink what you want so long as you don't get too wasted to do your job."

"It's like living in a dump out here, though. You feel safe sleeping underground in bunkers but I like to have windows where I can see the sun. But up here I'd really feel creepy if I had to sleep out where they could mortar you.

"It's worst during the monsoon. Sometimes you get no mail for two weeks and morale sure goes down."

It's what the GIs call "harassment" from career noncoms, the often despised "lifers," that bugs them and lowers morale.

"I didn't think you'd get harassment over here," said Cpl. Truman Hengesteg, 21, of Northwood.

"I can understand having formations, having to shave, getting a haircut once a week, policing up the area all the time, washing off the shells back in the States, but over here, that's for the birds.

"Those lifers, they mess with us too much."

"Harassment, that's our biggest worry," echoed Spec. 5 Thomas Roy Engel, 23, of Radcliffe. "Polishing your boots all the time, formations, that's what ticks me off."

Said E-3 Gary Haverman, 21, of Carroll: "It's a dismal life up here, all right. But when you get mail, a movie once in a while and good chow, they help a lot and compensate some."

We hitchhiked the 15 miles back to Quang Tri and spotted some of the names GIs had painted on Army equipment.

A 175-mm. gun bore the name "Birth Control." A tracked vehicle bore the name "Cannabis," one of the names for marijuana.

A captain just back from patrol said his tracked vehicle had hit a mine and one man, on his very first day in combat, had been wounded. He barely missed being hit by enemy automatic fire.

"Some days things go so bad you want to cry," he said.

A U.S. Car

We hitched several rides, on trucks and tanks, and rode through rice paddies and hamlets. Off in the distance we spotted an American car.

"Look at that," said an Army companion. "Bet it belongs to a province chief. He's fat on graft."

And then we saw a Vietnamese girl on the runningboard of a water truck and as we passed, the driver was taking military currency from a billfold and handing it to her.

"Pot (marijuana) sale," I was told.

The next day, it turned rainy, and I kept shivering from the cold, recalling that one reason I welcomed the Vietnam assignment was to escape from an Iowa winter.

Sunday, I hitched a helicopter ride to Khe Sanh, hub of the border build-up, along with a handful of other news and television correspondents.

The U.S. presence at Khe Sanh seemed skimpy at first. But we quickly discovered GIs were out in the bush, not far from the cleared runway area, forming a protective perimeter. The greatest danger was minefields left by the marines in 1968.

Bill Barton of the Associated Press and I followed fresh footprints along a trail, past the remains of an old U.S. truck with elephant grass growing from its planking, when someone yelled there was a minefield ahead.

But soon we found a group of GIs and three were Iowans—Pfc. Larry Schwenen of Nashua, Spec. 4 Jim McGough of Fort Dodge and Spec. 5 Ralph Mertz of Sioux City.

They seemed elated at the unexpected encounter with another Iowan and Schwennen even refused to yield to shouts from his platoon mates to join them for a move to another spot. He didn't want to cut short our chat.

"Go on," he yelled, "I'll catch up with you."

And when the shouts to him became more persistent, he called back, "What are you going to do about it? Court-martial me?"

All of them admitted to being scared and apprehensive, because the area around Khe Sanh is known to be the hiding place of Viet Cong troops.

Most expected to be shelled extensively before they got out of there.

They continued to patrol the barren area.

"We know they're out there," said Schwennen of the enemy. "We just haven't seen 'em yet."

After several hours, we climbed aboard another helicopter and stopped at Mei Lac where ARVN troops, looking so very small, and also impassive, were starting a long march, presumably to Laos.

Finally returning to Quang Tri, we found about 60 American newsmen—all of them anxious to get to Khe Sanh after they heard word of the build-up.

Whatever hardships and discomforts Gammack reported amongst the soldiers he met at Quang Tri, he himself endured no less. He was 61 years old and his health had begun to deteriorate, a fact he acknowledged only after his assignment was completed.

From Quang Tri he wrote to his editor: "It was unbelievably cold during the night and I shivered plenty after finding that my original bunk had been usurped and I had to find another. In the morning there was no water. There wasn't any until late this afternoon. Then I discovered that while slithering around in the mud and groping for a place to bed in, I had lost my notebook. I didn't come up here prepared so I had to send for my typewriter and that didn't arrive until this afternoon so I borrowed one from the information officer, Al Lamonica, and it broke down after two paragraphs. And as I was transcribing notes from my tape recorder, the batteries died."

In another letter, written February 1, he conceded: "I feel as though I've been sort of put through a wringer. Life at Quang Tri and points west was pretty grim but if you are happy with the results, it was all more than worth it.

"Naturally I'm anxious to learn the outcome of all the various aspects of the Khe Sanh story. God knows the networks went ape on it and spent thousands on chartered planes and all that jazz. I think I got some breaks because Lamonica et al., thought I rated preferred treatment as an 'old man.' He did give me every break the networks got."

TRIBUNE, FEBRUARY 8, 1971.

Iowan Guides Viet Attackers

KHE SANH, SOUTH VIETNAM—An Iowa soldier helped guide South Vietnamese troops to the attack area during the invasion of Laos.

He is Pfc. William R. Beecher of Dubuque, a member of the 101st Airborne Division's "Pathfinders" squad.

His mission: Precede the South Vietnamese troops into the barren Viet Cong areas of South Vietnam near Laos, then guide them across the border into attack areas.

The Pathfinders used red flares to warn of danger spots, and called in helicopter gunships to attack the opposition.

Did They Cross?

There was no immediate indication that Beecher and his fellow Pathfinders actually crossed the border. But United States helicopter gunships, manned by U.S. troops, were used in the operation.

Beecher was briefed secretly Sunday night on his invasion role, but I was told his mission involved the attacking South Vietnamese troops.

Beecher was in high spirits on the eve of the attack and said, "If I had it to do over, I'd still be right where I am. Back home all you got is career types giving you a bad time. Here at least you can ignore 'em."

Frightful weather undoubtedly was a factor in the stuttering delays of the Laos invasion. A trip to the Laotian border and back to Quang Tri that normally is completed in less than two hours took me 24 hours.

A helicopter slated to take six correspondents to Lang Vei near the border was grounded because clouds filled the gap in the mountains leading to Khe Sanh.

Directs Traffic

The only alternative was a truck convoy at a road junction where Pfc. Thomas Grant of Evanston, Ill., was trying to control convoys in driving rain as he longed for normal MP duty near Saigon.

Beecher and his fellow Pathfinders were nonchalant Sunday night about their upcoming mission, drinking can after can of beer, staging pistol-drawing contests and engaging in boisterous and profane chatter.

By and large the mood of U.S. troops at Khe Sanh was black as they wearied of the endless chore of digging foxholes and making sandbag bunkers.

The "highway" to Khe Sanh is more like a rocky lane leading to an Iowa farm, with hairpin curves as if it were winding through a mountain pass.

The trip was made in a truck loaded with heavy artillery ammunition. The driver, Pfc. Tom Karpiszka of Pittsburgh, Pa., a driver because he "sort of" got kicked out of Army electronics school, muttered and cursed as he maneuvered his huge vehicle through the slithering mud and over treacherously narrow prefabricated meshed steel bridges across gorges and ravines.

And he repeated "Oh, jeez" over and over when his brakes gave out and his truck barreled slowly but relentlessly into the back of the convoy lead truck laden with C-rations. We finally limped into Khe Sanh, forced to a snail's pace by locked front brakes.

The trip to Khe Sanh took nearly three hours with frequent forced stops while bulldozers and graders cleared clogged bypasses.

These are the kind of problems U.S. troops have been coping with for a week. Small groups of GIs along the road were heating rations over wood

fires, some were munching apples and many flashed the "V" peace sign to convoy drivers.

Sunday, a pea-soup fog descended on Khe Sanh, restricting vision to as little as 50 yards, and the attack into Laos seemed threatened by the foul weather, bitterly cold and raw.

GIs were uptight and in an ugly mood after having to sleep for up to a week on this ugly plateau, built into a drab city of tents and foxholes from the desolation of seven days ago.

Fidgety movements by U.S. helicopter pilots sharing one tent indicated all were affected by the wind and cold and apprehension of combat during the night.

Through the long night artillery barked incessantly while perimeter guards were alerted for possible enemy attacks.

Frequently the soft singing sounds of artillery projectiles could be heard as they sailed toward targets in Laos. And during the two hours before daybreak several flights of jet fighter bombers could be heard.

The clearing of the weather Monday seemed almost a miracle after Sunday night's fog. But an hour before dawn one pilot peered out of our tent and said, "I see stars in the sky; it's going to be a good day."

Gammack found the attitude of the military authorities toward the press dramatically changed in the year since his first visit. He sensed a "widespread hostility to the media." The escorts who had been accommodating a year before were now, by their own admission, functioning as on-the-spot censors.

Gammack explained, "The escorts have been good guys and helpful and they haven't peeped when G.I.'s have made strong anti-army statements. But the trouble is that G.I.'s are just bound to be inhibited and thus my mission has been constantly hampered."

TRIBUNE, FEBRUARY 10, 1971.

Tough Day with Our 'Censors'

MARINE FIRE SUPPORT BASE BALDY, SOUTH VIETNAM—Secrecy not only continues to shroud the South Vietnamese operations in Laos but there is also a shocking increase in attempts by some U.S. military men to control news about the mood and actions of our troops.

It's a subtle form of censorship about what is reported to people back home.

Other correspondents in Vietnam have griped about it, and I ran into it at Marine Corps units at this fire support base in the northern reaches of South Vietnam.

Here's how this "indirect censorship" works:

Upon arrival in Marine Corps combat territory, I was immediately assigned two escorts, Cpl. Bill Baldwin of Lubbock, Tex., and a new man who was being "broken in" as an information assistant in the field.

Baldwin or his assistant listened attentively to every question I asked marines from Iowa and elsewhere and, more important, to their replies.

How can a man express his true feelings when every word is being monitored and in danger of being relayed to high officers?

Finally, I asked Baldwin: "Suppose I wanted to talk to a marine privately?"

He replied: "Well, if it were really private and personal, I'd permit it, but not if it were an interview. You see, we have correspondents coming up here who are anti-military and who are against the Vietnam war."

He was asked: "I hear that the 101st Airborne grades the correspondents according to their attitudes about the war and the chances they'll write friendly stories."

"We don't do that," Baldwin contended, "but we have a pretty good idea about a correspondent's attitudes when he comes up here."

I asked him: "What would you do if a correspondent were interviewing a marine reconnaissance man and the marine said if he took 10 prisoners out in the jungle, he'd keep one for interrogation and kill the rest?"

I didn't mention that I had participated in such an interview (without interference) a year ago.

"I'd end the interview right there and report what was said to my commander," Baldwin replied. "Any marine dumb enough to say that, no telling what else he might say . . ."

TRIBUNE, FEBRUARY 11, 1971.

'Pot, War Don't Mix'

DA NANG, SOUTH VIETNAM—There is considerable grumbling about the war among some U.S. troops here, but if there is any outfit with high morale and minimum drug and racial problems, chances are it is a Marine unit.

And this makes the Marines' frequently absurd attempts at "indirect censorship" seem silly.

It is the rule, rather than the exception, that Marines talk articulately and with pride about their duty—and usually in support of our involvement in Vietnam.

One Iowan, for instance—Cpl. Carl Huber, 19, son of Mr. and Mrs. Zeno William Huber, jr., of Fort Atkinson—told unhesitantly about turning in a fellow Marine for smoking marijuana.

"I found him smoking it in a foxhole," said Huber. "He got busted. (Court-martial and dishonorable discharge.) If there's one thing I can't stand, it's pot. Not over here. Not any place, for that matter. Out here in the bush someone's on watch and if he isn't alert, it's easy as heck for a V.C. (Viet Cong) to crawl right into your perimeter."

Huber's company commander, Capt. Bob Tilley of Canyon City, Colo., added: "A man smokes pot and when his squad gets through with him, they put him on a bird for a medical evacuation to the hospital. Morale with my men? I've had just three disciplinary cases in the last four months."

Huber was finishing up a tour as a member of a CUPP (Combined Unit Pacification Program) team, operating in the hilly area south of Da Nang where the Viet Cong still have strong clout.

There are 10 such teams, operating as patrols by day, laying ambushes at night, killing up to 60 Viet Cong a month, living in the villages (vills, the Marines call them) and helping to strengthen the local militia called Popular Forces (PF). They cover an area about 14 miles long and often tangle with the enemy.

"There are acts of terrorism," says Huber. "One old man, he gave the land on which we built a school, and the other day he was found with his throat cut and three bullets in his head. His daughter was kidnaped and raped."

Huber added something that is heard time and again these days:

"Out in the country, in the rice paddies, the people just want to be left alone. They're friendly to us because if they're not, the PF's will beat them up. And if the North Vietnamese move in, they'll be friendly to them because they don't want to be killed."

Hootches

Huber says the PF's are getting firmer control in the villages, which are not much more than clusters of hootches with a store or restaurant or two along the road.

"We had one school just about completed when the V.C. blew it up," Huber said. "Next day, the village officials rounded up some parents whose sons and daughters were known to be V.C. They were forced to stand in formation and wave the South Vietnamese flag and they had to pay money to buy beans to make good the damage. Next time we built the school, it wasn't blown up."

Another CUPP team member is Lance Corp. Jerry Ozburn of Marion, 20-year-old son of Mr. and Mrs. Duane Ozburn. He says "there is no higher morale than in the CUPP teams because so few Marines have to depend on each other so much."

He also thinks that the teams are winning lasting friendship among the Vietnamese.

"Just two days ago," he recalled, "a mother came to us with her little girl who had been stabbed by a big water buffalo. The little girl was really gored right through the neck. I don't know how it missed the jugular vein. Our (medical) corpsman says he's amazed she lived, but he's the guy who saved her. Those people aren't going to forget a thing like that."

TRIBUNE, MARCH 5, 1971.

Why Viet News Is a Problem

SAIGON, SOUTH VIETNAM—In assessing reports of attempts to hobble newsmen in Vietnam, it is important to remember that these are efforts to deceive and mislead the American public. The harassment of individual reporters is relatively unimportant.

The war in Vietnam is my third. Previously, in Europe during World War II and in Korea, there was a mood of co-operation throughout the armed forces—an attitude that reporters were, in fact, the eyes and ears of the folks back home.

Almost everywhere a reporter went in Europe and Korea, he had the feeling that the welcome mat was out.

In Vietnam, a reporter constantly has the feeling of a hostile attitude by military personnel. In some areas it is more extreme than in others.

A top information officer with the 101st Airborne Division was reliably reported to have once said, "If every newsman over here were killed, it would suit me just fine."

Significantly, if an information officer had said anything of that sort in Europe during World War II and Gen. Dwight Eisenhower had heard about it, the officer very likely would have been disciplined severely—and almost certainly would have been transferred—because everyone in Eisenhower's command knew the general wanted minimum restrictions on the flow of information back home.

Set the Tone

That's the way it works, especially in a war.

The men at the top set the tone and it filters down through the ranks. Generals and privates alike in Europe knew instinctively that they could talk freely to reporters, within security limits, without fear of getting in trouble, because Eisenhower was a true believer in a free press.

But in Vietnam, generals and privates alike perceive a general hostility toward news media by President Nixon—and certainly Vice-President Spiro Agnew—and subconsciously they feel they can get by with an anti-media attitude, even to the point of wishing reporters personal harm.

Other factors, of course, are involved in the imposition of obstacles that reporters have to cope with in Vietnam.

One is the sensitivity resulting from a spate of unfavorable events—the My Lai deaths, refusals of men to go into battle, fake awards, bad morale, fraggings, the horrendous drug problem and many others.

In fact, it was the television report of a marijuana party, showing soldiers smoking pot, that led to the directive from Gen. Creighton Abrams' command that reporters must be accompanied by military escorts whenever they are with military units in Vietnam, a rule that makes it extremely difficult to get honest expressions of feelings from GIs.

"Let me take a look at that directive on escorts for reporters," I asked a lieutenant in the information office of the Americal division at Chu Lai.

He refused, claiming, "It's classified" security information.

Another reason for anti-newsman attitudes in Vietnam is that the military is frequently less than honest in the release of information to the American public.

Over the long haul, total casualty and helicopter loss figures may be reasonably accurate, but there is good reason to believe that reports are doctored along the way to make them more palatable back home.

26 Dead

I was at a military hospital one day when officers said that 26 dead had been brought in from a particularly savage battle.

The official report on that battle, however, said there had been 12 deaths. The other 14 were spread out and included in casualty reports for succeeding days, obviously to make the initial battle appear less bitter than it actually was.

There are reasons to believe that a similar policy is being pursued in connection with current helicopter losses in Laos. If they are particularly bad one day, only some of the losses are announced immediately and others are held back for days when actual losses are lighter.

As previously reported, if helicopters are recovered and brought back from Laos by other helicopters, they are not reported as lost, even if the ships are in shambles and crew members have been killed and wounded.

The credibility of the military in Vietnam is so poor that veteran reporters almost automatically doubt claims that U.S. military personnel are not involved in ground actions in Cambodia and Laos.

Some Army information officers with whom reporters are forced to deal have no conception of the news function. But there are exceptions to the rule and a few have been extremely helpful to reporters.

One is Maj. Al Lamonica of the 1st Brigade of the 5th Mechanized Infantry Division, which helped support the invasion. However, there also are reports that he was reprimanded for his co-operation.

Another is Maj. Frank Bailey of the Americal Divison. The division has had more than its share of bad news—My Lai, notably. But, refreshingly, it does not seek to hide its problems.

Thus, its information officers readily reveal that the division had 106 "fraggings" last year, that a survey shows one soldier in 10 uses heroin and that black troops marched on division headquarters to protest against alleged discrimination.

Work Harder

Muzzling a free press isn't easy and, by and large, the anti-news media attitude in Vietnam has served primarily to make the regular correspondents, those who report the war day in, day out, year after year, work just that much harder.

But the ominous thing about it all is that such hobbling attempts should not be a part of our free and open society.

In the latter portion of his trip, Gammack's focus shifted from spot coverage of the places where news was breaking to more comprehensive consideration of problems faced by the American G.I. in Vietnam. In particular, he dealt with drug addiction, fragging, and the morale problems of which they were symptomatic.

Part of the reason for Gammack's shift away from military hot spots was that he realized somewhat reluctantly his own physical limitations. "I don't feel entirely satisfied with my Laos border coverage but it was really a gruelling experience for a guy my age and the weather has continued to be absolutely miserable. I can handle the occasional hazards o.k. And they're increasing. But the constant scramble for chopper rides, walk after walk of a couple or more miles, carting cumbersome gear around, climbing up the back of trucks, putting up with the high decibel snoring of the TV crews, wrestling with C-rations and competing with some 60 correspondents for space available became damn burdensome. Also, there was inevitably a terrible waste of time between opportunities to get anything done."

There was a rueful tone to Gammack's expressions of respect for the front-line reporters. "I really have it soft compared to some of the competing agency people and my hat's off to guys who spend all day in the bush, day after day, and then often have to scream over the phone to Saigon for an hour to get their stories dictated."

But, whatever the motivation, Gammack's decision to focus in depth on morale and related problems precipitated some of the most interesting copy to come out of his Vietnam ventures. His article on a "lifer" who was despised by many of his men appeared some two weeks before his discussion of fragging but the two are clearly related. Two other articles which prefaced his five-part series on morale problems are also included.

TRIBUNE, FEBRUARY 9, 1971.

Ex-Iowa Sergeant Respected, Despised, a Murder Target

QUANG TRI, SOUTH VIETNAM—First Sgt. Gene Tingley, who grew up in Madrid, Ia., is trim, tough and every inch the Army man. He is respected by some of his troops, despised by others.

He's hated enough to be the target for murder by some of his men. In Vietnam, they call it "fragging" and it is becoming a problem.

It's obvious Tingley, 37, is an unusual man.

A skinhead by choice, he shaves his head regularly, leaving bare traces of stubble. His toothbrush mustache forms a triangle with his penetrating, stern eyes.

Tingley's family has moved to Michigan from Madrid, where he enlisted in the Army in 1951 after his junior year in high school.

But Korea is more of a home to Tingley now. He served four tours of duty there, married a Korean woman (she was his laundry girl), who waits for him to come back.

Last December his orderly room at the 14th Engineers Battalion here was bombed. It was only by chance that he wasn't in it—the attackers had every right to believe he would be there at 6 a.m. as usual. That day he was delayed momentarily.

No one has been charged with the bombing, but Tingley has firm ideas.

"I'm very sure I know who the men were," he said in an interview. "One of them is still in my company. Since it happened, I've had time to think about it and I've decided they didn't care whether I was in the room or not.

"It was a symbol, that orderly room, a military symbol. They wanted to intimidate.

"I'm sure they were crazy men, really crazy, on drugs—and real hard stuff, too. There was a conspiracy. I'm sure of that because the two men who planted the bomb aren't smart enough to have made it."

Is he worried about another attempt on his life?

"Worried, no. Concerned, yes. What's the difference? I walk when I want and where I want and I sleep well at night. I get up in the morning with a smile.

"But still I'm concerned. I have a wife and three children, a mother, a sister and a brother. I enjoy being with them and if I'm blown sky high I couldn't be there, so I'm concerned about that. But worry? That gets you nothing."

Q: How about your relationship with your men?

A: I judge men. I have good men. Some have tendencies to do things that are not right because they've never been taught the difference between right and wrong. Then there are those under the influence of drugs. They don't know what they're doing.

Q: How has the GI changed over the years?

A: The change has come in the home. He doesn't have the discipline I did. I wouldn't talk back to my father because I knew what it got me. I wouldn't talk back to my first sergeant because I knew what it would have got me. These young men will talk back to you today like you were nothing.

Q: Isn't this hard for you to take after all your years in the Army?

A: Very definitely. I believe I know what a military organization must be to accomplish its mission. Its mission is to win. Discipline is one of the most important things we sell. There are isolated instances of cruelty, misuse of authority. But stern discipline is a very necessary thing.

Q: Are you a stern disciplinarian?

A: I consider myself one, yes. When necessary, I don't hold back. Sometimes an order must be followed automatically without a question-and-answer period. Too many young men want answers right now. I try to make people who work for me know that my judgment is sound and when I require that something be done rapidly there's a reason.

Q: How do you rate today's GI?

A: He's not a bad guy. He's the same man I was but he's easy to lead astray because he's never had anyone tell him no. He does what he wants to do because there's no one to tell him that's not right.

These soldiers never have had any discipline and now we non-commissioned officers and officers have had the pressure put on us to not apply the necessary pressure to make a disciplined unit.

Q: So you've had to relax?

A: I've relaxed, yes, not because I think I'm wrong. I KNOW I'm right. But my commander sets the policy. My commander says I must relax. Therefore, I have."

Tingley is what the GIs here call a "lifer." There probably never will be a meeting ground between draftees forced into service and the career men who have accepted a stern, often ruthless, military as a way of life.

This is the core of what is widely discussed as the

morale problem in Vietnam. And when the basic conflict grows into hatred made wild and irrational by a dose of heroin that can be had easily for $2, the consequence can be ghastly.

Tingley can vouch for that.

TRIBUNE, FEBRUARY 27, 1971.

Morale Problems Behind 'Fraggings'

SAIGON, SOUTH VIETNAM—The repugnance the average GI in Vietnam feels toward commissioned and non-commissioned officers called "lifers" is very great indeed. At times it is murderous.

But when a "lifer" is adequately defined—not to include automatically all military career men—then some of this intense hatred is perhaps justified, or at least understandable.

So in studying this problem, a careful distinction must be made between the "lifer" and the career man. An Iowan, Lt. Col. James M. Timmens of Madrid, a social worker and a career officer himself, suggests these definitions.

The "Lifer"

He generally has a lower education and has made the military his life. Now, with retirement approaching, he is in a position of authority and responsibility and is almost entirely concerned with himself, his own interests and his own welfare.

He maneuvers to look good to his superiors by getting jobs done through subordinates. He has almost no concern for his men or their welfare.

In civilian life, he probably would have been a failure. Chances are he lost out in competition for desirable American women and turned to foreign women.

Often, he is a heavy drinker, if not an alcoholic.

The True Career Man

He is tolerated, at times accept 1, by his men and has a genuine concern for his troops. He takes care of them. He communicates with them and while the GIs don't like the system, they can at least respect this man, who has a job to do.

Soldiers who are mature enough to see that the man is trying to make the best of an unpleasant situation give him their respect. And the more mature soldier may say, "The Army's not my bag but if it is the career man's bag, let him have it."

Storm Trooper

A very astute Army chaplain from Iowa, a captain who asked not to be quoted by name, talked of one "lifer" who was the target of a "fragging."

"I'm surprised someone didn't try to get him sooner," he said. "He is an evil man. It's strange. He is a mamma's boy, writes to his mother every night, and yet in his treatment of men he is a sadist. He is an alcoholic yet has no compassion whatever for the GI who smokes pot.

"He has had at least two marriage failures and, you know, a man like that finally marries the Army and when a GI says anything derogatory about the Army, he resents it the way a normal man resents an insult to his wife. He is right out of the storm trooper mold."

The chaplain continued with observations about "lifers."

"GI's are always coming to me saying how the lifers are messing up their lives and I try to tell them there are lifers in civilian life, too. There are lifers in corporations and in the professions. And ministers can become lifers when they start believing their own B.S."

But there is the side of the problem as seen by the "lifers."

Career men all down the line complain that morale has been damaged by relaxed discipline many feel is ridiculously permissive.

"It's not like the Army of old, not by a long shot," complained Sgt. John Winbush of Jacksonville, Fla., who enlisted 18 years ago.

"We used to be strong and tough—a 40-mile hike in a day was nothing—and I loved it," he said. "But the Army's gone soft. There's no discipline any more and a GI can get by with just about anything."

Winbush has other reasons to complain.

He served a tour in West Germany and says there "is more discrimination against the black man within the American Army than you can find anywhere in the south. Over here a black man is treated pretty good, with exceptions. Germany's just awful."

And friends confide that because he is black, "lifers" deprived Winbush of additional sergeant stripes he should be wearing now.

Core of Problem

Nonetheless, the very core of the morale problem in Vietnam involves the "lifer" and almost always, he is the target and victim of fraggings—target of grenades and other explosives to kill, injure or terrorize.

First Lt. Michael Wolfe of Marshalltown, son of Dr. Otis Wolfe, operator of the Wolfe Eye Clinic in Marshalltown, is an Americal Division artillery officer who supports the Army system generally but has no intention of making it his career.

Explaining the origin of fraggings, he says "A GI comes over here and some lifer gives him a bad time. He gets drunk or high on drugs and says, 'I'll show that ____,' and some guy with him who doesn't have the courage of a mouse says: 'Oh, no, you won't; you ain't got the guts,' and the first guy says: 'Oh, yes, I have.' One thing leads to another and, Bang! something happens.

"It's often a case of weak people trying to make themselves strong. Society is built on masculinity, guns and weapons—being a hunter, the ability to fight well, things like that. And so, over here, when a man tangles with someone who has authority over him, he says to himself: 'I got a weapon, I can get that guy.' So he uses it."

What else motivates Americans to want to kill fellow Americans?

Says Maj. Ernest Jeppsen of Salt Lake City, an Army psychiatrist: *"People are sent over here to kill, people are taught to kill, people are taught it's the way to solve problems."*

"We think in terms of killing over here. A company commander asks a man, 'How many men did you kill today?' and if you've killed so many, you're a good boy. This is a way of life."

Many draftees with a higher level of education are especially critical of "lifers," although most don't go to the extreme of fragging.

One is Spec. 4 James Vigars, 22, son of Mr. and Mrs. W. H. Vigars of Eldora, a graduate of the University of Northern Iowa.

"In a way, I feel sorry for a lot of the NCO's," says Vigars. "They're supposed to be supervising lower enlisted men who have more education than they do.

"And college men aren't treated with the respect we think we merit. You know that your community respects you and your opinions. Then you come in the Army and all of a sudden you're a peon. You're put in a job and pretty soon you know more about it than the non-com over you. You do the job your way and he tells you it's wrong and you check it out and you find you are right and you are resentful.

"In a way, I feel sorry for the non-coms, the lifers. They feel their authority being undermined because people all around them are more qualified than they are."

TRIBUNE, FEBRUARY 16, 1971.

GI Morale Problems Extend to Rear Areas

DA NANG, SOUTH VIETNAM—There are increasing signs of serious morale problems among our troops in Vietnam.

These are more common in combat areas and have been widely reported. But even in rear areas such as this sprawling supply complex, there are ugly incidents—"fragging" and racial friction.

A "fragging," born literally of murderers' hate, gets its name from the throwing of a fragmentation grenade where it can kill, maim or—at the very least—terrorize the intended victim or victims, usually higher ranking superiors.

I sat in during the preliminaries of a general court martial of three GIs—from Oklahoma, Pennsylvania and Indiana—charged with a grenade assault against a non-commissioned officer, a warrant officer and a first lieutenant.

"It's so terribly hard to catch fraggers," a captain in the judge advocate's office remarked. "There are an awful lot of them—we had another just last night—but the odds are that you'll solve only about one in 20 fragging cases.

"A man tosses a grenade in a hootch at 2 a.m. and he has disappeared by the time it goes off."

Joseph Remcho, a civilian lawyer from Massachusetts and a member of the three-man Lawyers Military Defense Committee (privately financed by a Massachusetts group) is the chief counsel for the three accused men on trial here.

"We've had dozens of requests to defend fragging cases, so it must be very widespread," he said.

He added that civilian attorneys are badly hobbled in their military work in Vietnam because the military command, for the most part, denies them necessary use of military mails, telephones and transportation.

The judge advocate captain added: "A major problem these days is that high-ranking non-commissioned officers who are high school graduates at best have no concept of authority except to growl—and with GI draftees who are college men, it just doesn't work."

This doesn't mean that college men are the fraggers, but there are clear signs that the fragging pattern is becoming increasingly bold and systematized.

"A three-step process has evolved," one knowledgeable officer explained.

"First comes the smoke grenade, tossed into a noncom's or officer's hootch (home); absolutely harmless, no more than a nuisance, but the first warning.

"If that intimidation doesn't produce results, a gas grenade, one that causes vomiting, is next. The third one is the real thing, and I can't get over the fact that Americans are really trying to kill other Americans to such an alarming extent."

Two Iowans talked of the increasing racial friction they have observed at their base, through which combat veterans pass on their way home and which receives new men about to be sent into the fields.

Football Player

"Within our own units, we have no racial trouble at all," said Spec. 4 Robert Gibbs, son of Mr. and Mrs. J. R. Gibbs of Iowa City, a 1969 University of Iowa graduate who played defensive back and end on the 1966-68 Iowa football teams.

But many soldiers coming in from the field, Gibbs said, are on their way home and they don't care what they do here.

"They realize they can get away with more than they ever could back in the world," he said. "They're in a combat zone and figure no one's going to mess with them.

"It's a two-way street. Whites are as responsible as the blacks for provoking trouble.

"Morale—let's face it, it's low. Everyone's got a devil-may-care attitude. They say the hell with it. They know they're going to be leaving Vietnam in six or eight months and if they don't want to do something, they just say they won't do it. They have enough people who feel the same way, it's very difficult to set them down and say, 'You do this and get it done.'

"It's really tough," Gibbs continued. "I feel sorry for officers, I really do. Maybe it's the affluent society. We're all a product of it. I have a feeling it's going to get worse. No one wants to be here. It's dirty, it's hot, it's rainy, it's muddy, it's everything else and it's hard to tolerate . . ."

Both Gibbs and Spec. 4 Jim Dunlap of Davenport, whose wife, Cindy, of Fort Dodge, is a student at Iowa State University at Ames, work in the records divisions of a supply command.

Dunlap says he is frightened by "the hate that has developed between blacks and whites."

"I develop pictures late at night at the craft shop and I've decided it's just not safe to walk near the enlisted men's club when it's closing up," he said. "Anything can happen, men drunked up and black-white fights breaking out all the time. Call them what you want. I call them racial disturbances. Some times one group is to blame, sometimes another.

Mess Hall

"The other day, a man cut in line at mess hall, then decked another man for calling him on it. That night four or five guys jumped the man who did the slugging and he wound up in the hospital with four or five stab wounds.

"The next night a gate guard asked a soldier for his pass. The soldier reached into his pocket, but came out with a knife instead of the pass and stabbed the guard."

On top of the racial friction and the fraggings, commanders also are being forced to cope with "combat refusals," and even in the supply areas, some men are refusing point blank to go north from Da Nang to the danger areas where U.S. forces are supporting the South Vietnamese invasion of Laos.

TRIBUNE, FEBRUARY 24, 1971.

Hate, Bitterness Fill GI Viet Jail

LONG BINH, SOUTH VIETNAM—On the Army's sprawling supply base here, there is a huge rectangular area with fencing covered with canvas so those passing by can't see inside.

Inside the enclosure the atmosphere is in contant danger of exploding, mainly because racial feelings run high.

It's the Army's main jail in Vietnam, whimsically called the LBJ—Long Binh Jail.

Of the 375 prisoners now in the jail serving six-month sentences or waiting shipment home to face more serious charges, 62 per cent are black.

And many blacks serving here cite the jail as proof of racism being practiced by the Army.

Iowans on guard duty at the jail confirmed it is filled with hate and bitterness.

One Man's View

The first sergeant of a military police (MP) company on duty at the jail, a black from North Carolina, put it this way in a guarded interview:

"Don't use my name because I've only got a year before retirement and I don't want to stir up any more trouble than I already have. But see me in a year and I'll give you enough for a book.

"Don't tell me the black man doesn't get the dirty end of everything over here.

"Look! Most of the men in this jail are here on drug charges and the majority are black. I'm telling you 80 to 85 per cent of the men in Vietnam smoke pot. Twelve per cent of us over here are black.

"Now you tell me why the blacks are the ones who wind up in here for drugs. I'll tell you one reason. Less then one per cent of the Army investigators are black."

Official Army explanations make little difference—the blacks are satisfied the racial imbalance in the jail adds up to prejudice and racism.

One result is that inside the jail there is the constant potential of race riots, which break out from time to time.

Segregation then becomes the choice of the inmates. Guards, anxious to avoid trouble, encourage the separation into two color camps.

There is enough hate and bitterness in the jail that one MP guard from southern Iowa, Pfc. Dennis Bradfield, 22, asked that his hometown not be pinpointed "because there are enough crazy guys in there that one of 'em might want to track me down when he gets out."

Bradfield said no superior had laid down restrictions on comments about life inside the jail, "but I'm using my own judgment and I'll probably have more to say after I'm out of the Army."

There are three areas in the jail—minimum security, medium security and maximum security. Bradfield says men who behave "have it better than I do. It's an R. and R. (rest and recuperation) for them, it really is. No work and not much harassment."

Another MP Guard, Spec. 4 Gary Elings, 20-year-old son of Mr. and Mrs. Harold Elings of 3418 E. Thirty-third St. in Des Moines, has worked in both the minimum and maximum security compounds and he says "the prisoners give you a hard time and it gets on your nerves.

"They call you names, spit on you and I've even had cups of urine thrown on me," he said.

"A Bad Time"

"But," he added, "if I was them, I guess I'd do some of the same things. Some of the guards give the prisoners a bad time. If there's a senior non-com in the jail, a lifer, the guards really lay it to them."

Elings recalls once when a black prisoner was moved from medium to maximum security, the "box, with leg irons," other blacks staged a mass protest, shouting that if he were going to be put in they all should be.

And, says Elings, most of the protesters were. It happened more than a month ago and some of the demonstrators are still in maximum confinement because of the incident.

Prisoners judged guilty of violence in the jail are treated harshly, locked up, sometimes with leg irons, in what are called "conex boxes."

These are metal crates with openings for ventilation 6 feet by 5 feet by 8 feet. If a man is more than 6-foot-1, he can't stand up straight and is put elsewhere.

For sleeping, the best a man in the box gets is a cot and a blanket. Well-behaved prisoners have sheets and blankets for their bunks.

Pfc. Michael Potter, 19, of Cedar Rapids, son of Mr. and Mrs. Talbert Potter, is a maximum security MP and he recalls the time a caged prisoner reached out, grabbed a guard and attempted to cut his throat with a sharpened tin-can top.

The wound was not serious, however.

Another Iowan on duty at the jail is Sgt. John Buchholz, 24, of Carroll. He handles jail records in an office just outside the compound.

Most of the prisoners, he said, have a record of prior military offenses of some sort.

TRIBUNE, FEBRUARY 25, 1971.

Drug Problem in Viet: 'Everyone Depressed'

CHU LAI, SOUTH VIETNAM—The enormity of the drug problem among American soldiers in Vietnam scarcely can be exaggerated.

An absolute minimum of one in 10 GIs is using heroin that carries a clout stronger than usual because it is 95 per cent pure.

Responsible estimates indicate at least half of the men in Vietnam smoke marijuana regularly or have experimented with it.

The Americal Division, with headquarters here has just completed a survey on drug usage among its men. Many would not be reached, but 3,000, ranging from general to private, completed the questionnaire. It's considered a fair sampling of the troops.

Psychiatrists and other officers who supervised the survey were aware that many would not, and did not, trust the Army's promise of anonymity and say the actual number of drug users is higher than shown in the survey.

Even so, 40 per cent of the men said they had used one type of drug or another in Vietnam.

Ten per cent said they had used hard narcotics—heroin in almost all cases.

"These are rock-bottom figures," says Maj. Ernest A. Jeppsen of Salt Lake City, Utah, a psychiatrist with the division. "I think actual usage, especially with marijuana, is somewhat higher."

The study showed that drug usage was much lower—about 10 per cent—in the field where contact with the enemy always is likely.

Jeppsen believes few men start on drugs to allay their combat fears. Rather, he says, the most often heard excuse is an approximation of the GI expression: "The lifers (career men) are messing with me."

Drugs become an escape because men are harassed, not treated as individuals, feel deprived, are denied normal outlets and miss their families.

"Everyone over here is depressed, either a little depressed or a lot depressed," says Jeppsen. "You're supposed to be depressed in Vietnam. There's no reason to be happy here."

One bright spot in the drug picture is suggested by Lt. Col. James M. Timmens of Madrid, a career social worker with the 935th Medical Detachment of the 93rd Evacuation Hospital at Long Binh.

Timmens feels a majority of the men who become addicted to heroin in Vietnam are able to shake the habit when they go home. This, of course, is in sharp contrast to the United States figures indicating that 90 per cent of the hard-core addicts in the States return to the habit after treatment in government institutions.

"When a soldier comes over here he plugs into a primary group," says Timmens. "It becomes his little world, a sub-culture and he tends to adopt peer group attitudes, value systems and behavior. With this peer group, drugs may be a part of the culture.

"But about the tenth or eleventh month, he begins to think about home, going back to Dubuque or Boone or Adel or somewhere. He thinks of his family, his girl friend, his future. Drugs are not a part of that values system. So he unplugs from his peer group and plugs in to the atmosphere of his home town and starts adopting these values. He starts to abandon the drug habit."

Can he shake it that easily?

"It takes motivation, just as with smoking or drinking," says Timmens. "Sometimes there is the withdrawal period and our rehabilitation program helps him through this. But it's easier, perhaps, than giving up alcohol. Back home everyone may drink, it's part of the culture, but there is no drug subculture in the average guy's home town."

Timmens has worked with hundreds of heroin addicts but, he says, not one has been an Iowan, to his knowledge. Based on averages, only one in every 100 GIs in Vietnam is an Iowan and, further, heroin is not the problem in Iowa that it is in major metropolitan areas of the nation.

The division survey revealed that of the men using heroin in Vietnam, half had used it before coming here.

"With marijuana, we found no background pattern," said Jeppsen, the psychiatrist. "It was a general one, including proportionate numbers of college graduates and high school graduates, rich and poor.

"But the heroin users are less educated; there are more dropouts, more law violators, more people invited to join the Army to avoid prosecution."

Following are Jeppsen's answers to two questions on the drug subject:

Q. What indications are there that marijuana leads to hard drugs?

A. That's part of the marijuana controversy. Make that statement before drug users and you've got a red-hot argument. There are lots of pot users who never touch heroin and those who start on pot probably used alcohol first. All I can say is there is an association. If you're the type of person who is going to experiment with drugs, you're going to take what's available.

Q. How serious is the problem?

A. If you have 10 per cent of a company not working to capacity, you've got a problem. What we see here reflects what's going on in the U.S. There is more drug usage here because it's easier to get and there are more frustrations.

The drug user is a peculiar person, does a lot of imaginative thinking, starts off saying to himself: "I'll try it once; won't hurt me." So he tries it and likes it. He uses it time after time then and tells himself: "As long as I use it occasionally, I'm not going to get addicted." But when he uses it more and more, he tells himself he can stop any time. Then he finds he needs it and he makes excuses to himself, he doesn't feel so good. Finally he tells himself, "I can stop as soon as I leave Vietnam and go home."

When men approach their DEROS (date of estimated return from overseas service), they are most likely to accept the Army's amnesty program and try to get off drugs.

In the Americal Division, the system works like this.

A soldier gets amnesty when he goes to his commanding officer, and says, "I have a problem and want help."

He is given a built-in guarantee he won't be prosecuted. The man is examined by a physician who determines whether withdrawal in a hospital is necessary or whether an out-patient basis is adequate. It takes three days, either way.

The man then returns to his commanding officer who counsels with him and decides whether anything can be gained through a change in job, associates or living arrangements.

Early in the amnesty program, it was used by malingerers. Soldiers left dangerous positions in the field in droves, saying they couldn't go on a patrol or some other combat mission because they needed treatment for drug addiction.

That's not possible now. When the man goes to a doctor in the field, faking is spotted quickly and these soldiers are promptly returned to their units.

"I've been pleasantly surprised by the reception I've been receiving by company and other unit commanders," says Jeppsen.

"Some, of course, just aren't interested, don't want to be bothered. As far as they're concerned, the only way to handle a drug addict is to get him out of the Army.

"But others see it as a problem that's got to be handled—you just can't ship the addicts home because you'll just get another shipment of potential addicts in return.

"The Army has better capabilities to develop drug abuse programs than civilian organizations because it is more structured and organized and the financing is automatic.

TRIBUNE, FEBRUARY 26, 1971.

GIs in Therapy Swap Stories of Their Addiction

CHU LAI, SOUTH VIETNAM—Eight U.S. soldiers—four white, four black—whose lives had been on the verge of destruction from heroin sat in a circle and swapped stories about their addiction and attempted salvation from it.

It was group therapy, a Saturday afternoon ritual at the mental hygiene section of the Americal Division here.

The addicts talked openly and honestly of "smack," a name for heroin, "caps," the vials it comes in and of being "strung out," a term meaning that a man is deeply under the influence of heroin.

How much is accomplished by unburdening one's soul at these sessions is questionable. Few addicts return week after week. But the sessions do provide evidence of the severity of the drug problems with the U.S. military in Vietnam.

Common Thing

"The idea of sticking a needle in your arm used to be horrifying, send shivers down your spine," said one of the men at the session.

"It's not like that any more, it's a common everyday thing. You know these Coke-kids, those boy-sans coming around selling you Coke? They sell more'n Coke. Those kids get you anything you want."

"Yeh," said another. "Bet you I can approach eight out of every ten hootch maids, and get them to bring me in stuff, anything I want. And those kids you see, they'll bring you anything. Their sisters even."

The conversation rambled on.

The men seemed to get satisfaction from confessing their drug addiction.

Unlike some civilian convicts who proclaim penitence and discovery of the path to virtue in the hope of parole or some other "angle," these men had nothing to gain. They were part of the Army's amnesty program that offers help, without penalty, to drug addicts who turn themselves in.

Only one man, white, sat in silence. His blue robe and pajamas indicated hospitalization for his withdrawal from drugs. His eyes were glassy. His face was blank. He chain-smoked endlessly.

A psychiatrist and two aides gently led the discussion and steered it from problem to problem.

"Has anyone explained the amnesty program?" inquired the psychiatrist.

"A group of black NCO's (non-commissioned officers) practically broke my door down yesterday," said one especially talkative group member.

"They came into my hootch and spoke to me for about an hour, telling me, 'Get off, get off, get off, it's going to ruin you,' because they knew how I was when I first came here and could see what dope had done to me. They gave me a pass to come here to Chu Lai and I'm going to do my best."

"How heavy are you?" inquired the psychiatrist.

He replied: "I'm not gone, three caps a day. First I started shootin' and then I started sniffin' as you can probably tell by the sound of my voice. Some people say to a guy, 'I'm better'n you because you're shootin' and I'm sniffin'! That's ridiculous because it's still the same stuff, still a habit."

The medical men wondered what could be done to help addicts break the habit.

"That's what I'm trying to do now," one man volunteered. "I came here from Duc Pho to stop the habit and when I go back to Duc Pho and my buddies see I'm not messin' with drugs any more, I know it will encourage more and more of them to stop.

"If just one guy will say, 'All right, why don't you get me into the program,' then he'll show a friend and that guy will come back and show another friend that the habit can be broken."

"Trouble is," said another," "the guys who are using it every day aren't interested in stopping it, they just want to control it."

"Yeh," the conversation continued, "I was trying to encourage a couple of fellows to come with me to stop these habits and there were guys saying, 'Don't go, don't go, don't go, you'll get drugs on your records.'

"It sounds more reasonable not to trust the establishment, so these guys say, 'Yeh, I might get a record,' and the habit increases, and before you know, it's out of hand."

"Lie to Yourself"

The men talked of how they become addicted and one said, "You know you shouldn't do it, but you talk yourself into it, you rationalize, lie to yourself. It's weird that the stuff will do that to you, but it does."

The psychiatrist inquired, "Does the drug do it or is it the type of person you are?" One replied, "A lot of people say it's just psychological, just saying you're not going to get caught, get addicted. But you're just fooling yourself until you're greasy and grimy and you've lost everything you have and you realize you're gone."

Said another: "It's more of an experiment at first. You get high real easy, don't need very much. You're high and that's fine. Well, time goes by and you need more. You're not addicted yet but it takes more and more to get you high—and pretty soon you're hooked.

"You keep hearing guys say they're doing it because they're in Vietnam and as soon as they go home they'll quit and it won't be a problem. But if you get strung out over here, it's going to stay with you."

(But some military social workers, including Lt. Col. James M. Timmens of Madrid, Ia., disagree with this.

Timmens feels many users and addicts in Vietnam can shake the habit when they return home because narcotics are a part of the Army culture and value system in Vietnam, but not in most cities and towns in the United States. Thus, the pressure from peers to use drugs will not be great in most cases, Timmens explains.)

Another man added: "The stuff here is so much stronger. In two months you're a hard-core junkie."

Some of the men participating in the session said they knew of men in their outfits who died from heroin overdoses.

"A lot of guys think this stuff against heroin is a lie. And if an officer says it, they put it down as propaganda. But if they see an O.D. (overdose death), it becomes real, it can happen to them."

"Trouble is not everyone sees an O.D.," one man suggested.

Don't Do Jobs

Several men said they started on heroin thinking it was non-addictive cocaine.

One explained, "I was in the hospital, hit by shrapnel, and when they let me out, there was still plenty of pain. I was smoking pot and that helped some. Then a friend says, 'Here, man, try this, it is THE pain-killer.' I got high and didn't feel no pain and he said it was cocaine, that's what the boy-san had told him. But it was smack."

The psychiatrist said that drug users had told

him repeatedly that they can do their jobs completely satisfactorily while on drugs.

"Then I talk to their C.O.'s (commanding officers) and they say that all of a sudden these men aren't doing their jobs right," said the psychiatrist. "The drug user thinks he's doing a good job, regardless of what he does. It's very hard to point this out. If a C.O. does it, it's just more harassment."

Several of the addicts suggested that the full repercussions in the United States from drug addiction in Vietnam won't be felt for a year or two, maybe three, when addict veterans will be committing crimes, wholesale, to finance their heroin habits.

TRIBUNE, MARCH 1, 1971.

Morale in Viet— It All Depends . . .

SAIGON, SOUTH VIETNAM—Generalizing about morale in Vietnam can be tricky.

Morale sometimes is surprisingly high in active and select combat units, especially when troops actually are fighting the enemy. When troops began moving toward the Laotian border to support the South Vietnamese invasion, for example, the morale among some forward elements perked up noticeably.

But in non-active support positions, and in rear bases, the morale may deteriorate into drug abuse, fraggings, racial tensions. More often, there are non-violent—but still serious—protests that go beyond the normal GI grumbling.

Winding down the war has contributed to the problem. So has the peace movement back home.

By and large, men here are frustrated, unhappy—and often angry—during the year they are "in country," which is anywhere in Vietnam.

Anywhere else is "The World" and you get there on a "freedom bird."

Individual War

For each GI in Vietnam, it is an individual war, so unlike wars of the past.

In World War II, men went through basic training and joined a unit. They became a part of that unit. They went overseas together. They fought together.

There was pride in companies, battalions, regiments and divisions. There was camaraderie that lingers to this day.

They knew that, save for death or crippling wounds, they were in it—a united effort, the good guys against Hitler and Tojo and the other bad guys—for the duration. Then they would come home together. Fond memories took root, and were nourished by jovial reunions.

Even in Korea, there was the feeling that the Red Chinese and North Koreans had to be defeated to save that country. Most believed in the war.

Now, men go through basic training and board a plane to Saigon, sharing the cabin with strangers. Ironically, they travel in style a shiny commercial airliner, pretty stewardesses, soft seats, juicy steaks.

And when they arrive in Vietnam, they are shunted off in many directions and ultimately join a unit. Again they are among strangers, at least some of whom are near the end of their tours and couldn't care less about the problems of new men.

Almost immediately, a new man begins counting the days until the end of his individual war.

When he has less than 100 days left, he's a "two-digit midget."

At last he does go home, if he survives, and quickly is absorbed into a community that has paid scant heed to his service.

This guy isn't going to go to any reunions of the Americal or the 25th or the 1st or the Fifth or the 1st Cavalry.

He has known no bond of that sort. He wants to forget Vietnam.

Because there are so many reasons for a soldier not to measure up in Vietnam, it is a wonder his morale is not worse.

Finest Ever

I was walking along a dusty road near Chu Lai with a West Virginian, infantry Lt. Jim Jordan, and he said:

"The American GI is a funny sort of a guy. This man in Vietnam has to be the finest ever put in the field, considering all the abuses he's had to put up with—back home, everywhere.

"It's remarkable there aren't more combat refusals, it's such an unpopular war back home.

"Guys come over here after their parents tell them, 'Just stay alive,' and in a way that's the worst thing you can tell a soldier.

"He should be told: 'Look, son, do your best. We're behind you, you're fighting for your country.' At least, let him think so, because he'll stay alive longer.

"But these guys get almost no support from home. You'd be surprised how many don't even get mail, and all they hear about are college deferments and protests. It is incredible that they do a job and do it remarkably well."

TRIBUNE, MARCH 2, 1971.

Project HELP Gives Morale Boost to GIs

CHU LAI, SOUTH VIETNAM—Several weeks ago a band of black soldiers marched to the Americal Division headquarters building and demanded to see the commanding general, Maj. Gen. James Baldwin.

General Baldwin was out in the field but the assistant division commander met the soldiers. They complained of discrimination—they were being sent on hazardous rifle company assignments when most of them had already been in the bush with other divisions.

The assistant division commander replied, apparently to the complaining soldiers' satisfaction, that there was simply a shortage of riflemen and most new men assigned to the division had to go to the field. The question of color was not a factor, he told them.

It was a peaceful demonstration and, reportedly, there was no ugly aftermath. But it spawned discussions among top division officers that something has to be done about the misinformation and misunderstandings that often lead to morale problems.

The result was Project HELP.

Any soldier in the division now can write to "HELP," or telephone by dialing H-E-L-P, and request information about his military life, complain that he is being abused by a superior, gripe about not being promoted, enter a protest against the food, inquire about home leave, family allotments, legal matters—anything under the sun.

And an answer is guaranteed within five days.

There have been some odd results in the project.

A Navy Seabee called in he wanted transportation on a helicopter to get beer to his outfit. He not only got it—but also a jeep to carry him and the beer to and from the chopper.

One non-commissioned officer, a 10-year veteran with a fine record, said he had developed an urge to kill his troops. Another GI said he would kill himself if he couldn't take his Vietnamese girlfriend back to the States.

Both men were steered to division psychiatrists and presumably helped.

Flag Pin

One letter that got solid results was from a GI who wanted to wear a miniature metal replica of the U.S. flag on his uniform.

"Never before have I been so upset and disgusted with the Army," he wrote to Project HELP.

"I was ordered by the sergeant-major to remove the pin-on flag from my uniform. It was a gift from a patriotic organization back home with the notation, 'Wear It Proudly.'

"I sought an appointment with my commanding officer. He told me the same thing—not to wear the flag, the flag for which I am serving and for which many of my fellow Americans have died and are dying.

"I'm really afraid to guess the true aim of the U.S. Army when, after they preach patriotism and love for God and country, they turn around and order a replica of the flag of the United States of America to be removed.

"I sincerely hope that personnel other than myself will take the initiative and strive to fight against such a regulation . . ."

A couple of days later a directive went out to all members of the Americal Division. The general had approved the wearing of the pin-on replica of the flag—at the corner of the flap of the upper right pocket of the fatigue jacket.

Sgt. First Class Jimmy Ray Miller of Louden, Tenn., in charge of the HELP program, says it is particularly helpful because, "Non-coms are going up the ladder so fast, many of them lack the experience to have the answers to a lot of questions."

Between 25 to 30 questions are received daily. There have been nearly 1,000 so far this year. The Los Angeles earthquake prompted many from GI's who wanted quick assurance their loved ones were safe. These queries were passed on to the Red Cross and the chaplains.

Sergeant Miller says a surprisingly large number of single GI's want to adopt Vietnamese babies and take them home. The reply: Both U.S. and Vietnamese law forbid it; perhaps the adoptions could be handled through the families of the soldiers who want the children.

In covering the return of war prisoners from Vietnam, Gammack demonstrated just how effectively the expertise he had gained in covering three wars could be utilized. His accomplishments at Clark Air Base in Manilla were summarized by Frank N. Hawkins, Jr., then chief of Middle East Services for the Associated Press, in a letter to Drake Mabry, January 24, 1974, in support of Gammack's nomination for several journalistic prizes.

"Gordon's performance at Clark can best be summed up by a comment one newsman made after the dust cleared in the wake of the release of the first batch of POWs. 'That Gammack certainly showed all these young bucks what it was all about.'

"Gammack was one of nearly 100 journalists who showed up at Clark, most of them of Vietnam War vintage. These journalists represented some of the best reporting talent

in U.S. journalism including Peter Arnett of the AP, Don Oberdorfer of the Washington Post, Liz Trotta of NBC, Peter Jennings of ABC, Bernie Kalb of CBS and many others.

"The U.S. Air Force, which was running the show, did its best to prevent this group from learning anything beyond the official press releases and off-the-record briefings.

"We were prohibited from interviewing or having any contact with the POWs under any except the most controlled circumstances. This, the Air Force said at first, was to shield them from initial exposure to contacts that might be harmful. There was a question of their health, they said. When it was learned the health of the returned men was much better than expected, then the line became that any stories told by the men of the experiences in the camps might create hardships or endanger those still held captive. This also proved to be nonsense. After Gordon's stories began breaking (carried abroad by the AP), the North Vietnamese virtually ignored the matter. They knew the stories would come out and frankly didn't care.

"All of the returnees had a story to tell and most of them were anxious to tell it. It was the end of a long, dreary, bitter experience. The American people had paid dearly for it in blood, emotion, money and national pride. Many of us at Clark believed that no matter what the Air Force said, the American people who had put up with and supported this conflict for so long, deserved to know what had happened. There was no good reason to hold back the truth from the American people.

"One of those who believed this was Gordon Gammack. There was one difference; Gordon did something about it. After his arrival at Clark, Gordon made contact with those in the hospital (which was strictly off limits to newsmen) who could help him. He simply found a couple of Iowa boys who were in a position to pass along what the returnees were saying. This had its comical aspect because shortly after Gordon's arrival at Clark, the Air Force looked him in the teeth and told him with a straight face they regretted there were no Iowa boys among hospital personnel for pre-release interviews.

"The rest is now history. Within two days of the arrival at Clark of the first batch of prisoners, Gordon was filing stories about what some of the POWs had undergone during their years in captivity. In particular, he was able to get the story of Michael Kjome, a story Gordon followed up in depth when they both returned home. He was alone in digging out this copy. It was a brilliant scoop and a terrific piece of journalism.

"The Air Force went crazy trying to patch up the leak, but they couldn't do it. Because it wasn't just Gordon who believed the story should be told. So did those in the hospital who helped him.

"In my mind it was an example of American journalism at its best. A good reporter, who knew a story had to be told and went out and got it despite all the curtains and obstacles the Air Force could throw up in his way.

"It is this kind of work that keeps a free press alive and deserved to be recognized."

Gammack was immediately aware of the protectiveness of the authorities and, in early reports on the preparations for the returning prisoners of war, he alluded to the resentment felt by medical personnel which was to become essential to his coverage.

Two weeks later, having devised a way to circumvent the official restrictions, Gammack commented at greater length on what seemed to him the excessively cautious and protective attitude of the military authorities towards the returning POWs.

TRIBUNE, FEBRUARY 8, 1973.

Sees 'Overkill' in Homecoming Plans for POWs

CLARK AIR BASE, THE PHILIPPINES—Freedom will come gradually to returning U.S. war prisoners, even after they are finally liberated by the Communists.

Some grumbling about "overprotection" is beginning to seep through the tight security ring thrown around the details of the prisoners' homecoming.

A few of those involved are privately calling it "Operation Overkill" instead of "Operation Homecoming."

If, for instance, returning POWs ask for cigarettes or shots of whisky to steady their nerves on boarding freedom planes at Hanoi or in South Vietnam, the answer will be no.

FEBRUARY 12, 1973. Returning American POWs walk along the red carpet and are greeted by military commanders and a color guard upon their arrival from North Vietnam. *(AP)*

And they probably won't be allowed a beer, highball or cocktail until after they reach the United States.

At Clark Hospital here, the chances are they'll be surrounded by as many guards as—or even more than—in any of their prisoner-of-war camps or stockades.

But the hospital guards—one for every stairwell on every floor, for example—will be assigned to protect the returnees from outsiders rather than to confine them to the hospital.

Returning prisoners nevertheless will be confined to the hospital during the minimum of three days they are here.

At one briefing of medical officers, a senior U.S. officer made this statement—recalled verbatim by a medical officer from Iowa who was there:

"There are anti-war types who are saying that the returnees will be exchanging one type of confinement for another, but that's not true. We're keeping them inside the hospital here for their own good."

4 Questions

There are 50 or so armed forces public information officers here (commissioned and non-coms). Four questions were submitted to them dealing with the amount of freedom in non-security areas where the returnees will be allowed. Three days later the answers were provided after an Air Force captain submitted them to two Air Force full colonels for approval. They are:

Question: If a returnee boards a plane at Hanoi and asks for a cigarette, will he be given one?

Answer: Probably not because during the short flight to Clark (about two hours), the condition of the other returnees on board will not be known and smoking may cause discomfort.

Q. What if he wants a shot of whisky to steady his nerves?

A. No, if a sedative is indicated, appropriate medication will be available.

Q. How soon after his arrival at Clark will he be able to make the choice—to smoke, have a beer, a highball, a martini.

A. In the hospital at Clark there will be no attempt to deny a cigarette to a returnee. Alcohol may influence body chemistry in such a way as to confuse the biochemical measurements of the blood. Therefore, the consumption of alcoholic beverages is not normally allowed in any hospitalized patient, and is not permitted in outpatients for a period of 12 to 48 hours before taking blood tests.

Q. Has there been any thought of trying to persuade the returnees, assuming they have had few if any chances to smoke in captivity, that this would be a good time to quit for health reasons?

A. It is not anticipated that time would permit any in-depth counseling regarding the desirability of quitting cigarettes. However, this is not to say his physician (here at Clark) would not suggest that it would be in his best interests to take this opportunity to quit smoking.

One of the striking factors about the preparation for the reception of the returnees here has been the extreme reluctance of the public information structure to make available medical personnel for interviews.

Col. John W. Ord, hospital commandant, made a 30-minute appearance before reporters, but when asked if other medical officers would be available he replied that they are "too busy."

The fact is that many of the normal hospital activities have been suspended—no elective surgery at all, for example—and the medical people have so much time on their hands they've been leaving work early.

3 Iowans

At least three key medical officers from Iowa are at Clark Hospital: Maj. J. P. Westra of Jefferson, a "primary" homecoming physician; Maj. Addison W. Brown, jr., of Des Moines, an opthalmologist who will be checking the eyes of the returnees, and Maj. Robert Beckman of Mount Vernon, anesthesiologist who will be on call.

At an after-dinner gathering at the Clark base, attended by a number of medical officers, the reasons for attempts to muzzle them became abundantly clear after many of the officers spoke cynically and critically of the extraordinary plans to "protect" the returnees and other arrangements for their homecoming.

These, almost without exception, were officers in service against their personal wishes and itching to finish their tours of duty. They are secure in their rank and relatively immune from attempts to throw roadblocks to their careers.

And so, while not eager to court trouble by being quoted by name, they felt free to speak their minds, even though they revealed that each daily briefing concluded with the directive, "Don't talk to the press."

"Paranoid"

On the other hand, the career officer who says the wrong thing, makes the wrong move, can seriously jeopardize his future.

It was the consensus of the medical men that many of the returnees will be in reasonably good physical and mental condition and that these men still will be subjected to overprotection for some time.

One doctor said the planners have been "almost paranoid in this operation. I'd call it overkill rather than homecoming."

And he wondered if some of the things that would really help and please the returnees hadn't been overlooked—the problem of the extremely cold air-conditioning in the hospital for men long exposed to the tropics, for example.

"And why haven't we chartered a 747 (commercial jetliner) that would get these men back to California from here in comfort and at about half the time of those lumbering, noisy military planes?" he asked.

Another medical officer was critical of the program calling for each returnee to be assigned an escort on arrival here and for the return to the United States.

"Baby-sitters, that's what they are," he said. "They've all been given all sorts of information about the returnees, their family situations, any bad news that might be in store for them—although the brass insists we call it 'sensitive information' instead of 'bad news.'

"How would you like to suddenly find yourself with a constant companion who knows a hell of a lot more about you than you know about him?"

TRIBUNE, FEBRUARY 21, 1973.

Undue Fears for POWs?

CLARK AIR BASE, THE PHILIPPINES—While American prisoners of the Vietnam war are coming home, the public still has only sketchy information about what they went through in prison camps at Hanoi and in the jungles of Vietnam.

The official reasons for the government-controlled blackout of such news and extremely limited access to the returning POWs are given as:

The protection of the mental and physical health and welfare of the returnees.

Concern that the North Vietnamese or the Viet Cong still holding American captives would become upset, thus posing a threat to the release of those still held captive.

Both reasons have strong basic appeal—as difficult to argue against as motherhood and apple pie—but judging from those already returned, there may be undue concern and little justification for such fears.

First of all, the generally good health of the great majority of the returnees who flew here from Hanoi and South Vietnam was quickly established.

Plans for special bland diets to nurse the men slowly back to strength were quickly abandoned in almost all cases. The happy warriors started right off eating pizza, ravioli and steak, topping them off with apple strudel and banana splits, sometimes with second helpings.

Medical officers were astounded by the generally good condition of the men and how little treatment was required.

Fears about the mental health of the men were even more empty.

The psychiatrists on hand at Clark Hospital for Operation Homecoming had absolutely nothing to do, except for one case of odd behavior that apparently predated the man's capture.

The really surprising aspect about the government's insistence on keeping the returnees isolated is the fear they might say something that would endanger prisoners not yet released.

Career Officers

Look at the military ranks of the men who have been released, especially those from North Vietnam—Navy captains, commanders and lieutenant commanders; Air Force colonels, lieutenant colonels, majors (very few below the rank of captain), and Marine colonels and lieutenant colonels. Most were career officers.

It is an insult to their intelligence to suggest that they don't have the judgment to talk about their prison experiences without jeopardizing security and the welfare of those still being held.

The name of the government's game is not to make public anything that might offend the North Vietnamese.

But it can be argued that reports of the prisoners' seemingly almost unanimous support of President Nixon's war policies might be as irritating to the North Vietnamese or the Viet Cong as a story of a guard's brutality to a U.S. prisoner.

In any event, it is about as illogical to deny reporters access to these liberated air officers as it would be to forbid war correspondents to talk to regimental and battalion commanders, lest the officers reveal battle secrets to the enemy.

Some information about the rigors of prison camp life was, of course, clandestinely leaked out, including the brutalities to one Iowan—civilian Michael Kjome of Decorah, held by the Viet Cong for six years.

In the first place, many of the returnees talked freely to medical officers who examined them at Clark Hospital—a clear indication that the men want to discuss their experiences.

Most Interesting

And although medical officers have been ordered almost daily not to talk to reporters, some of them have, passing along the most interesting information to come out of Operation Homecoming.

Other information about prison camp life has come from families of returnees.

The information certainly is the type the American public is entitled to without endangering security or anyone's welfare.

The stories yet to be told promise to be fascinating, even fantastic.

One of the folklore heroes of the prison years likely will be Col. Robinson Risner, the returnee who phoned President Nixon on his liberation.

There have been second-hand reports on his strong leadership among the prisoners, his tremendous concern for the welfare of the men, and the inspiration he gave to help other prisoners keep going when their spirits faltered.

Colonel Risner was emphatic when he said, on being questioned about the propaganda statements: "I ask you to consider the source."

The fine physical and mental condition of the prisoners undoubtedly was due in large part to the insistence of the prisoners and their leaders on programs—a variety of educational classes and physical fitness—that would keep their minds alert and their bodies fit.

The Homecoming operation here was a major triumph for the Pentagon. There was much miscalculation about the condition of the returnees and the care they would need, and there was a lot of overplanning in the Pentagon.

Smoothly

But the start of the operation went smoothly and the military had almost complete control of the flow of information.

The bulk of the information about the returnees was fed to reporters by armed forces information officers. Thus, one of the greatest stories of our times was "covered" by men without the training or qualifications of cub reporters. Information officers were on the planes from Hanoi to Clark Air Base to coach the returnees on what to say in future public appearances.

As Operation Homecoming continues, the pattern likely will remain the same. What the returnees have to say will be tightly controlled by the military until the last man held by the North Vietnamese is free.

Then the full story will begin to unfold.

The stories Gammack filed blended what he had observed directly with information obtained through his medical contacts inside the hospital where the returning prisoners were cloistered. Gammack had established an inside track and he loved it. "This has been a ball," he wrote to his editor. "As you know, my day-to-day work isn't particularly competitive so it's real fun to have the chance to play tricks and games again."

TRIBUNE, FEBRUARY 10, 1973.

High Spirits, an Air of Pride, Big Smiles

CLARK AIR BASE, THE PHILIPPINES—The skies were overcast, gloomy and gray when the big white U.S. hospital planes came from Hanoi with their freedom cargo.

The faces of the American prisoners who got off the planes were mostly without color, too—a prison pallor.

Some of the men limped. A few had withered hands and arms.

Three—but only three—of the 116 liberated Vietnam war prisoners were carried on stretchers from the plane that brought them here from prison camps in North Vietnam.

But that was the extent of the surface sadness to the long-awaited day called homecoming.

Mostly, the liberated prisoners appeared in good physical condition and exceedingly high spirits, especially the two Iowans who arrived on the third of the three planes from Hanoi—Navy Lt. Cmdr. Larry H. Spencer, 32, of Earlham and Air Force Maj. Charles G. Boyd, 34, of Rockwell City.

A third Iowan, Marine Lt. Col. Edison W. Miller, 43, now of Tustin, Calif., was on the first plane.

The fourth Iowan in the first group of prisoners, civilian Michael Kjome, 36, of Decorah, was released from captivity by the Viet Cong in South Vietnam and arrived at Clark Air Base on a later flight.

Spencer, the fourth man off the third plane, stood erect and smiling.

Faith Never Wavered

Navy Capt. James A. Mulligan, jr., the senior man aboard the plane, made a short talk in which he said the prisoners all had faith in "our God, our country and our families," a faith that never wavered.

There was an air of pride in the stride of Spencer as he walked to the bus that took him to Clark Hospital for the start of physical tests, a phone call home and the beginning of a new life.

He was followed shortly by Major Boyd, who seemed to have a little more color in his cheeks than many of the returnees. He, too, was smiling broadly.

Of Spencer, Boyd and the other 35 men aboard the third C141 medivac plane used in homecoming, an Army information officer aboard the return flight said: *"The morale of the men is so overwhelming it is difficult to talk to them without being engulfed with the total magnetism of their complete joy and delight in being free. Words don't describe it."*

A bulletin from Clark Hospital said that the scenes in the wards were ebullient for the most part and scenes of great celebration. Preliminary examinations showed that no emergency medical treatment was required and most of the men asked for and were given a regular diet for the evening meal. The men were in the process of getting acquainted with their escorts.

Monday's homecoming was bursting with emotion from start to finish.

There was the story about one released prisoner, a senior officer, who on boarding the plane at Hanoi told welcoming officer Lt. Col. Richard Abel: "You know, Dick, I couldn't have made it if it hadn't been for Jesus Christ. Always, I could look up and see him."

And there was the crude sign carried by one of the men aboard the first plane: "God Bless America and Nixon."

Was the making of this sign a daring act of defiance before the men were free?

Dr. Roger Shields, in charge of the prisoner release program for the Defense Department, was asked about the sign and a few other similar ones. He replied:

"They were, er . . . I think, well, maybe I'd better not comment on that. But I don't think they were made on the way back."

Then there was the story of the exchange between two prisoners as they boarded the plane at Hanoi. The first one clenched his fist as he made a vigorous thumbs-up sign and cried out: "Do you believe it now?"

And the other man thrust his thumb skyward and replied: "I believe it . . . I believe it."

As the men boarded the planes, they hugged each other and slapped each other on the back. Some said reverently: "Thank God."

A few knelt and prayed.

"Smell That Perfume"

As one man spied a pretty flight nurse, he shouted: "Wow, smell that perfume!"

On the flights to Clark, the returnees peppered members of the flight crew and escorts with questions. Although they were reasonably up to date on major U.S. news—they knew for instance, of President Johnson's death—they wanted to know about a multitude of every-day things: Sports, bell-bottom trousers, the latest military and civilian fashions, long hair and, yes, women's lib.

They eagerly read copies of the Stars and Stripes, the U.S. military daily newspaper, and paid special heed to the list of the prisoners being released.

Contrary to earlier information put out by homecoming officials, the men were permitted to smoke cigarettes on the flight and many jumped at the chance to have an American cigarette.

The first plane touched down at 2:11 a.m., Iowa time. It edged very slowly to its parking spot in front of the batteries of television cameras and newsmen and welcoming brass.

Multitude of Emotions

Observers wondered what a multitude of emotions—joy, hope and surely some fear—were packed into that white airship bearing the numbers 60177 and a bright Red Cross on its tail.

The noise of the four jet engines was deafening as the C141 wheeled around in front of more than 1,000 air base personnel, including many children who started chanting, "Welcome Home," and unfurled a banner that read, "We love you."

The plane stopped. A ramp was wheeled up to the exit for the ambulatory while an ambulance eased backward to the open rear end of the aircraft for the three litter cases.

For the ambulatory, a red carpet was rolled out

to the buses standing by with red lights flashing. A color guard was there, one man from each of the services.

The first man off was the senior officer of that group of returnees, Navy Capt. Jeremiah Denton. He exchanged salutes with the welcoming admiral and general, stepped to the microphone and said:

"We are honored to have had the opportunity to serve our country under difficult circumstances. We are profoundly grateful to our commander in chief and our nation for this day. God Bless America."

Then the first parade of returnees started from the plane. First, after Captain Denton, was Lt. Cmdr. Everett Alvarez, jr., the first American to be shot down in the Vietnam war—on Aug. 5, 1964.

Then came the first of several signs that the returnees carried.

The men marched from the plane smartly and in the precise order in which they became prisoners (except for Captain Denton's opening appearance).

Expressions Restrained

Watching the returnees walk from the planes to the buses prompted the thought that some of the expressions of greatest joy are restrained—the slow shaking of the head from right to left that seems to say: "Dear God, this is wonderful," and the soft smile that never leaves the face.

And it was thus with this group of Americans. Some gave the thumbs-up sign; others waved with the fingers of their right hands wide apart; a few spotted friends in the crowd and waved vigorously to them; a few seemed to be looking without success for familiar faces.

TRIBUNE, FEBRUARY 12, 1973.

Yell, Slap Backs at U.S. Hospital

CLARK AIR BASE, THE PHILIPPINES—The returning American prisoners are in remarkably good health and talk freely of their treatment and experiences as captives, including the recent bombing of Hanoi, a medical officer reported from the hospital here Monday.

The physician, an Iowan, said they slapped each other on the back and yelled like a winning football team after reaching their hospital wards out of public view.

"By and large, both the physical and mental health of the liberated men is very good and I've heard of almost no cases in which permanent serious harm is likely," he said.

"The spirits of the men are remarkable. The wards are like a football locker room after a tremendous victory, with guys slapping each other on the back over and over again.

"There was much more exuberance in the hospital when the men were with each other than when they made their public appearance getting off the planes."

The Iowa medical officer reported that the returnees are talking freely about their experiences.

One story: The guards in the Hanoi area became angry during the B52 bombings, pointed their guns at the prisoners and ordered them into corners.

But when the saturation bombing attacks came last December, the guards became terror-stricken and "ran for the tunnels."

One returnee said he knew of no American prisoner wounded by massive B52 bombing attacks in December except that "concussion knocked a big hunk of plaster from a ceiling and hit one guy on the head."

The men told a few stories of harsh treatment, of salt being rubbed in the wounds of a badly burned pilot, for example, and men being suspended by their arms.

The Iowa major doubts that many of the returnees will get bad news they don't already know about, or have suspected. They've received an average of about one letter a year and have been brought up to date regarding many of their personal affairs in this manner.

The returnees said they have wondered what was in some of the North Vietnamese cigarettes they were issued, that sometimes when they smoked them they received relief from pain.

The medical officer has neither observed nor sensed anything except harmony among the liberated men, no sign of the type of bitterness and recrimination that were prevalent among Korean war prisoners, some of whom were accused of collaborating with the enemy.

The Iowa medical officer, who also talked with other doctors checking the men, gave his interpretation of the arm and hand injuries that were obvious on some of the men as they arrived home.

"I think most of these arm, elbow and shoulder injuries resulted from fractures caused when ejected from planes at supersonic speeds," said the doctor.

"The legs usually came through these ejections OK, but some of the arm, elbow and shoulder fractures did not heal well and were inadequately treated.

"In most of the cases, even ones that look quite bad, I think surgery performed a few weeks from now, plus therapy, will do wonders. There'll be a few lasting injuries where nerve damage is involved."

The Iowa officer thinks eye problems may be the most troublesome.

Vitamin Deficiencies

"Quite a few of the men complained about their eyes and asked about glasses," he said. "Their ailments may have come from flash fires when their planes were hit or the result of vitamin deficiencies in captivity. But some of the eye trouble may be difficult to correct."

On arrival at the hospital the returnees wanted, almost demanded, immediate showers. They wanted to feel clean. They also wanted cigarettes and American food.

Scented Soap

They said they loved the smells in the hospital, not only the smell of perfume and the scented soap from the nurses, but even the antiseptics.

"They loved everything that smelled of cleanliness," said the doctor.

They were handed disposable paper towels, the fancy kind that have a woven appearance and are commonplace in American kitchens and bathrooms. Some of the men were puzzled by them.

"What's this? What's it for?" some of them asked.

The Iowa medical officer said he was told that at least two of the three litter cases from the first plane from Hanoi were not necessarily serious, but involved back and buttocks injuries that made sitting painful.

The doctor believes that tests will show that the returnees are suffering from infestations—hookworms and roundworms, for example, but that medication will cope with this satisfactorily. Also, the men probably have head lice, which will be eliminated with one proper washing.

One story they told indicates they didn't lose their sense of humor in captivity:

In at least one prison camp, a prisoner was given a party on the anniversary of so many years in captivity. Other prisoners hoarded their rations to make it a special occasion.

At Clark Hospital, one of the returnees feigned disappointment that he just missed one of these special parties.

"Eight more days and it would have been my seventh anniversary," he said.

His chums booed and one of them said, "Wanna go back? There's a plane leaving for Hanoi tomorrow."

TRIBUNE, FEBRUARY 18, 1973.

Grudging POW Respect for North Vietnam

CLARK AIR BASE, THE PHILIPPINES—The framework of the Vietnam prisoner of war story emerged last week, but the full story, and it promises to be a fantastic one, probably won't unfold until the last U.S. prisoner is free and the fear of retaliation by the North Vietnamese is removed.

The fear that the North Vietnamese would retaliate against remaining prisoners if reports of cruel treatment were publicized are generally regarded as remote if not fanciful. But by and large, the returnees are maintaining silence about their prison experiences.

They've either made this decision on their own, collectively perhaps, or on orders from the Pentagon.

It has become clear that Americans held in North Vietnamese prison camps were an elite corps— proud, brave and determined—with precise, hard but compassionate leadership. That's why most of the returnees arrived at Clark Air Base strong in body, mind and spirit.

Their performance was in sharp contrast to that of many returnees from North Korean POW camps 20 years ago.

But if the Korean War POW experience was sometimes inglorious, it has been put to good use. Lessons learned from it, according to the Pentagon, led to a rewriting of the Military Code of Conduct and to the drafting of new training manuals on survival.

The new code and the survival training are given much credit by Pentagon sources for the way American POWs have come through in Vietnam.

Dr. Roger Shields, deputy secretary of Defense for POW affairs, who was in Hanoi to escort the first freed POWs out, said later that the men had organized a command structure.

"When the first prisoner got off the bus in Hanoi," he said, "the senior officer called them to order—and they stood tall. They just weren't a bunch of guys coming off pell-mell."

This structure, it was reported, goes back to survival courses that were instituted following the Korean War and are mandatory for all men who are to be in combat.

The training stresses ways and means of staying mentally alert and in good physical condition. "It gives a very good grounding on how to stay alive in most situations," said the Pentagon spokesman.

Political Views

In addition, a glimpse of the POWs' political outlook has emerged in their comments of the last week.

For instance, one POW told a medical officer about the December B52 bombings of the Hanoi area (the prisoners seemed assured our air command knew where the POWs were and wouldn't hit them) and of seeing and hearing the bombs land.

"We got up at night to watch it," the returnee said.

"It was the greatest show on earth.

"It was worth waiting for—because I didn't want to come home a loser."

Statements of this sort help to explain the seemingly almost unanimous support of the returnees for President Nixon.

The great majority of the returnees are professional, career military men, and, like their counterparts through the U.S. military system, are hawkish, conservative, Republican, and disdainful of long hair, campus protests and most of the activities associated with liberal causes.

After visiting the base exchange here, Air Force Maj. Charles Boyd of Rockwell City stressed that the slacks and shirts he bought were "the most conservative I could find."

How were the American prisoners really treated by the North Vietnamese and the Viet Cong?

Well, we're going to hear the "good" side until Operation Homecoming ends because of the fear of retaliation and it's going to make the enemy sound rather benevolent. Undoubtedly, there will be stories of frightful barbarism later—most of them dating back to before 1968. And it already is clear that the prisoners held by the Viet Cong fared worse than those in the north, partly because of conditions in the jungles.

On the positive side, though, Col. John W. Ord, the Clark hospital commander, said that the condition of the returnees on arriving here forced him to conclude that they had been treated well by the North Vietnamese.

One of the orthopedic surgeons at Clark told a medical officer from Iowa: "Some of the surgery done by the North Vietnamese was excellent. The results were at least as good as I would have hoped for if I had done the surgery myself.

"Apparently, some of the surgeons were very well qualified. Sometimes the American prisoners had a very difficult time persuading their captors they needed hospitalization but once they got in the hospitals they received even better treatment than the North Vietnamese civilians."

"Correct" Behavior

The enemy was "correct" in a number of small ways. Michael Kjome, a civilian from Decorah, could scarcely believe it, for instance, when the Luther College class ring taken from him when he was captured five years ago was returned to him last week.

Another civilian had with him $140 in military scrip when he was captured by the Viet Cong. It was in seven $20 bills. Apparently, some Viet Cong "borrowed" from it during the American's captivity because the money was returned to him in five $20 bills and four $10 bills.

Clark hospital dental officers were surprised by the generally good condition of the returnees' teeth. Prison diet apparently was such that not many cavities occurred.

There were some chipped teeth, mostly the result of biting on pebbles in rice fed to the prisoners in pitch darkness. And two men needed repairs resulting from a gruesome experience.

The two prisoners held by the Viet Cong were in awful pain from abscessed teeth. It was the same tooth with each man. In their desperation, they took a nail and a rock and took turns hammering at the teeth to make a large enough penetration for the abscesses to drain.

One medical officer here says that whenever the enemy guards mistreated our men they were careful and clever enough to do it in such a way no evidence would remain.

An ear, nose and throat specialist at Clark commented: "Some of our men had their ears cuffed severely, for instance. The guards did it with cupped hands and with enough force to fracture the eardrums. But in every case but one that I saw, the injuries healed by themselves."

Operation Homecoming has been loaded with super security and much downright deceit from the Pentagon in dealing with the news media.

One highly important returnee confided to a friend: "When the full story is told, neither side is going to like it."

Long-Term View

In other words, both the United States and North Vietnam will have difficulty producing propaganda value from those long years of imprisonment for the Americans who now have been freed and the ones who will be liberated in the coming weeks.

But there is a growing feeling here that the North Vietnamese will be pictured finally as reasonably benevolent captors by Southeast Asian standards, that CIA agents and career Foreign Service officers, long disdainful of the South Vietnamese and admiring of the North Vietnamese, will develop warmer contacts with the north and that further friendliness will grow from our reconstruction efforts there.

And the final irony—a friendship will develop with a former enemy following a span of madness that cost some 50,000 American lives.

Because of the information network he had established, Gammack was filing stories with the Des Moines Register *and* Tribune *that contained a wealth of details on the returned POWs unavailable in any other newspaper. Peter Arnett, special correspondent for the Associated Press, also a Vietnam veteran, hit the same roadblock of secrecy all other correspondents there struggled against and leaned heavily on Gammack's files for details in his reports. This cooperation carried one condition—Arnett was to wait until the next cycle to use the material, thus preserving the exclusive material for the Des Moines papers.*

Gammack also submitted routine requests to military and state department officials for interviews with returned POWs from Iowa. In most cases, these were automatically denied. But one POW, Michael Kjome of Decorah, requested that he talk with Gammack. During this routine conversation, just before Kjome returned to the United States, he agreed to tell Gammack his entire story on the condition that the narrative would not be published until the last POW was out of Hanoi.

The result was an illustrated, detailed account of Kjome's five years with the Viet Cong, prepared in advance and published within minutes after the last POW plane landed at Clark Air Base from Hanoi.

Gammack spent more than a week interviewing and tape recording Kjome's review of the five years, which ran about 120,000 words.

This was transcribed onto paper. Gammack then organized the mass of material and quotes and wrote the narrative. Kjome was actively involved in the organizing and editing process.

Nobody could better appreciate the scope of Gammack's triumph than the other newsmen who were his colleagues. Their response was very gratifying to Gammack.

"The night I was writing the bootlegged Kjome story, Tom Pepper, a swell guy with the Baltimore Sun, *sat down beside me and with no intention of trying to crib anything scanned the first few paragraphs of the story. The next morning Oberdorfer says, 'I hear you got a hell of a story.' And the following day, the guys from the big magazines, NY* Times, *etc., were asking if they could see it. It was all very amusing because some of the characters had been giving me the brush-off reserved for the little people from the sticks and all of a sudden I was one of 'them' and the NY* Times *was asking my age and experience and whether I was in the Washington bureau. If you'll forgive the immodesty, I think we had more success than anyone in penetrating the military's iron curtain on this."*

TRIBUNE, MARCH 29, 1973.

A POW's STORY: 5 YEARS WITH THE VIET CONG

A Whispered Warning—Then Capture

About midnight on Jan. 31, 1968, Michael Kjome of Decorah, a civilian teaching in South Vietnam, was surrounded by the Viet Cong during the Tet offensive and captured the next day. He spent five years in captivity in the jungles of Southeast Asia.

Kjome (pronounced: CHO-me) told his story to Tribune columnist Gordon Gammack, a veteran war correspondent who reported on Iowans at war in Vietnam and more recently covered the return of the POWs at Clark Air Base in the Philippines, where he first met Kjome.

The returning prisoners, military and civilian, had agreed not to tell details of prison camp life and treatment until the POWs listed by the enemy as held in Southeast Asia were safely home. They feared such stories would bring retaliation against those still captive, or delay their release.

Now, the last listed POWs are safe in American hands and the full story can be told for the first time.

Future daily stories by Kjome, now 36, will appear exclusively in The Tribune. They will include how he endured intensive interrogation and was nearly murdered; his treatment in prison camps, ranging from unusual kindness to utter brutality; forced marches; the food on which he survived; the loneliness; escape plans and attempts; the personalities of his Viet Cong captors; how increased U.S. war activity affected the treatment of POWs, and, finally, the road to freedom and home.

MARCH 1973. Michael Kjome, wearing the clothes he wore as a Viet Cong captive, recreates his jungle life-style. *(Register and Tribune)*

Cho An Nhon is a quiet, peaceful village on the outskirts of Saigon. I taught school there in a French villa surrounded by orchards.

There had never been any trouble with the Viet Cong in the village. Duty there had been carefree.

So it was a shock to be awakened by pounding on the front door about midnight of Jan. 31, 1968, the eve of Tet.

At the door were three of our South Vietnamese employes, all frightened and trembling.

One of them said hoarsely, "VC!"

I didn't know it then, but that midnight message was the beginning of a nightmare—my capture by the Viet Cong (VC), five years of endless solitary captivity in leg irons, a diet of rice laced with barnyard filth, small rations of meat from jungle animals—monkey, snake, tiger, leopard and rancid elephant—brushes with death and disease, long, grim night marches through the jungles, and endless spells of boredom and despair.

Hindsight is useless now, of course, but I did receive warnings that day and I ignored them.

A Korean friend had told me that three Koreans had been shot on the streets of Qui Nhon, a city in the northern part of South Vietnam that was considered very secure.

He thought it was ominous and told me to be careful.

Tet is a major Vietnamese holiday, and I thought it strange that only two or three students came to class that night. Their native instructor didn't show up at all.

Had they received some sort of warning, at least to stay off the streets?

Nonetheless, I shot some firecrackers for some neighborhood children, gave them some Cokes and went to bed about 10:30 p.m.

I was reading Winston Churchill's "The History of English Speaking People" when I heard some small-arms fire and that fateful rattling at the front door to deliver the simple message, "VC."

I started getting a little nervous. Then there was a loud burst of machine-gun fire only about 60 or 70 feet away. Awfully close!

I locked the front door and told the Vietnamese, "Sit down and rest and don't worry. They'll go away." But they shook their heads and one of them said, "No, beaucoup VC."

Suddenly it became like daylight. U.S. helicopters had started dropping flares for C47 gunships that were spraying the area with machine-gun fire. We called such armed planes "Puff the Magic Dragon."

Then there was a great explosion—WHOOMPH—and part of our roof fell in. I don't know if we were hit by gunfire from our own planes or from the Viet Cong.

I tried the telephones, but they were dead.

A few rounds of fire came into the building, probably from the Viet Cong. So I piled books and papers on top of two steel desks and a steel top table. When the shooting was close, we got under them for protection.

The shooting kept up all night, and in the morning I decided I'd better try to get some help.

First, I used a mirror to try to flash a signal from the sun to one of our helicopters overhead.

Then I used Scotch tape to tape together sheets of paper to form letters spelling out "HELP" about three feet high. I crawled out on the front porch and slid the message off on the concrete walk.

No help came.

About noon, I sat down and wrote a letter to my folks. Whatever happened, I wanted to let them know as much as I could.

Later, I realized the night duty man at the school was supposed to make a record of incidents that occurred. There was one entry listed for "Incidents or Disturbances."

I put down simply, "HELL YES" and signed my name.

Sometime after 4:30 p.m., there was a great rattle at the front gate. I peeked through a crack in a frosted window and I could see men out there.

They Were VC!

I told one of our men to look and see if they were VC. He came back white as a sheet.

Then there were nine or 10 people on our porch. One of them had a bazooka with a rocket sticking out of one end.

They were Viet Cong.

I was going to suffer for it later, but I had taken off my shoes—to make less noise walking around the building—so I was in my stocking feet. I threw on a nylon jacket, with no shirt underneath, when I went to the door.

I unlocked the door. By this time there were about 15 men there. Most carried Russian-made AK47 automatic rifles.

They were dressed in shorts, sort of like gym shorts, with black rubber sandals—made from auto tires—on their feet.

All wore neckerchiefs, sort of like those Boy Scouts wear, made of camouflage parachute nylon. The neckerchiefs apparently were a special recognition mark because all the Viet Cong I was to see in the weeks ahead wore them.

None could speak English. But they poked us with their guns and bound our arms to our sides with parachute cords.

I couldn't understand them except when they said, "Di," which means "go." When they said, "Di," I went. They pointed in the direction they wanted us to go. There were four of them in front of us and four in back.

We had to dodge U.S. helicopters overhead. We'd run for a while, then hide against a building. We weaved in and around a bunch of buildings and suddenly I saw something I can never forget.

We came up to a little house and in front of it was a young fellow with his right leg blown off about five inches above the ankle. It was just hanging there, bleeding. He was just sitting with an AK gun in his hand and a stunned look on his face.

I felt sorry for this guy because it crossed my mind there was no way this kid could live—he needed immediate surgery and there was no way he could get it.

One of my guards knew it was hopeless. He pulled a hand grenade from his belt and handed it to the wounded boy and said something in Vietnamese. The kid nodded. Then the guard took the kid's AK.

We starting running again. I saw some bodies that appeared to be South Vietnamese soldiers. I noticed women and children hiding underneath some tables.

We came back through the same area later. There had been an explosion, and now there were just arms and legs and other parts of bodies. I don't know if the wounded Viet Cong used the grenade, but I've had nightmares about what happened to those children.

We finally came to a pagoda, just one large room. One man was sitting at a small table in the center. To one side were three Buddhist monks in orange robes.

The man at the desk spoke English. He asked my name. I told him, and added that I was a schoolteacher and a civilian. He said, "Do not worry. If you do not try to run away, we will not shoot you."

He gave me a card with printing in English on one side and Vietnamese on the other. It said that I was a prisoner of the National Liberation Front and that if I behaved I would not be harmed in any way. I would be taken to a prisoner of war camp and treated humanely.

He let me keep my ring (my class ring from Luther College) and my watch, then pointed to two guards and said they would take me to a safer place.

Only One Remains Alive

I don't know exactly what happened to the three South Vietnamese captured with me, except that only one is alive today.

The guards took me to a small house. A young Viet Cong, not more than 14 years old, was left to guard me.

Viet Cong kept busting in and out. They had rocket launchers and rockets. They would rush into the street, fire at our helicopters and then duck back in.

Toward morning I was trying to get some sleep when there was one hell of an explosion and a brick wall started to fall toward me.

The young guard dived on top of me, covering my face with his body. Bricks and tile came cascading down, but this kid took the brunt of it and was pretty well bruised up. But, thanks to him, I didn't get a scratch.

I thought to myself, "Gee, these people are really human; not the awful VC I'd heard so much about."

I continued to think this until my first intense interrogation. Then things got a lot tougher.

At daylight, we kept moving from one building to another. I was given some chicken and beer and a chance to rest.

As I lay there, I said the Lord's Prayer, prayed for my parents and everyone at home and for the strength to get me through whatever lay ahead.

I had done an awful lot of running since my capture—perhaps five miles—but now, just a little more than 12 hours after my capture, I didn't think I was much more than a half-mile or so from the school.

My rest was interrupted by U.S. helicopters spraying nearby streets with gunfire.

Finally, two guards in civilian clothes took me and we headed into farming country. At a farmhouse we were given coconut candy and tea.

About midnight—about 36 hours after my capture—we ran into an angry group of 15 or 20 Viet Cong. They were raging mad about something and they started shoving and poking at me while they waved their guns and yammered in Vietnamese.

I have a feeling some of their friends had been killed and they wanted revenge. Anyway, they made it clear they were going to take me with them. They outnumbered the guards, of course, and so I went with them in the direction I had come from. My original guards tagged along behind.

Suddenly we encountered four men. One of them was an officer with a pistol in his hand and he appeared to be a man of considerable authority.

He took me away from these angry VC and led me into a nearby house.

I'm sure this man saved my life. I grew to know him only as Major Blanket.

TRIBUNE, MARCH 30, 1973.

As U.S. Planes Hit Viet Cong, He's Captive in Enemy Foxhole

After the Viet Cong major rescued me from the angry soldiers, he led me into a house where a bowl of big flowers and pictures of the Viet Cong flag and Ho Chi Minh were on a table in the main room.

I looked out the window and saw some Viet Cong (VC) with a group of South Vietnamese prisoners, 15 or 16 perhaps. The VC who had taken me in tow were there, too, and pretty soon they all disappeared into a bamboo thicket.

A few moments later, I saw and heard a burst of machinegun fire. And then another . . . and then one more.

Soon the VC came back, but the South Vietnamese weren't with them now.

Obviously, they had been murdered with their arms tied behind their backs.

I bowed my head, recited the Twenty-third Psalm ("The Lord is my shepherd . . .") and prayed that they wouldn't come and get me and do the same thing.

I never knew the major's name, but I think of him as Major Blanket because while I was with him he saw that I was cold and took a brand new blanket from his pack—blue with red, white and yellow flowers—and gave it to me.

It was an act of kindness I'll never forget.

Major Blanket was obviously important—apparently he was in charge of the rocket attacks on the huge Tan Son Nhut Air Base near Saigon.

He said something about going to "liberate Tan Son Nhut" and that I was to go along with him. We moved along a trail and Major Blanket waved his arms and said, "We go liberate Tan Son Nhut."

He seemed to be in a hurry because he ordered us to start running.

We came to a large dike with a canal running past it. Near the canal were small bunkers or foxholes, not more than two or two and a half feet deep. There was a hole about every 20 feet. There were lots of Viet Cong around, carrying boxes that I assumed contained ammunition.

Major Blanket ordered one Viet Cong to get out of his foxhole and pointed for me to get in it and stay there.

From my hole I could see people moving into a sugar cane field with rockets—big ones, each man carrying two, one on each shoulder.

Major Blanket came along and gave me a full package of cigarettes, a Vietnamese brand called Ruby Queens, and a book of matches from a U.S. Army "C" ration. He indicated I should stay in my foxhole. I indicated I had to go to the toilet.

It's funny, this was the first time I had to go to the toilet.

He pointed to a tree.

They loosened my bonds so I could move a little better. I could smoke and climb in and out of my foxhole.

I was looking for ways to escape, but I could see no hope.

All of a sudden, wham! Out of the sugar cane field came a lot of gunfire—mortars and rockets. Apparently they were shooting at the Tan Son Nhut Air Base.

Soon, our jets started coming in. F100s, I think. They started shooting into the sugar cane field with rockets and machine guns and, boy, I stayed in that hole and hugged the dirt!

The jets would zoom in, pull out and up and then they'd come back and do it again.

But they seemed to be putting their fire about 50 yards beyond where the VC had their rockets and mortars. But if they'd been much shorter they'd have been hitting right where I was. I remember repeating the Twenty-third Psalm over and over again.

Major Blanket Directed

This kept up, off and on, all morning. When the U.S. planes went away for a while, the Viet Cong would let loose with the mortars and rockets. From what I heard later, it was a major attack on Tan Son Nhut.

And Major Blanket directed the operation.

About noon, when there was a break, he sent me his canteen full of hot milk—the kind of canned milk sweetened with sugar that is popular in Vietnam.

That afternoon he sent me another pack of cigarettes.

The firing kept up and when the jets were gone I could see people coming in with more ammunition, big boxes carried on bamboo poles by two men.

Every so often, Major Blanket would come to check on me and then go back to a field telephone a short way down the dike.

Every time U.S. planes came in, the poor guy whose foxhole I was in would get down from the dike and stand in the canal with water up to his neck, holding his AK weapon over his head.

About 4 o'clock that afternoon, the Viet Cong seemed to have run of of ammunition. Major Blanket came and motioned me out of the hole. He shook hands with a number of people he had been with and then put his pack on.

We started out again—Major Blanket, two guys with AKs, another with an empty rocket launcher—heading across some rice paddies.

I was still in my stockings and my feet were a little sore, but not too bad.

I tried to use what little Vietnamese I knew and asked Major Blanket, "Di Hanoi?" meaning were they taking me to Hanoi. I thought all prisoners were taken to Hanoi. He smiled and nodded his head, so I thought that's where we were going.

After a while, we turned north and Major Blanket said, "Di Bien Hoa." He said I'd go to Hanoi later. I said, "OK, I'll go and talk to Ho Chi Minh. Maybe he'll let me go."

We kept on walking, I don't know how many miles. It seemed endless, through rice paddies and on scrubby ox cart roads. Finally we stopped at a farmhouse for some rice with a fish sauce and a short rest. When we started walking again, a girl 18 or 19 years old was our guide.

It was dark now, but the moon was bright. Major Blanket gave me his parachute-cloth neckerchief and made me tie it around my head as a disguise. I put it on like a woman's head scarf.

They wanted me disguised mainly because if I was recognized as an American, others might think I was a U.S. adviser with a South Vietnamese unit and start shooting at us.

Once we came across a file of about 100 men with weapons, sneaking along a fence.

Major Blanket pushed me down and the guards got down, too. These men came to within about 40 feet of us and I didn't know whether they were South Vietnamese or Viet Cong.

I didn't dare yell out on the chance they were on my side. But finally they spotted us. They crouched down, their weapons ready, too.

I'm sure Major Blanket didn't know who they were, but he stepped out from behind a tree and walked about 20 feet right toward them. He put his hands on his hips and just looked at them. Then one of their men came out and he put his hands on his hips.

It took a lot of courage for Major Blanket to do what he did. If it had been a South Vietnamese patrol . . . well, that would have been it. But they were Viet Cong guerrillas.

Cup Filled with Tea

Our next rest stop on the way northwest was an old farmhouse. An old woman, she must have been 80, looked at me carefully, then went back in the house and returned with a plastic cup filled with tea and sugar.

I kept that cup all through my captivity and have it to this day.

She also gave us bananas. When my cup was empty, she refilled it with coconut and ginger candy. It's a Vietnamese custom to give visitors some tea and something to eat. She was a very nice old lady.

Shortly after midnight, we came to the outskirts of a camp in a bamboo grove. I could still see the lights and flares over Saigon. I don't know how far we had walked, but my feet were getting awfully sore.

I was forced to stay on the edge of the camp with two guards. They brought a bamboo sleeping mat for me.

This was just a stopping place for the night. In the morning they brought us rice for breakfast. I only ate a few bites. A guy came out from the camp with a bottle of Merthiolate to paint the bottoms of my feet. My stockings were wearing out.

We had walked through dried-out rice paddies, which was like walking through an oat field after harvest—the stalks were like hundreds of needles poking at my feet.

We walked all day and at dusk a guard said "Bien Hoa." Apparently we had come close to the perimeter of the big U.S. base and air field at Bien Hoa.

We kept walking and came to a big river. Major Blanket started taking things out of his pack. He had about eight wrist watches, Japanese types that the Vietnamese wear, so I imagine he had taken them from dead people.

At the bottom of his pack was an inner tube, a small one, and it occurred to me that we were going to have to cross the river and that he had the inner tube because he couldn't swim.

I thought this might be a chance for me to escape because I am a good swimmer. But eventually a boat came for us and took us across the river.

Finally, we came to a densely wooded area concealing a Viet Cong field hospital.

We stayed there a whole day. Major Blanket brought an interpreter and told me he was going to leave. He asked me if I was sick, and I told him I wasn't feeling too good—I was having stomach trouble.

They brought me a can of sardines, some rice and a can of milk. They also gave me aspirin and quinine. They put me in a bunker and told me to crawl in and go to sleep. There was just room for me to curl up.

I slept most of that day. Then a medical worker took my temperature and thought I was getting malaria. I had headaches, my stomach was upset and I couldn't eat the rice.

Major Blanket told me that others would take me to a prison camp. It was the last time I saw him. I really would like to see him again for he had saved my life.

I now had three new guards. We walked at night and slept in the daytime. They could always find some sort of a secure Viet Cong camp to stay in. I began to lose track of time.

At one camp, an officer had a camera. Each of the officers there wanted to have their pictures taken with me, an American prisoner. I guess they wanted pictures to send home. They wanted me to smile, but I wouldn't—I just made faces. But once I laughed because one officer looked so darn funny.

My three guards were never mean. They'd push me if I slowed down, but when I got real weak and was just dragging, they'd stop.

My feet were getting bloody.

They finally found a fresh pair of stockings and tried cutting out some pieces of cardboard to protect the soles of my feet. But it didn't work.

It must have been about seven days since I'd been captured and I had the feeling we were in the area of Tay Ninh, not far from the Cambodian border.

TRIBUNE, MARCH 31, 1973.

Tied to Tree by Chain 12 Feet Long

Although it still was going to be a long time before I was in a prison camp with other Americans, as our plodding journey continued we started coming to camps that were rather well organized.

There was one camp, for instance, where there were 15 or 16 South Vietnamese prisoners. This camp had a couple of big underground bunkers with buildings above them.

The prisoners were shackled at night, stretched out in a line on straw mats. Every day they got political lectures, and I was told that most of them had decided to defect to the Viet Cong. I had no way of knowing if this were true.

I ate with the Vietnamese prisoners and, in a strange sort of way, played cards with them. One guy would sit behind me. I'd hold the cards and he'd show me which one to play.

They put up a hammock for me to sleep in and a mosquito net that belonged to a Viet Cong nurse in the camp.

The nurse also made me a set of black pajamas. She measured my arms and legs with a stick. She had a sewing machine and made a good fit.

She gave me quinine and figured I was coming down with malaria because I wasn't eating very much. I was losing weight fast and the bottoms of my feet were nothing but scabs because I had walked more than 50 miles without shoes.

They had no meat in this camp. One Viet Cong shot a bird with a slingshot. They added it to some sort of soup they made with vegetables and fed it to us with rice. We were given all the rice we wanted to eat. The nurse also was the cook.

They took me to a stream and gave me soap so I could wash myself and my clothes. They tried to find some rubber-tire sandals for me, but the sandals were all too small. They put some sort of salve on my feet every day.

One day a Viet Cong came into camp with a white sack with things like doughnuts. They gave me three of them, but I couldn't eat them. I couldn't eat anything, although I drank a lot of tea with sugar.

Learning to Roll Cigarettes

We got a handful of tobacco every day and a big piece of cigarette paper and I had to learn to roll cigarettes. My feet started healing, and one day two guards and an English-speaking officer said they were taking me to another camp. We were joined by a young woman guide.

We seemed to travel west and north again through a large rubber plantation.

We stayed one night and a day at a camp where a Viet Cong propaganda radio station for South Vietnam was located. I understand information to Hanoi was relayed from there.

There were several large underground bunkers, very well fortified. They asked me to repair an American typewriter, but the ribbon was missing and there was nothing I could do.

I had my first hot bath at this camp. In fact, it was the only hot bath I had while I was a prisoner.

They wanted me to make a tape recording condemning the war. I told them I couldn't do that, although I was against all war as a matter of Christian principle.

I am against all needless killing in a war—My Lai, for example—and believe there are other ways to solve world problems. When war has been necessary, and when it may again be necessary, it should be to protect individual rights and freedoms.

The morality of this war is difficult to determine even now—after all, I've been isolated for five years and have a lot of catching up to do.

Anyway, they weren't too insistent about my making a statement.

At the next camp I had my first real experience with leg irons—but many, many months would pass before I was freed from them.

In a large bunker, about 8 feet by 10, there were upright poles to attach hammocks to. There was room for five or six men to hang their hammocks.

A guard came with a chain about 12 feet long, a fairly heavy chain, like a log chain with links about a quarter of an inch thick. He told me, "We have to chain you up."

They chained me to a tree, but there was still room for me to get into the bunker.

One end of the chain was locked to my ankle. I'd never been chained before and I was real unhappy. But they removed the nylon cord I'd been trussed up with along the trail.

When the time came to leave this camp, the guards unlocked my chain and told me to put it in a carrying bag I had been given.

I had to carry my own chain with me!

We started out on the trail again, this time with three young guards.

I think we traveled north and west again, but we weaved back and forth through the jungles constantly.

In the moonlight I could see huge holes where U.S. B52s had dropped bombs.

The guards were careful that we weren't spotted by any planes. But even more, they didn't want the civilians to know that an American prisoner was in their area. Whenever civilians approached, they'd hide me in the jungles.

Once we came to a hilly area and all of a sudden I heard an American radio. It couldn't have been more than 300 yards away. Apparently an American artillery outfit had moved in quickly.

The guards stopped me and, oh, God, how I wanted to yell out.

But they made it good and clear that they'd shoot me if I made one false move. So we turned around.

We came to a small camp and they chained me to a tree. A little later they came with a half-dozen bananas.

The next day my three guards were joined by two others. One seemed to be a senior non-commissioned officer. One of them kept saying, "B.S."—for no particular reason.

Rice Bowl from China

I kept adding items to my sack. A medical worker who painted my feet with Merthiolate gave me an ink bottle full of it. Another man gave me a crude spoon made out of a piece of aluminum that had been hammered out over a wooden mold. They gave me a rice bowl made in China.

At one camp I was approached by a Viet Cong officer. A guard ordered me to get up when the officer came to me. The first thing he said was, "Why do you not stand at attention?"

"I don't know how. I am a civilian," I said.

"You will always stand at attention when you speak to an officer or a guard. I have come to take you to a new prison camp. Are you well?"

I told the officer I thought I had malaria and I showed him my feet. They were a mess and he said they'd find me some shoes.

A little later I got a pair of rubber sandals, like shower shoes. I figured I could wear them only if I dragged my feet a bit. It was better than walking barefoot anyway.

The officer had a habit of scratching his nose constantly. Whenever he spoke, he would stop every few seconds or so and scratch his nose. I never knew his name. He wouldn't tell me. But to me he was, and always will be, Itchy Nose. That's the name I gave him and I grew to respect him.

Not long before we finished another long march through jungles, we came to a road intersection that must have been the scene of a real battle.

Some bunkers had been blown to bits.

There were tank tracks and an armored vehicle had been wrecked. American ration cases were scattered around and it looked like good old American food to me. I was about to grab it when Itchy Nose said, "Don't touch it. It may be booby-trapped."

'Your New Camp'

About a half-hour later we came to a thick jungle with dense bamboo growth underneath.

Itchy Nose said, "This is your new camp."

This was the first of several "permanent" POW camps I was to be in, each for several months. It was located in Cambodia along the border northwest of Saigon.

I told Itchy Nose I was sick to my stomach. He said a doctor would see me the next day. And they chained me to a tree.

The next morning, I saw a fellow wearing a black uniform like mine. He was an American and I asked Itchy Nose, "Do we have another prisoner?"

He said, "Yes, he came in during the night, but you must not speak to him."

We were about 60 feet apart and shortly he noticed me. Although I was sick, my spirits rose: Here was another American and I wasn't going to have to walk any more. I had lost at least 20 pounds.

Itchy Nose came to talk to me again and asked me questions. I told him I was a schoolteacher and he said, "That is an honorable profession if that is what you are. We shall see."

I told him I was very sick to my stomach and couldn't eat. He sent for a medical worker who gave me a thermometer. My temperature was 103 and he said I had malaria.

They gave me an injection of some sort. I slept a while and they gave me some food, but I took only a few bites and threw up. So I just lay down.

I could see the other American prisoner's hammock. Guards were talking to him and I heard Itchy Nose ask his name. He answered, loudly, what sounded to me like "Patton." Later, I found out he was Tom Van Putten.

I tried to smile at the guy, but I was damn sick. He waved at me and I lay back down and went to sleep.

All that night I sweated and had chills and I kept vomiting. The medical worker gave me some shots, quinine I think, and some vitamin pills.

I was to have many more sieges of malaria, some severe, but I had been a prisoner for nearly three weeks now and, at last, my regular prison life seemed to have begun.

I had been treated reasonably well; at times with extraordinary thoughtfulness. But truly terrible days lay ahead.

TRIBUNE, APRIL 2, 1973.

Interrogation— Gun at Head, Grave at Feet

At one ghastly time during my captivity by the Viet Cong, I was certain I was a split second away from death with a cocked pistol at my head.

This came at the end of two days of interrogation, the worst two days of my five years as a prisoner.

Up to the end, the Viet Cong were certain I was either a spy, a CIA agent, or a high-ranking military officer.

Whether the Far East headquarters of the CIA is on Okinawa or not I don't know, but the Viet Cong were certain of it because they kept trying to trick me into admitting I'd been to Okinawa.

They'd ask a bunch of questions, for instance, about places I'd been and then, suddenly, "How was the swimming in Okinawa?" They'd use that device time after time—but, of course, I'd never been to Okinawa.

It was because they were so convinced I was with CIA or something similar that they were particularly determined to keep me isolated from other prisoners.

It was the same with Douglas Ramsey, a top-ranking official for the United States Agency for International Development, who was in the same prison camp with me for some time. They were doubly careful to keep Ramsey and me apart.

The interrogations were tough and there aren't many things about my prison experience I think back on with amusement. But the business with my jacket was really funny.

It was a maroon nylon windbreaker I'd thrown on just before I was captured. On one shoulder there was a patch of the Northeast Iowa Fox and Coon Association, a conservation club I belonged to in Decorah. On the other shoulder was the patch of the Norski Run Ski Club from Decorah.

On the back of the jacket was a round patch, yellow and maroon and about eight inches in diameter and it said "Wasioja Conference Champions, 1965-66," and there was a design of wrestlers.

The wrestling team I coached at Pine Island, Minn., won the conference championship the first year I was there.

These patches really bugged them. They would stare at them and important people in the camps would be called to come and look at them. They'd have huddles to try to figure out what military outfit they were from.

One day they took the jacket away from me and gave me an old green shirt that was too small to wear and sent the jacket off some place. Several days later they gave it back to me but they kept on being curious about those patches.

They took them off, apparently to send to some sort of a headquarters, and finally they took the jacket away from me altogether. I think I saw parts of it on a jacket that had been made for a child in one of our camps.

The first time I was subjected to a thorough interrogation was at one of the temporary camps before I reached my first regular prison camp.

There were three interrogators. One of them was about 60 years old with silver-grey hair. He spoke no English. Then there was a young man, 26 or 27, who was the interpreter. And there was a man I recall as "Gold Specs." I'll hate him until the day I die.

But he didn't reveal his true nature that first day.

He was about 40 years old and wore gold-rimmed spectacles.

One afternoon they unchained me and took me before the three. They sat in chairs behind a table made of bamboo and some other wood. I sat on a bench six to eight inches below their level. It was arranged that way deliberately so that they could look down on you and they thought you would feel small.

They had a small pot of tea, three cups and a package of cigarettes. Some one came in with some papers and they shuffled through these.

The man in the center, the young interpreter, spoke to me in English and said, "We are the Viet Cong."

I replied, "I am an American and I am not very glad to meet you."

'You Are an Officer'

The Gold Specs asked my name and what my job was. I said I was a teacher for Pacific Architects and Engineers and he said, "No, you are not. You are an officer."

And so the interrogation began. I told them about my life in Iowa and how I happened to come to Vietnam and they asked me what I thought about the war.

"All wars are immoral and I don't like to see people killed," I replied.

They kept asking what military unit I belonged to, what my rank was, and I kept replying that I wasn't military. This kept up all afternoon. There was no real harassment this time.

Of course, they asked about the patches on my jacket and they thought that the wrestling patch might mean I was an expert in judo and karate. One of them said, "That's why we have to chain you so you won't kill one of our guards and run away."

I said I didn't want to kill anyone, but I would like to run away.

I asked when I would be able to communicate with my parents, if they would be informed that I had been captured and if letters I had written would be sent to them.

They said that as soon as I reached a regular POW camp and showed a good attitude I would be allowed to write home.

"But you are showing a bad attitude now," they said. "You will not tell us your rank and what unit you belong to."

They asked me about military information and I said that in the first place I didn't have any and, second, if I did have military information, I would say nothing that would lead to harm to fellow Americans.

Finally, they took me back to my bunker and chained me up.

The worst two days of my life came several weeks later. It was the latter part of May, 1968.

It started when Itchy Nose, the commander of my first POW camp said to me, "You will go to a meeting today."

A guard took me to a building with a plastic roof. I could see that inside were two men at a table with a pot of tea, two cups, a package of cigarettes and some folders. One of the men was my old adversary, Gold Specs.

The guard told me to bow when I went in. I said I didn't bow to anyone, but I greeted the men politely. I saw that there were two .32 automatics on the table.

Gold Specs started right in, "You say you are a schoolteacher. You are not. You are an officer or CIA."

I said no, they were wrong, I was a teacher. They sent me away at noon and said that I would be back at 1 o'clock. They were getting very ugly.

I went back to my hammock and rested. I wasn't given anything to eat. When the questioning resumed, they told me again I was lying and Gold Specs said, "You will kneel down in front of us and talk to us on your knees."

"Why should I do that?" I asked.

"You will kneel down," said Gold Specs. He motioned to a guard who came toward me with his gun and bayonet. So I knelt.

Gold Specs and the other interrogator had their hands on their automatics.

And then I noticed that there was a big hole in the dirt floor, sort of like a grave, and a plastic sheet hung beside it. Apparently it was a psychological trick—to make me think that when they shot me, the blood would splash on the plastic shield.

They kept me on my knees for two hours. They had a lot of information in their folders. They knew about my family. They had a complete U.S. military and civilian directory for Saigon—names, units, assignments. They had a list of all the departments of Pacific Architects and Engineers. They asked me to name them; then they checked them off. But they still insisted I was CIA or military.

Late that afternoon they dismissed me again.

"You will be back tomorrow," they promised.

They gave me a little dried fish and rice that night and in the morning I was back at the interrogation shack—on my knees.

The interrogators referred to other people. I heard the name "Ramsey" for the first time. And they tried to whipsaw me. Gold Specs said, "Ramsey is a CIA agent who has crossed over to our side and he is protesting the war and he says you are a CIA agent."

I said, 'B - - - s - - -! I have never heard of this Ramsey." At that time, I knew nothing about him.

Ramsey was captured on Jan. 17, 1966, while delivering rice and medical equipment to a Vietnamese hamlet. He was released with the same group of prisoners with me.

When I had a chance to talk with him, I determined for sure he was not a CIA agent, and knew he had not really helped the Viet Cong in any way.

Once again, no food at noon, and by afternoon, on my knees again. I was getting angry.

I said, "You are asking questions about things I know nothing about. If I did know, damned if I'd tell you. According to the Geneva Convention, I don't have to tell you anything."

Gold Specs said, "We are the Viet Cong and if you do not tell us we are going to shoot you."

I said, "Then that's the way it will have to be."

Gold Specs replied. "You will think about this. We will give you 30 minutes. You will face that wall right there."

And they made me face the plastic sheet beside the hole. It seemed like I was there three weeks.

I thought, well, by God, they are probably going to shoot me. Finally, the heat, lack of food, no water since morning, got the best of me. I passed out. I went head first into the hole. When I came to, I couldn't get up because my arms were tied behind me. The hole was five feet deep and there I was, upside down. A guard helped me out and they gave me water.

Then they started their damn questions again. They kept saying they were going to shoot me. I was hungry and I was sick.

About 4 o'clock they stopped and Gold Specs said, "We will give you until 6 o'clock. When you decide to tell the truth, tell the guard. If you don't talk by 6, you will be shot tonight."

'You Haven't Answered'

About 6, Itchy Nose came to me and said, "I'm sorry, you haven't answered the questions. If you haven't told us by midnight who you are and what you do, you will be shot."

Then they chained me up differently—in spread-eagled fashion so I could barely move.

I was ordered to get into my hammock. They put one chain on my left ankle, fastened it to a post so my leg was up in the air. Another chain was put on my left wrist and fastened to a tree so my arm also was up in the air.

I couldn't get out of my hammock. I was real weak and didn't know what to think. It was the worst moment of my life, so far.

Finally, I went completely to pieces. I started to think about my mother and dad and I started to cry. I cried for about two hours and then, about 8:30 or 9, I started to pull myself together.

I said to myself, "Hell, if they're going to shoot you, there's not a damn thing you can do about it." I tried to wipe my face.

A guard came over and kicked me a couple of times and I started shouting at him. It was the first time I'd had rough treatment from a guard.

I said a prayer. I asked God to help me recover my senses, to come through this some way or other. That helped and I settled down.

At midnight, Itchy Nose came with four guards and he said, "I'm sorry. We are going to shoot you." They led me off into the jungle, 300 yards perhaps. By God, they had dug a hole, a grave, sure as hell—six feet long, five feet deep and two feet wide.

"Have you changed your mind?" Itchy Nose asked.

I said no, I didn't know anything.

"You are a military officer or CIA."

"I could tell you that I am but then you'd ask questions about it and I'd have to lie and you would know," I said. "I am a teacher."

"I am sorry," said Itchy Nose. "Would you like to pray?"

I knelt down by the hole and they stepped off about 15 feet. I just made my peace with God. I believed that I was going to be shot but I figured I was going to some place that they weren't. Then I stood up and said, "I am ready."

"Kneel down by the hole," said Itchy Nose.

He put the pistol to my head. I heard him cock it. I wasn't afraid any more. I think I was as close to God as I have ever been.

Nothing happened and I said, "Go ahead and shoot."

"Will you change your mind. Will you tell us who you are?"

"I've told you who I am. Go ahead and shoot."

Itchy Nose stood there absolutely still for two minutes with that gun at my head. Finally, he said, "I will give you some hours to think about this."

He released the hammer and put the gun back in his belt. They chained me up in the normal way that night. At first, I started to sweat. Then I came to the firm conclusion they had been bluffing.

I said the Lord's Prayer and went to sleep.

I slept well.

TRIBUNE, APRIL 3, 1973.

A Barbaric Isolation in Life of POW

Prisoner life was naturally grim, but actually it was more barbaric—a sort of primitive existence—than brutal.

There wasn't much physical punishment and little torture.

The isolation gets to you—we had only clandestine communications between fellow Americans.

Often the food was not fit for humans. While the Viet Cong usually were indifferent to minor sickness, they became extremely concerned when they thought a prisoner might die. On at least one occasion, this extreme concern came too late.

Some captors were evil men and I'll hate them until I die. Others were fairly decent. A handful, usually those of higher rank or very low rank, were extremely considerate at times.

By Oriental standards, treatment of prisoners in the jungle camps was severe but within survival limits.

But by Western standards, the treatment was unspeakable.

Itchy Nose, my first camp commander, was quick-tempered, but although he was the one who held a pistol at my head trying to make me admit I was a CIA agent, he was often quite considerate.

When he left my first camp after two years, conditions there got worse.

Another officer once gave us a ration of tobacco when the Viet Cong's supply was virtually exhausted.

But one Viet Cong I really hated was an interpreter named Hua. He was an evil man who made trouble for me whenever he could.

If he disagreed with our slightest act—even a word—he wouldn't hesitate to hit us or, if on the trail, punch us with his rifle.

He'd steal our tobacco and once stole a prisoner's shoes.

He was just pure mean, that's all.

Usually, there were no more than eight prisoners in one camp, but about 60 Vietnamese. Their prime function seemed to be gardening, probably raising food for Viet Cong guerrillas and hospitals.

Actually, prison life is best described with a series of unconnected vignettes. Life was extremely monotonous and only special incidents stand out.

Itchy Nose gave us a list of Vietnamese words to use—how to ask to go to the toilet, for food, for a doctor or the camp commander, how to say thank you and how to address women and children.

The Vietnamese worship children. Usually there were children in our camps and the guards played with them constantly. The children didn't have any real toys, but the guards made slingshots and other things for them.

At first, the only other prisoner in my camp was Tom Van Putten, who later successfully escaped.

Itchy Nose told me, "You must not talk to the other man or you will be punished."

But Tom and I managed to communicate. I said at Clark Air Base that I had talked more on my first day of freedom than in all the five years I was a prisoner. That was a bit of an exaggeration, but not much. In some cases, prisoners shared cells and could talk to each other. But I was always alone until Jan. 1 of this year.

Tom and I started to communicate by hand signals—one finger for A, two for B, three for C and so on. For "W" we'd flash all 10 fingers twice, then show three—to indicate the twenty-third letter of the alphabet.

Other times we'd form letters with our hands. But we'd have to do it all when the guards weren't looking.

Sometimes it would take a whole day to send one or two sentences.

I found out in this way that Tom was from Michigan, had a girl friend, was an Army Spec. 4 and a heavy equipment operator who was captured when his convoy was ambushed.

Also, when interpreters talked to us, we would talk loud and in that way pass on information about each other.

I hadn't been in prison camp long when an interpreter handed me a razor blade and said, "Here, you can shave." I asked how I could shave without a mirror, so they brought me a mirror.

I took the bare blade in my hand and tried to get off a few whiskers. Finally, I got a small plastic razor and, using water from my rice bowl, I tried to shave. But I cut myself in about a million places. After that, we didn't shave—they just trimmed our beards.

Itchy Nose talked with me quite often. I suppose he hoped to catch me off guard and get some intelligence. He told me he had been a prisoner of war of the South Vietnamese government for two years.

He'd give me tea and ask about the United States, our holidays, and I'd tell him about schoolteaching. He talked a lot about Ho Chi Minh and started bringing me papers printed in English.

They were propaganda, of course, and once I asked him, "How come we never see anything in here about your people being shot and killed; just the Americans and South Vietnamese?"

He'd reply, "That's not important."

We got up at sunrise, went to bed at sunset and had a nap at noon. It was that way all the time I was a prisoner. I got used to it—and it's been a little hard to change, going to bed later and missing the noon nap.

I said a short prayer every morning when I woke up—and again just before I went to sleep. So much of the time the only person I could talk to was the Lord . . . I'm not a religious fanatic, never have been, but prayer helped and I thought a lot about my past life.

While in one camp, there was a sudden great roar from a U.S. jet only about 200 feet off the ground. It was followed by a flight of C124s and they were spraying defoliant to clear the jungle cover.

The guards panicked. They'd been fed the propaganda that these defoliants were poisonous. I was amused by the way they'd wrap cloth around their faces and run back and forth. It just smelled like strong DDT to me.

Within two days, leaves started falling off the trees, but they just moved us to a new spot that was hidden from the air.

They went to a lot of work to build bunkers for four prisoners. They were about five feet deep, with trap doors that were locked at night.

We were chained up day and night as well—we were never without those 12-foot-long chains for the first 2½ years.

I was in a one-man bunker and once asked why I couldn't share a two-man bunker with another prisoner. They said, "You will poison his mind."

During one June, a Vietnamese artist came into the camp and made some charcoal drawings and water color paintings of life in the prison camp. I don't know why, and never saw the results.

What little we knew about what was happening back home we'd get from Itchy Nose. He would listen to the British Broadcasting Company radio and would pass along the news—our moon landings, Eisenhower's death, the assassinations of Bobby Kennedy and Martin Luther King.

Anything bad that happened in the States, such as racial disturbances, the Attica prison revolt, assassinations, Angela Davis and the charges against her, anti-war statements, we'd get from Radio Hanoi.

I had what I called my ten factor. I divided anything I heard on Hanoi Radio by ten, so I believed about one-tenth of what they broadcast.

When Ho Chi Minh died in 1969, there was a big stir in camp. Viet Cong leaders brought us his life history to read and asked two or three of us to write what we thought of him.

I felt—and wrote—that he wasn't as terrible as some made out, and in fact was a hell of a lot better man than some of the people they have up there now.

In September of 1969, I had a letter from my mother—my first letter from home—that my father was very ill in the hospital (later his leg was amputated but he is in good condition now).

I became distraught and tried to figure out some way to communicate with my family. I knew they didn't know whether or not I was alive and that this could have an effect on my father's condition.

I asked to write a letter home and they said I could if I would write about the CIA. I said again that I knew nothing about the CIA.

By this time, I think Itchy Nose was beginning to believe me, but the interpreter Hua kept insisting I was an agent.

"Your father is very sick and you must tell us about the CIA if you want to write home," Hua said.

When I repeated that I knew nothing about it, he asked me if I would write a condemnation of the war.

"I cannot condemn the actions of my government," I said. "I believe in fighting Communism."

They kept trying to tempt me. They said that because of my father's health I was being considered for release.

Finally, they brought me a piece of paper and an envelope and told me I could write to my mother. I told her I was fairly well and hoped the war would be over soon and that Dad was all right.

I actually thought they were going to mail it, but they didn't.

At one camp, a Viet Cong guard went berserk. Apparently some member of his family had been killed in the war. He got hold of a gun and acted like a madman.

He shouted that he was going to kill all the prisoners and ran down a trail with a whole bunch of other guards chasing him.

They subdued him and I think they tied him up because all night long we could hear him shouting. The camp commander kept running back and forth, very concerned.

It made us all nervous. We realized that some guard could go off his rocker any night and kill us all.

At another camp, one guard said to me, "You like to make things. We will let you make many things here." He showed me how to make a round, tightly woven basket of bamboo strips, the kind used to store boiled rice. The guards got other prisoners to cut some of the strips for me. Every so often a guard would stop and help me.

I had a feeling something was up, especially when they brought us cookies and more meat. I was right.

Soon, a five-man camera crew showed up at camp. They had modern, fancy equipment, both movie and still cameras. They took movies of the camp, including me working on my basket.

After they left, a guard took away the basket I'd been working on and added, "You don't need this; it isn't a very good job anyhow."

In September, 1968, nine months after my capture, a camp officer asked about my aunt and uncle: "Who are Jim and Jennie?" I told him and he said, "They are having a celebration of some sort." I said, "Yes, they are celebrating their fiftieth wedding anniversary this year."

Obviously, mail had come for me and they had been reading it.

The next day, the officer gave me a letter from my dad. It had been written Apr. 10, his birthday. I think they'd had it since late in April but here it was September. They let me keep the letter for 30 minutes, then took it away.

The next day, he gave me a letter from my mother, mailed April 9. My folks didn't know whether I was alive and had written to me in care of the National Liberation Front's Cambodian ambassador.

I got a total of six letters from home. The last one, from my mother, was written Jan. 5, 1970. I was given it in April. I carried that letter around my neck the rest of the time I was a prisoner and read it over and over and over.

Many times, camp officials let me write letters, but they never sent them. They just wanted to see what information they could get out of them.

The Viet Cong never could figure out how I could be a teacher of English in Vietnam and not know Vietnamese. Some thought that I was faking and that I knew Vietnamese well.

I tried to explain that under the system we used to teach English, it was preferred that the teacher not know Vietnamese. Thus, the students would be forced to use English words.

A few guards taught me some Vietnamese and I taught them a little English. They had little notebooks on which we would draw things like hands and feet and I would repeat the English word for the picture.

But then Hua—my enemy—would come along and tell them I spoke Vietnamese and they'd get mad.

They thought I'd been playing tricks on them and got very belligerent.

Hua pretended to be pleasant but he was a snake. I had one way of bugging him. Whenever I wrote anything for Itchy Nose, Hua had to translate it and copy it in triplicate. So I'd make everything just as long and wordy as I could to make him do more work.

We changed camps periodically, and one in Cambodia didn't have underground bunker cages—they were cells above ground, about 5 feet high, 6½ feet wide and 9 feet long. We were locked in our cells—unchained for the first time in months.

And we had wooden beds. They actually felt good after months in hammocks—which are OK except for having your feet and head higher than the rest of you.

At this camp, the guards slept and lived in the areas above our string of small cells but under the big roof over our complex—sort of an attic. Top bars of our cells separated us. They made flooring of bamboo mats for themselves.

We called these guards our "landlords."

We tried to get on good terms with our landlords to get extra favors from them.

They'd write and study in their little cubicles above us and often brought bits of food up there with them. Sometimes they'd share food—sometimes we could steal it.

My first landlord I named Spider Legs because his legs were so skinny. He was a filthy dirty fellow who came in without taking the mud off his feet. He never swept his bamboo mat floor and dirt kept filtering down into my bed.

So I made a broom from bamboo sticks tied together, gave it to him and asked if he would sweep. He didn't get mad, and actually swept his place and laughed about it.

He would have bad attacks of malaria that would last three or four days. He'd shake so badly with chills that the building would shake, too.

We became quite skillful at stealing from our landlords.

In spite of all their Communist talk about principles and their training, they'd steal from each other. So when prisoners stole from them, they usually suspected their fellow guards.

They were almost all terrible thieves. We became pretty decent thieves ourselves.

The guards knew we stole food but took this in stride and just tried to keep it out of reach. But we'd steal other things, too—thread, bits of cloth to patch our clothes, needles, tobacco, paper to make cigarettes.

There were various ways of stealing. The guards put things under their beds and we could reach up outside the cell and get to them. They didn't realize how long our arms were, because theirs were so much shorter. We'd also use sticks with snares at the end of them to snag the booty.

Once I was reaching up to see what I could find and mistakenly grabbed Spider Leg's foot. I thought I was a goner. He woke up but didn't realize what had happened.

Then, funny things would go through my mind. I could look through cracks in that bamboo mat and see the feet of my landlords. I don't know how many times I had that childish but almost irresistable urge to tickle their feet.

At times I had a feather and then the temptation was even greater. Once I almost did it—I had the feather an inch from Spider Leg's feet.

After Spider Legs, my next landlord was a youngster I called Baby Rabbit. He was only 15 years old or so and appeared scared to death.

Later, we started calling him Baby Snookens because of his "overtures" to the other boys in the camp. He'd take some of them up to his room with him.

But some guards were stupid and sadistic. The way they treated animals infuriated me. They'd take lizards and frogs and deliberately burn them with cigarettes to make them squirm.

One day a guard had a baby monkey with a black skinny face who was really sick. Someone had been jabbing lighted cigarettes into its head and neck. It was almost dead.

Another guard we named "Stick," because he walked as though he had a stick up his back.

Two other prisoners drove Stick absolutely nuts because they were the loudest snorers you've ever heard.

Stick put up with this until a new guard came into camp, and then persuaded him to take his place as landlord for the loud snorers. The new guard took it as long as he could, then persuaded another newcomer to take his place. And that's the way it went. The snorers had many different landlords.

There was another guard, Porky, who spent every noon hour in his shack masturbating. He didn't realize we could see him. This gave us a club to hold over his head. Any time he made it rough on us, we'd protect ourselves by threatening to tell the commander what we knew — and he'd shape up.

Dealing with our captors required restraint and judgment. After all, we were at their mercy and we had to reckon constantly with the consequences of our actions, not only to ourselves but to our fellow prisoners.

But it was always a game of wits — and I like to think that we were better at it than our uneducated Viet Cong guards.

TRIBUNE, APRIL 4, 1973.

A Challenge: How to Keep Minds Busy

Merely passing the time was a great challenge during the five years I was held by the Viet Cong. Monotony, boredom and loneliness were among our greatest enemies.

That's why I welcomed work details, unless I was extremely ill, no matter how hard the work was. Work meant something to do and, occasionally, a chance to talk to fellow prisoners.

There were times, however, when a sick prisoner was forced to work, as punishment, or if his captors thought he was faking.

With all our stress and misery, we found ingenious ways to occupy our minds with other things.

For instance, a few of us worked out a way to play chess, although we were 50 feet apart and had to communicate by hand signals.

With various materials we scrounged, we made chess boards. Then we worked out a system of transmitting signals of our moves by hand.

Unfortunately, we were caught eventually. The guards thought it all was an elaborate escape plan.

We also "talked" to each other by singing. The guards couldn't understand English, so we'd make up tunes as we went along and carry on conversations with the words.

We'd use singing to pass on information: An inspection was coming or, if one of us was able to find out, what we would eat at the next meal.

If a guard was approaching and someone was doing something against the rules, someone close by would whistle the Funeral March or "Look Out for Jimmy Valentine" — the signal to stop.

Sometimes a fellow would be dozing when the guards started making one of their five daily trips to light cigarettes and we'd rouse him by whistling "Winstons Taste Good Like a Cigarette Should."

Battered Deck of Cards

In 1968, I got a deck of cards and used them right through to the end. I've still got them, battered as they are.

One rainy day they got wet and the deck swelled up three times its proper size. Over the years I nursed those cards along, sewing them up and putting on new backs. Of course, it didn't wind up being a very legitimate deck because there were telltale marks on each card.

I'd play bridge by dealing out four hands, trying to figure out the right bidding and then play each hand in turn.

We'd also play a gambling-type of solitaire. I still owe one prisoner $2.80.

One year I planted some orange trees. We were given a couple of oranges and I kept the seeds and planted them just outside the bars of my cell where the sun would hit them.

I watered them every day. Finally, I had 27 or 28 little trees growing, some of them six inches high.

I used dirt for all sorts of things. I made a screen out of bamboo and sifted all the dirt in my cell to get rid of the stones and lumps of clay. Then I'd smooth out the fine dirt and draw things, such as designs for houses and buildings I remembered back in Decorah.

Many times, instead of just doing nothing, I'd take a small strip of cloth and try to guess how many threads were in it.

Then I'd pull out one thread at a time, carefully counting them, to see how close I had guessed.

It sounds ridiculous, but it did pass the time and kept one's mind occupied. Incidentally, I became pretty good at guessing the number of threads in those small patches of rags.

We were hungry most of the time, and we'd dream up all sorts of food concoctions — new ideas for pizza and other crazy things.

One dish I came up with was to take ground beef and mix in crushed black walnuts and grated Swiss cheese. I kept thinking about that combination for a long time and it sounded better all the time.

I finally tried it just the other day. I came home late one night. All the ingredients were on hand; I mixed it up. It really tasted good.

Constructing with Bamboo

We'd construct small items that would seem unimportant to most people but were significant to us. I'd split pieces of bamboo with my teeth, and use the thin strips to build little boxes for cigarettes I rolled and mats for my cup and dish when I ate.

I'd devise ways to trap and kill small animals — rats and mice mostly — that created a lot of problems in my cell.

But I wouldn't kill frogs or toads because they'd eat the insects and keep them away from me.

I occupied myself by watching ants and termites.

One kind of ant liked to eat night crawlers. I watched these ants for many months. They'd send out scouts, one or two ants at a time, and when they'd find a night crawler they'd disappear and return with a whole army of ants.

Then they'd all attack the night crawler, stinging and biting. They'd work on the crawler until it could hardly move and then start dragging it back. If it was too big, they'd come back with more ants. Those little ants could handle a crawler as big around as your little finger. I often wished I'd had a magnifying glass and notebook to keep some sort of record of this fascinating life.

There were some termites that could sting you like a bumblebee.

Sometimes on the trail I'd step on them barefoot at night, and they could really raise a welt. But they gave a warning. They'd get under dry leaves and you could hear their vibrations if you got real close. They'd flick their tails against a dry leaf and it would make a rattle, almost like a rattlesnake.

One noon I went down into my bunker and there was a large group of termites, about a quarter of an inch long, marching from a hole somewhere in the bunker, across my hammock, up the hammock strings and then out of the bunker.

There were millions of them.

The ants were miserable. If you spilled a little bit of food, they'd come in hordes. You'd likely wake up with a blanket full of ants. And some of them could bite viciously.

I spent lots of time watching the birds and squirrels and chipmunks. I'd catch scorpions and tie strings on them and play with them.

Sometimes I'd kill time just by peeling bark from logs. One kind of bark was real soft and could be split apart in layers. I tried weaving things with the pieces—mats, little baskets, things like that.

At one time, the Viet Cong gave us baby chicks to raise. Most of the men got one, but for some reason they gave me two. I really enjoyed them and trained them so well that when I whistled, they'd come to me.

At night I hung the chicks up in a basket in my cell so snakes and rats couldn't get at them. Of course, I had to share my rice with them, but I was glad to do it.

I'd feed them other things—little lizards, for instance—and they loved them.

I even took the chicks with me when we moved from one camp to another, even though it was a chore lugging that basket with them in it along with my other gear.

Eventually, the chickens were big enough to kill for food. I cried about that, for it was like losing a favorite pet dog, but when they fed me a few bites, I didn't hesitate to eat. Any kind of meat was too precious to pass up.

At one time, I was given a project that used up a lot of time. Itchy Nose, the camp commander, said, "If you are a schoolteacher, you can tell us about American schools."

So I wrote all the good things I knew about American schools. I used 180 huge sheets of paper to do it. It was damn near a book. I wrote about courses offered in high schools and colleges. I remember writing out the entire curriculum of a couple of schools.

Then Itchy Nose asked me to do the same thing about religion—and I did that.

There Were Differences

I'm not going to say there were never any differences or arguments between prisoners because, from time to time, there were. But I'm not going to talk about them in any detail.

These differences were really quite minor because whenever the going was tough, we stuck up for each other without question.

Sometimes we'd get into arguments and two fellows wouldn't speak or communicate with each other for a month.

They were mostly silly arguments—like who wrote a certain piece of music.

And we'd make bets. I owe one prisoner $200. They were silly bets, too—who wrote the Nutcracker Suite (I said George Gershwin and, boy, was I wrong!); who played the lead in "Cat Ballou" and who played the drunk in the same show.

But all this gave us something to do. After all, we had all the time in the world.

TRIBUNE, APRIL 5, 1973.

Escapes: How Several Failed, One Succeeded

The Viet Cong went to extraordinary means to prevent escapes, and yet escape and the chances of getting away with it were constantly on my mind. I'm sure all other American captives were preoccupied by the same thoughts.

During the first few days I was a prisoner, I thought I had an excellent chance to get away, and was confident I could make it.

That's when I was with Major Blanket and we had come to a good-sized river near Bien Hoa.

Blanket had sent out a couple of scouts—to investigate the area, I thought—and from his pack he took a small inner tube and had me blow it up.

I figured he either couldn't swim or was a poor swimmer and was going to use the inner tube to help him cross the river.

I'm a good swimmer and I said to myself, "This will be my chance. When we start across the river, I'll make a break for it, swim underwater like mad and get away."

It was a first-rate idea, except for one thing. To my despair, a boat was soon coming our way carrying a Vietnamese and a small boy. The two Viet Cong scouts were with them.

They ferried us across the river—and that escape chance went down the drain.

Another time I thought I might be able to get away if I could get my leg chains unlocked.

At one of the temporary camps, I was in my hammock out in the open and the guards were off to one side, sitting by an open fire, sipping tea and eating rice. They thought I was asleep.

I tried to pick the lock open or break it in some way.

I took the top of a tin can and twisted and bent it with my teeth until I made a narrow probe out of it. Then I started working on the lock. I thought I just about had it picked open when the metal strip—my probe—broke off in the lock.

I couldn't get it out. I realized that if the guards found it that way, they'd know what I'd been up to and I'd be in deep trouble. So I went to work with another piece of the same can, made another probe and tried to get the first one out.

When the guards came by I played possum. Along about dawn I finally got that probe out. I kept on trying to pick that lock—but I never made it.

Chained to a Log

There was one hospital camp where we stayed only a short time because too many local people were curious about whom the Viet Cong were guarding.

There was no big tree close enough to chain me to, so they drilled a hole through a log about a foot and a half in diameter and four feet long and fastened my chain to that.

I pretended I could just barely get it off the ground. Actually, I could lift it without any trouble. I thought maybe I could carry it and escape at night.

Just about then, I noticed a guard we called Bull Moose carrying a big bag of Claymore mines—the kind that pop up, explode and spray deadly shrapnel about waist high when tripped.

He walked to the edge of the jungle and started setting out these mines around the camp. They'd be connected by thin trip wires hidden in the jungle floor, and if anybody happened to hit one of the wires, several mines in the network would go off.

They'd take them in every morning, but lay them again at night.

I gave up the idea of trying to pick up that damn log and walk away with it. There was little chance of getting through all those mines without hitting a trip wire you couldn't even see.

Two Army POWs—Tom Van Putten and Jim Ray, who was in military intelligence—tried to escape in the summer of 1968.

By playing up to their guards, they were allowed to have their chains on quite loose at night. The chains were merely wrapped around our ankles, then fastened with a padlock. Those on Van Putten and Ray were loose enough so that by using a lot of soap they could slip out of them—losing only a little skin in the process.

Anyway, they started digging a short tunnel from inside their locked bunker to the outside. They hoped to escape on the Fourth of July.

They had the tunnel about three-fourths finished when one night there was one hell of a rumpus in camp: The Viet Cong were all over the place. They had caught Van Putten and Ray digging in their tunnel.

The Viet Cong chained them up tightly and kept their arms bound behind their backs at night after that. They threatened to kill them if they tried it again.

They did the same thing to the rest of us—sort of like a 30-day sentence for all.

They also rebuilt the bunkers to make them tunnelproof. They dug a trench about three feet deep around every bunker, then filled it with huge logs and boulders to make tunneling through that impossible.

Bull Moose the guard was especially rough with me for some reason. He tied my arms down. And when I got in my hammock, he'd pull the leg chain up until my left leg was about a foot in the air. Then he'd fasten the chain on the top of my bunker so I'd just have to lie that way, one foot in the air and my arms bound.

I had a mild case of malaria at the time and was having diarrhea. It was just plain awful.

I had to lie that way all night. I started yelling, and yelled all night. I was really mad. The guards came and told me to shut up or I'd be shot.

Within a few days I worked out a way to beat this method of raising my chained leg up in the air.

When I went into my bunker, I'd rig my hammock so it just barely touched the ground. Then Bull Moose would pull the chain up tight with my leg in the air. I also worked out a way to loosen the ropes on my arms so I could raise my hammock a couple of feet.

After Bull Moose pulled my leg in the air with the chain, I'd raise the hammock and there would be enough slack in the chain so I could be half-way comfortable.

There was a time in 1969 when I became overwhelmed with despair.

I had been hopeful of being released in one of the Viet Cong's propaganda gimmicks, but finally realized there was no chance at all.

For the second time in my captivity (the first time was when I thought I was going to be murdered) I broke down completely.

I lay in my hammock and cried through half the night.

Toughness of Mind Vital

After that, I pulled myself together and from then

on managed to keep myself in line emotionally through the rest of captivity.

You've got to have a certain toughness of mind and spirit to survive what prisoners of war went through in Vietnam.

I began to think about escape again and decided the first thing I had to do was get rid of the chain I was locked to day and night.

That meant I had to work on the padlock. I discovered that two small brass pins held the top hinged part of the lock secure inside.

I knew that brass was relatively soft, so I started pouring a little dust inside the lock for an abrasive, then clicking the locked hinge against those soft brass pins—thousands of times a day—to wear through them.

If it took a million clicks against those pins, I was willing to do it. I had lots of time. I kept at it day after day when the guards weren't looking.

I'd do it 1,000 times with one hand, then 1,000 times with the other.

Eventually, I had those pins about three-quarters worn through.

But it all went for nothing when a guard happened to look at what I was doing and put on a new lock.

I also started to scrounge items for a jungle survival kit. It wasn't much—a little sulfa powder, some bandages and a bit of quinine.

I kept the kit buried about six or eight inches in the ground so they couldn't find it. They never did, and I brought it home with me.

Whenever Tom Van Putten, the Army prisoner, and I had a chance to talk (we were kept about 60 feet apart), we discussed the possibility of escape. In the spring of 1969, in a camp that wasn't surrounded by mines, we saw an opportunity.

We had gone to a lot of effort to butter up two of the guards to make them think we were good guys who were completely co-operative with the camp rules and routine.

One of the guards we called Pock Mark because of marks on his face; the other, we called Jake the Barber, because he gave us haircuts.

They would escort us to the toilet one by one, then bring us back to our underground cells and snap the locks back on our ankle chains. But they got in the habit of trusting us and letting us snap our own locks shut. Also they liked to go off some distance from our cells and talk to each other.

"I think we can get by with it," Tom signaled one day after the toilet trip.

There was quite a lot of artillery activity in the area. U.S. guns were shooting over us from east to west. In fact, a few rounds fell in our camp.

One smashed a bunch of the Viet Cong's bicycles. Another hunk of shrapnel smacked into a post right beside me, missing me by only six inches. I dived head-first through the trap door of my bunker.

Tom suggested using the artillery for a guide.

It would be impossible to head straight east because that meant going through a part of the camp where capture would be certain.

"We'll go west for one hour, north for two hours and then head east toward the sound of the artillery," Tom suggested. "If we can flag down a helicopter, we will."

The circumstances for escape seemed to be right, but unfortunately I was extremely weak from malaria and had serious doubts that I could make it.

It would be tough getting enough to eat to stay alive, although there were some jungle weeds we'd seen the guards eat and some edible roots we could recognize.

Locks That Weren't Shut

Pock Mark unchained me, accompanied me to the toilet and then he did the same thing with Tom. Pock Mark didn't snap the lock shut when he brought me back to my cell and failed to notice I didn't do it.

I signaled this to Tom. He signaled back that he wasn't locked up either.

Soon Pock Mark came toward me and he was close enough I felt sure he'd catch me with my chain unlocked. This could ruin the escape for both me and Tom. So I snapped the lock shut and went down into my bunker. The chain always made a loud clatter as I did this.

Pock Mark then started in the direction of Tom's cell, but was distracted and went off to join Jake the Barber.

Tom, still unlocked, lowered his chain into his cell and made sure it made the kind of rattle it did when he went down himself so the guards would think he was in his cell.

But actually, he stayed on top of the shelter, out of sight behind the slanting roof.

(With a sense of the dramatic, he snapped the chain lock shut so the guards would find it that way when they discovered his escape, leaving them puzzled over how he got out.)

Tom started tip-toeing away, carrying his sandals in his hands. As he passed my shelter, I told him, "I hope you make it, Tom. I will pray for you until I know you are safe. God go with you."

Despite my weak condition and sickness, I would have gone with Tom if I had been unlocked. And I know if there had been any way for Tom to help me out of those chains, he would have.

Tom got a two-hour start before the Viet Cong guards discovered he was gone.

The sergeant of the guard,—Boston Blackie, we called him—came by. He had taken Pock Mark's place.

He looked into Van Putten's cell, then pulled up the empty chain and saw the ankle lock that was still snapped shut on the chain. He yelled into the cell, "Putten." There was no reply. He reached down and shook Tom's hammock.

Boston Blackie left in a hurry. He didn't yell or blow his whistle as I thought he might do. He walked rapidly down the trail and out of sight. In about three minutes he came back with about 15 Viet Cong. They all pulled out the empty chain and looked at it, puzzled.

An interpreter came up to me and said, "Where's Putten."

"I don't know," I replied, acting innocent. "Isn't he in his house?"

"No," he snarled and slammed down the lid on my cell and locked the trap door, which they normally did only at night.

A whole flock of guards rushed off into the jungle, but they came back in about 10 minutes. Thirty minutes later an interpreter came by and said, "Put everything in your pack. We are moving to a new camp."

And so I knew Tom had made it, at least some distance away from the camp, because obviously the Viet Cong were afraid he would find U.S. or South Vietnamese troops and they would attack the camp and rescue us.

Tom never found that artillery unit, but I later learned he survived 18 days in the jungle before he was picked up by an American helicopter.

I don't think I could have lasted that long, sick as I was.

Pock Mark and Jake the Barber disappeared from camp for what I assume was some sort of punishment.

He Attacked a Guard

There was one escape attempt that ended in tragedy.

Jim Ray, the Spec. 5 from Army Intelligence, just about had his mind and spirit broken by the Viet Cong after they discovered his tunnel escape attempt. Jim was young, 18 or 19, and he wanted to be free more than anything else.

One day, in what was really a courageous but not well-thought-out escape attempt, he attacked a guard. He had the wild idea of setting us all free.

He was subdued, of course, and badly beaten. Then suddenly, he disappeared from our camp and I never saw him again.

We heard later that a young man of Ray's description was brought to another camp and chained by both legs in a dungeon.

Medical workers brought him food, but he wouldn't eat. Apparently, having suffered too much and being a wild, freedom-loving spirit, he stopped eating, just as many of God's wild creatures will do if we humans pen them up. Soon he was free of the misery of his life.

One day an ox cart came to the cell and something bulky was put in it and taken away. The next day, the cell was empty.

The Viet Cong have since reported that Jim Ray died in captivity.

He was a good man. I am wearing his POW bracelet today.

TRIBUNE, APRIL 6, 1973.

For 5 Years, Teaspoon of Meat Daily

Few people know how desperate you can get for food when a prisoner of war.

One time, a fellow prisoner became gravely ill. We didn't think he was going to make it. Finally the guards moved him some distance away from the rest of us, but we could hear him coughing.

The days passed and the coughing continued. Then one day we didn't hear him any more and we thought he had died.

Somehow the word got around that when a prisoner died the Viet Cong served the remains to the survivors.

Later, when we were given bits of meat, some of the prisoners wondered whether it was from their late fellow prisoner.

I knew enough about anatomy to know that it was monkey meat, but two fellows thought it might well be their former friend. One refused to eat the meat. But the other did. He was that desperate for food.

The food was never good. (Understandably, it was best when the Viet Cong started "fattening us up" for release). Usually it was unspeakably bad.

Over the five-year span, I doubt that I averaged more than a teaspoon or so of meat a day.

And what meat! Imagine thinking of monkey and tiger meat as delicacies. But I actually grew to like them.

What we got most of was rice, of course—and that doesn't mean the kind of rice served in American homes.

The rice we got was coarse and usually filthy, with little rocks and worms in it. Often it was stored where rats, mice and chickens walked over it and fouled it.

I just ate the rice without looking. Otherwise you'd spend half your time picking out the worms and other stuff. Also we adopted a bit of the philosophy that what you don't know won't hurt you.

The little meat we got was limited to what the Viet Cong could get from the jungles. During captivity I ate not only monkey and tiger but elephant, water buffalo, leopard, lizards and snakes.

Once in a long while we'd get chicken—but that wasn't anywhere near as good as it might sound. The prisoners got the heads and the feet; the Viet Cong got the rest. One chicken would make two meals for nine men. About the best we ever got were chopped bones with whatever shreds of meat were left on them.

I remember once eating rancid elephant meat. It smelled just awful. But once I got it past my nose, it didn't taste too bad.

Getting animal meat from the jungles wasn't

always easy. After we'd been in a camp for a fairly long time, the available animals would be pretty well cleaned out.

Also, if the Viet Cong thought there was the slightest chance that U.S or South Vietnamese troops were within hearing, shooting was forbidden.

In the summer of 1971 in Cambodia, the Viet Cong shot an elephant no more than 200 yards from our camp. That gave us a good supply of meat—fresh meat for three or four days, then smoked or dried elephant.

Every day, each of us would get the equivalent of a small meatball. That summer we also had string beans, black-eyed peas, tensil beans, boiled cucumbers and boiled pumpkin, which I hated. Occasionally, but not very often, they'd cook vegetables with a little pork fat to give them some flavor.

The Viet Cong basically were lazy, especially if their labor involved the prisoners. For instance, they'd try to avoid feeding us anything that would give us diarrhea—and thus force them to escort us to the toilet more often.

They also were so lazy that if one prisoner left some food, they wouldn't take it to another who really needed it.

Rice Soup

After one of my bouts with malaria, I found that plain rice soup didn't bother my stomach as much as other things. I hated plain rice and wanted rice soup instead. I refused to eat the rice. I ate rice soup for 18 months.

Then a doctor told me I had to stop this. I said I wouldn't, so they gave me soup that was plain water except for a few kernels of rice. That cured me. I went back to eating plain rice.

From the very start, I said a little blessing before each meal. I was brought up that way in Decorah, and even if I got no more than a little rice I wanted to thank God for that much. I don't think I missed asking a blessing more than three times in five years.

Most of the time I ate with a spoon made out of scrap from a U.S. helicopter. The spoons were made of soft aluminum and the handles would break easily. I'd use chopsticks until I could make another spoon.

Next to food, tobacco was important. Most of the time, we got a tobacco ration but paper to roll cigarettes was a problem. I'd use anything I could get my hands on—even peeling layers off cardboard.

Holidays are important to the Vietnamese. Thank God for that. We got our best treatment, especially food, on holidays—both theirs and ours.

We thought so much about eating that when one holiday was over, we would think about the next. Like . . . it's only so long before Tet and then we'll get a good meal. And then only so many days until May Day. Then the Fourth of July, and so on.

Christmas always was a big day in our camps. I made a Christmas tree of some sort every year.

Itchy Nose expressed an interest in Christmas and asked me to write something about it for him. So I wrote about 15 pages about our customs, our songs and our meals and the Christian meaning of Christmas.

Itchy Nose told us we would be able to enjoy Christmas.

"It is National Liberation Front policy to let prisoners enjoy their great national holidays," he said. They took the same attitude about our Fourth of July and New Year's. They wouldn't recognize Easter or Thanksgiving.

Made Christmas Trees

About a week before Christmas 1968, I was able to communicate with Tom Van Putten and we both decided to make trees. He made one with a cone-shaped bamboo frame, and pinned leaves and twigs all around it.

I made one by taking a long stick and then collecting leaves. Every time I went to the toilet I collected leaves and graded them by size, and then I braided them and fastened them to the stick to form a tree.

I decorated it with little strips of colored paper, the red cap from a toothpaste tube and icicles and stars from the same tube. Every year I made a cross from bamboo strips.

That first Christmas in captivity we had meat and vegetables with our rice for breakfast, little sausages and real chicken—not the heads and feet we usually got—at noon. We had a loaf of bread, some fancy noodles and some egg dish for supper.

They released half of us from our chains on Christmas day. On New Year's they released the other half. But we couldn't go more than 12 feet from our bunkers and we weren't allowed to talk. They also doubled the guard.

They gave us three or four real cigarettes each and let us share a bottle of wine. They played the radio throughout camp and along with some propaganda was a recording of Bing Crosby singing "White Christmas."

We sang Christmas carols—"Silent Night," "Deck the Halls," "Hark the Herald Angels Sing" and others. When we didn't know all the words we'd whistle.

I always asked Itchy Nose if we couldn't sit together at Christmas but he said we'd "poison the minds" of each other.

You can never completely stifle the Christmas spirit among Americans. We even exchanged gifts among prisoners.

The Viet Cong wouldn't let us do it openly, but we'd pass things along to each other when we went to the toilet. We had hiding places where we left things, then passed the word for others to pick them up.

I made tobacco pouches from scraps of cloth and plastic for some prisoners. One fellow made me a cigarette-rolling machine from a piece of plastic and a stick. It took me two months to learn how to use it. Another found an old buckle and made me a belt.

We also shared other precious things, such as soap, cigarette papers and sewing needles.

TRIBUNE, APRIL 7, 1973.

The Constant POW Battle with Illness

Throughout my captivity, I was repeatedly ill—gravely at times—but Viet Cong doctors and medical workers pulled me through many crises.

The Viet Cong always seemed determined to keep their prisoners alive. It was near panic when they lost one of us.

Perhaps they were conscious of our hostage value in peace negotiations. Perhaps they wanted to establish a record of being kinder and better captors than the South Vietnamese.

I don't think they were motivated by compassion, but the sanctity of life conceivably was involved.

The Viet Cong had medical equipment and supplies, and treatment certainly was better than primitive. But by our standards, it often was unorthodox.

Once I got a horrible infection from a dirty hypodermic needle. An abscess developed and it kept getting bigger. One day it erupted and great globs of infected liquid came out.

A doctor lanced it with a razor blade and then took forceps and pulled out another mass of infection. It was a grim experience, believe me.

Then the doctor filled the hole with wild honey. On following days, he cleaned the wound and put wild honey in again. I'll say this: The wound healed perfectly.

Some of the Viet Cong thought if you had an upset stomach, you could cure it by eating spiders. (Their doctors didn't share this theory.) Another theory some had was that you could cure a headache by pinching your nose until it was black and blue. Others felt pulling three or four hairs out of your head would cure a headache.

One fall we were in a large camp that had once been a hospital. Civilian prisoners were in one part of it and, though we didn't know about it until much later, U.S. military prisoners were in another section.

Suddenly, we were all called in for complete physical examinations. The food became much cleaner. You could get medical treatment faster—and it was better. If you had the slightest complaint, you got prompt attention.

The reason was that in the military section of the camp, a U.S. Army captain had died because he didn't receive proper medical attention. They didn't believe he was as sick as he said he was and refused to give him medication—until it was too late.

He didn't have to die.

Malaria and Beri-Beri

Malaria plagued me all five years of captivity. I'd have a mild attack about once a month and then a serious attack two or three times a year. I suffered from beri-beri about half the time and that, of course, was due to a vitamin deficiency, the result of the miserable food we were fed.

At our first regular prison camp, not long after I was captured, I became very ill with malaria.

We had just arrived at the camp when Itchy Nose, the Viet Cong commander, said, "We are very busy building this new camp. You must try to get well. A doctor, a real doctor, will come and see you tomorrow."

They brought me food that night, but I couldn't eat it. I kept vomiting. I thought that maybe from fear and worry I had a small ulcer. The medical worker gave me more injections, but my legs and feet started to hurt a lot. My arches were cramping. My legs were swelling and I could hardly stand up. I had chills so badly I lay covered up all the time with all the clothes I had.

Then Itchy Nose came with the doctor, a handsome young Vietnamese.

"This man will take care of you," he said. "He has come here from a hospital."

The doctor took my temperature and pulse, gave me some injections and ordered some medication and vitamin pills. And he ordered the guards to remove the chain from my ankle.

I was in no condition to walk far. I could walk about four feet to go to the toilet and then come back and lie down again.

Day and night, they kept bringing me different foods, rice cakes and bread. I could eat a little bit of the bread, but for 13 days I lay there and ate little.

The doctor and a nurse, quite pretty and 22 or 23 years old, came twice a day and gave me injections.

From time to time I could hear Tom Van Putten. Once he shouted at a guard, "Don't I ever get any cold water?" It was hot in the daytime and cold at night and every time his water would be cool enough to drink they'd fill it up with hot water.

Guard Clowns

One guard tried to cheer me up. He was a funny looking fellow, a little like Stan Laurel of Laurel and Hardy. The radio was playing some American music and he made like he was dancing, just kind of danced around in circles, trying to cheer me up.

The tenth or eleventh day I started feeling a little better. I could eat a little banana and a little rice. They killed a chicken, mostly for me, and gave me some chicken broth.

On the fourteenth day I could get up and move

about pretty well. The doctor said, "You must try to take a bath." So, with two guards I went to a stream, took a bath and washed my clothes.

Sometimes we all had bad trouble with beri-beri. At night my legs would ache so badly I'd get up and bang them with my fists. It was just a lack of proper diet.

Near the end of the U.S. offensive into Cambodia, I again became desperately ill with malaria. One morning the guards told everyone to pack up and be ready to move, but I was to stay. They left behind with me a doctor, the Butcher we called him, an interpreter we called the Tobacco Man, and a guard we named Loud Mouth, an ornery, quick-tempered fellow with napalm scars on his chest—but at times he was quite softhearted.

I got so sick that for three days I don't remember a thing. They told me later I threw rocks at the doctor.

On the fourth day I woke up in my hammock and thought I could see my mother sitting on a log across from me. I started talking to her and the doctor came over and asked who I was talking to. I told him I was talking to my mother, I was that delirious.

Then she "disappeared" and I screamed at the guards, telling them they had chased my mother away.

They gave me some injections of quinine and some vitamin pills. I asked where I'd been, where everyone was. Then I started to remember that they had gone. They checked my temperature and apparently the quinine knocked the malaria. On the evening of the fourth day they got me up and tried to get me to walk back and forth. I could go about 30 feet every 10 minutes.

Quinine, Vitamins

On the fifth day, they brought me some jungle boots, a pair of stockings, a can of milk, some large ampules of glucose and quantities of quinine and vitamins.

The guards had some Vietnamese tobacco they'd cut. It wasn't completely mature or dried, but they gave me one cigarette and asked if I could travel the next day. I said I would try.

"We have to get to camp with the others," an interpreter said, "because we only have enough rice for two more days."

I said I could never make the 17 or 18 miles to the camp in one day, but might be able to do it in two.

So we started out. I walked with two canes and with a man on each side of me. We'd walk 20 minutes, then rest 10, I couldn't make the hills alone. They'd take me by the arms, and one would push and the other pull. They were quite kind about it.

On the way, one of the men shot a monkey, so we did have some meat.

We also met a unit of about 300 Viet Cong guerrillas, about a third of them women. They were moving back into Vietnam from Cambodia.

This was at a fairly large river, and the two tallest men in our group picked me up and more or less floated me across the river.

Finally, we made it to camp.

I continued to have hallucinations from malaria. I kept seeing my brother John and talking to him. Half the time I knew what was going on; half the time I didn't.

Jim Rollins, a fellow prisoner, said that for more than a month after that he would hear me talking, both in the daytime and at night. At times he yelled at me and asked me who I was talking to and I would reply, "My brother John."

John is my younger brother. In my hallucinations I never saw my older brother, Nels, or my father, but I'd keep on seeing my mother.

I finally returned to normal, though occasionally I would have hallucinations of the same type when I would have an attack of malaria.

Since my liberation, American doctors have told me that in spite of all my prison illnesses I'm in pretty good shape.

They don't think I will have recurrences of malaria. My kidneys aren't in the best of shape and my central vision is blurred a little from vitamin deficiency due to the lousy diet. My vision problem probably will be permanent.

But when I think of how sick I was at times and how, night after night, I had to go on those cruel jungle marches, I marvel at what punishment the human body can take.

TRIBUNE, APRIL 9, 1973.

POWs Suffer as Reds Flee U.S. Invasion

Forced marches during captivity were frequent and tough, but they were especially bad during the American invasion of Cambodia in 1970, when the Viet Cong constantly feared being overrun by U.S. forces.

Those were desperate days for us. The Viet Cong, running low on food vented their frustrations on us.

They were brutal during the marches. When Americans were too weak to continue and fell, the Viet Cong strung wire around their necks and pulled them along the ground—a test to see if they were faking or really ill. The guards kicked us a few times, too.

The invasion of Cambodia forced us to flee 100 miles to a safer camp. After four days, some prisoners, including me, dropped out—we just didn't have the strength.

So they put us on bicycles. The Viet Cong moved all sorts of stuff by bicycle—livestock, rice and people. Sometimes they'd push us while we were on the bikes.

We were on a jungle trail I'm sure was part of the Ho Chi Minh supply trail.

Usually I was pushed by Tay, a medical worker. In addition to his medical equipment, we carried my 40-pound pack, his pack, two chickens in a basket and his weapon.

One night, a prisoner on a bicycle was being pushed by a guard we called Hardnose. We were going down a long hill and Hardnose lost control of the bicycle. He had to run just to keep up with it. Down the hill they zoomed, with a pig they were carrying on the bike in a box oinking like mad.

They went all the way down the hill, around a corner, onto a narrow bridge and then off into a stream. There was sand in the bottom of the stream and nobody was hurt.

Artillery Piece

Often we passed North Vietnamese units and equipment on the trail. Once an artillery piece was being moved and they tried to blindfold me before we passed it.

The piece was pulled by oxen or water buffalo, which I could smell as they passed by. More than 100 men followed, each one carrying a single artillery shell.

The Viet Cong carried their wounded along this trail, too. We'd see them—a hammock with a wounded man in it suspended from a long pole carried by two men.

One night we met 11 vehicles coming down the trail, each with only one headlight burning. They were all empty, so one of our officers got them to turn around and we all rode a while.

We later resumed walking, and on the tenth night of the march, other prisoners started dropping out. They were completely exhausted. Instead of the usual rest of 10 minutes every hour, one group had to rest 30 to 40 minutes.

One prisoner had malaria and couldn't go on. He just refused to move. The Viet Cong put wire around his neck and started to pull him to see if he was faking. Despite this he still wouldn't move. Finally, they put up a hammock and let him rest several hours.

Another time, I'm sure a prisoner's life was saved when another gave him mouth-to-mouth resuscitation.

Finally, we reached our new camp inside Cambodia.

All during the Cambodian invasion, we were the victims of confusion resulting from the U.S. and South Vietnamese attacks. Often we knew we were in the path of attacks because we'd find propaganda leaflets dropped by our planes. The leaflets infuriated the Viet Cong, but we loved them and picked them up as fast as we could.

The Red Cross couldn't send us packages, but those leaflets made wonderful toilet paper and cigarette papers.

But we had to keep moving.

The Viet Cong became increasingly nasty. They were in unfamiliar territory, worrying constantly about being found by American troops. They were far away from their normal supplies and had to live on what they could find in the jungle.

Normally our ration was about 2½-bowls of rice three times a day, but now we got only two bowls—one at 8 in the morning and another about 4 in the afternoon. There was no meat. We ate that way for more than three weeks.

VC More Stingy

The Viet Cong became more and more stingy. They'd get wild fruit from the jungle, but we'd never get any. One time they brought in nine monkeys. We didn't get a bite.

We'd ask to go to the toilet, and they'd make us wait 45 minutes.

They were surly about everything. One reason, we found out, was that they were having to go on long marches of their own, to get supplies and bring them into camp.

And all the time they were scared to death of being caught in B52 bomber attacks.

Artillery rounds fell into our camp now and then. A number of times I got down in my foxhole as deep as I could with my face almost in water. I'd pray I wouldn't get hit.

I'm sure some of the Viet Cong were getting killed and wounded. They never would tell us about this, but sometimes they would leave and some never came back.

Water became scarce. There was no quinine or other medicine. I became ill and my fellow prisoners had to protest for me before a medical worker came and gave me medication.

After the Cambodian invasion ended, our conditions improved.

The Viet Cong shot an elephant and brought what seemed like a ton of meat into camp. They must have divided it among 1,000 men in the area.

I guess the Cambodian venture may have been successful for the United States. It was a nightmare for us.

TRIBUNE, APRIL 10, 1973.

Peace Hopes, Care Ebbed and Surged

We had one sure sign the Communists were ready to release American prisoners: The treatment and food improved. They wanted to fatten us up, so to speak, to make it appear that we had been treated well.

In October of 1972, when it appeared a peace agreement might be reached, there was an astounding improvement in the food.

They started giving us vegetables with every meal and a beef calf was slaughtered for us. Fresh tomatoes were boiled with our fish. We got oranges and bananas, and anyone who was ill got double rations. The rice was washed—no longer were there worms in it.

If you got the slightest scratch, a medical worker would come on the run. We got baths every three days instead of every six. They gave us medicine to get rid of the jungle rot we had accumulated.

The word was around that we'd be home by Christmas.

The Hanoi radio let us follow the U.S. election campaign and we listened with a great deal of interest.

I don't want to suggest that I was either for or against Senator (George) McGovern, but the fact is that in our prison camps we had the feeling early in the fall that if McGovern won, the war would end and we'd go home.

With our sketchy understanding of what was going on in the States, almost all of it fed to us by the Viet Cong, we thought McGovern had a 50-50 chance to beat President Nixon.

Well, the election came, McGovern lost and on Nov. 5 all the good food stopped. No more meat. No more fruit. But the medical care continued to be good, and the rice stayed clean of worms.

We were told that Nixon had gone back on his word and that the peace talks had broken down.

But they also said not to worry, the North Vietnamese and the Viet Cong would win the war in 1973 and they would protect us from everything except the B52s. There was nothing they could do about that, they said.

Work Made Us Stronger

The Viet Cong started using us for construction work. We didn't mind because the exercise made us stronger.

We got a new camp commander straight from Hanoi and he was quite friendly. We nicknamed him Cream Puff because he seemed shy. He and a political officer, Horse Face, again tried to make me admit I was a CIA agent.

There was nothing nasty about the interrogation this time and camp conditions weren't too bad. Cream Puff told us we could talk with the prisoners we worked with. The guards became less and less security minded and would wander off, leaving us without armed guards.

In mid-January of this year we found out that 11 other American prisoners were in our camp. The Viet Cong had kept us apart, but now they let us all mingle and talk.

Some hadn't been prisoners very long and from them we learned a lot of things about home—the new cars, the hippies, the long hair, who won the World Series and the football championships, that sort of thing.

We heard, of course, about the renewed bombing of Hanoi, but they told us the President had stopped the bombing so the peace talks in Paris could continue.

The situation brightened again. We felt the end certainly was coming. Then on Jan. 27, I think it was, one of our familiar Viet Cong officers told us a treaty had been signed and that we would be freed within 60 days.

The next day, the full text of the peace agreement and the accompanying protocol for the release of all prisoners was read to us.

The Viet Cong also gave us lectures. One officer asked us to think of the good things that had happened to us, that we were still alive, and to forget the bad things.

"You should all go home and join the revolutionary movement," he said. We chuckled about that.

But we knew we had to remain civil and cooperative to a degree. After all, we weren't free yet. There was always the chance someone would be taken away and not come back. The Viet Cong could say that he'd been bitten by a snake or died some way.

On Feb. 2, a guard said we were going to move in 10 days. He hit it right on the head, as it turned out.

Doctors Made Rounds

Doctors made the rounds twice a day, giving us shots and vitamins and asking us if we needed anything.

The afternoon of Feb. 10, we were told to pack up and get on some trucks. We were along the Mekong river deep in Cambodia at the time, and headed toward South Vietnam on Highway 13.

After riding all night, we finally arrived at Loc Ninh, just across the border in South Vietnam.

The next afternoon, a flock of Vietnamese photographers with both movie and still cameras showed up and started taking pictures of us—but only after we'd been given razors and told to clean up.

The Viet Cong allowed us to hold a party that night and stay up as long as we wanted. They brought tea, candy, cigarettes—and even butchered a pig for us to eat.

I was given back the Luther College class ring and Timex watch that were taken from me after I was captured. The watch didn't work any more. Some fellows got back military currency and actual U.S. dollars that had been taken from them long before.

The next morning, American helicopters arrived to pick us up and, God, they were a wonderful sight.

As reported at the time, a delay developed. The Viet Cong argued that the South Vietnamese weren't releasing Viet Cong prisoners according to the peace agreement.

It was a tense situation and it filled us with all sorts of worry. We felt better after those American helicopter pilots told us, "Don't worry. We're not leaving here until we leave with you."

At last that long-awaited moment came when we boarded the copters.

They lifted off the ground and I started that wonderful journey that would take me to Saigon, Clark Air Base, the U.S.A., and finally, to my home and loved ones in Decorah.

As the helicopter rose skyward, my spirits soared with it.

I thought they would burst.

TRIBUNE, APRIL 11, 1973.

Kjome Reserves Judgment on Issues of Vietnam War

After five years as a prisoner of the Viet Cong and isolation from national and world events and incidents, Michael Kjome is reserving judgment on the issues that have divided and excited the American people, especially the Vietnam war.

"I want to get involved in a lot of reading, study and reflection before I arrive at any conclusions," he says. "I'm keeping an open mind. After all, I've been in a hermetically sealed atmosphere for five years."

Kjome is ambivalent about the Vietnamese, both North and South.

"I liked especially the common people who weren't corrupted by the war," he says. "I love the Vietnamese children and if I ever marry and find I can't have children of my own, I'd like to adopt some Vietnamese."

When Kjome went to Vietnam in 1967 as an English teacher for Pacific Architects and Engineers—a Los Angeles based firm that handled a variety of housekeeping chores for the U.S. military overseas—he supported the American cause in Vietnam.

Disillusioned

"I thought we were doing the right thing, fighting Communism and saving South Vietnam from aggression," he recalls.

But soon he became disillusioned about the South Vietnamese.

"I was shocked to see the tremendous amount of graft, bribery galore, money being passed under the table to government officials even for a thing like a passport.

"And the gross inefficiency, the incompetence of the police, their inability even to control traffic was shocking."

Kjome was distressed also to hear reports from American soldiers about barbaric behavior of our own forces in Vietnam villages—the destruction of everything and everybody in communities suspected of harboring Viet Cong and VC sympathizers.

This was before the world heard about the My Lai massacre.

With the reports of such atrocities in the back of his mind after he was captured, "some of the propaganda put out by the Viet Cong seemed more believable."

It is Kjome's view that no partisan groups in Southeast Asia have a monopoly on virtue. But he is especially critical of Americans who have taken the view that the Viet Cong and the North Vietnamese can do no wrong.

"The American people should always be free to speak out, but perhaps they should do it with restraint," he says.

"What I really dislike is the action of the people who have gone out and have raised the Communists to such a high level of perfection with the high and mighty attitude that they're so good and we're so bad.

"Isn't True"

"This just isn't true. They've got just as many faults as we have. They say the South Vietnamese treated prisoners horribly, and I believe this is true.

"But also there are Americans who say that we were treated well—and that is not true.

"I don't want to see anyone walking down the streets in my home town carrying a Viet Cong flag."

How does Kjome rate the morality of the Viet Cong?

"There's dishonesty among the VC all right," he says. "There are thieves among them. And they're guilty of racial prejudice, even among their own people.

"I'd find this out when I tried to have an interpreter help me establish the identity of a guard. And he'd ask me, 'What's the color of his skin? Is it light or dark.' He and the rest of his Viet Cong from the north considered themselves superior to the people of the south.

"And the educated Viet Cong held themselves above the uneducated.

"Some Viet Cong I hated, others I felt sorry for, others I liked."

Guard Gave Name

Kjome found it significant that one Viet Cong guard wrote out his name and address several times and gave the information to several of the American prisoners.

He thought the Americans would return to Vietnam, and he wanted to maintain contact in case he came to the United States some day.

"He and the other Viet Cong had so many misconceptions about our country," says Kjome. "They really believe that all American communities, even our little towns, are overrun by prostitution and that there are race riots every day everywhere."

How has five years in prison affected Kjome?

"It made me realize how terribly necessary it is for a person of this country to really find out what the people are thinking and doing.

"I don't want to be like the people who holler and scream about conditions in this country, as so many do, and still are too lazy to pay attention to what their congressmen and legislators are doing."

Is he bitter?

"No, not really. It was a long time out of my life. And I'm not going to put myself in a position where it can happen again."

But Kjome may go overseas again, perhaps even to Southeast Asia. His employers have offered him a new position with the company.

Meantime, he's going to catch up on international, national and state affairs.

"Good grief," he said, "I didn't know Iowa had lowered the voting age to 18 until just a couple of days ago."

Born a Reporter

BY Donald Kaul, COLUMNIST FOR THE DES MOINES **REGISTER** AND **TRIBUNE**

FOR THREE YEARS of my professional life I shared an office with Gordon Gammack. It was more of a cubicle, really: a 9-by-10 space crammed with two desks, an extra chair, some shelves and two egos sharing one telephone.

It was close quarters. When one of us reached into a pocket, the other had to stand up.

A situation like that is like a marriage; you either grow to hate your partner or love your partner. With Gordon and me, it was love.

He was 25 years older than I and we were of dissimilar temperament and background but we liked each other—a lot.

Most often, we showed it by trading insults.

Every daily columnist has days he'd like to forget, days on which his muse has a headache but on which he has to produce something anyway. Generally, he produces a turkey.

On my turkey days, Gammack was absolutely unforgiving. He'd sit there across his desk, reading my dullest passages aloud to me. When he was done he'd take off his glasses and twirl them around in his characteristic way and say:

"You know, Kaul, you have a clever typewriter." Someone had once written me a complimentary letter using that phrase and I had had the bad judgment to show it to Gammack. He never let me live it down.

He could take it as well as give, though. He had what seemed to me an excessive admiration for trivial coincidence. Once he wrote an item detailing the experience of an Iowan who sent off a package to a relative and, on the following day, received a package from that relative.

And, Gordie wrote, the incoming and outgoing packages had both carried the same postage!

It was a dumb item and I didn't let him forget it, either. Every time he'd give me a hard time I'd come back with "Same Postage." It also served as the descriptive catchword for the kind of simple coincidence story he remained forever addicted to.

In a sense, Gammack was miscast as a columnist. Columnists tend to be full of opinions and speculations and high-flown phrases. Gordon was more at home with facts and flesh-and-blood stories.

He was a master of the reporter's trade. He could walk through a strange town and three stories would run up and jump into his pocket.

His secret, I suppose, was that people talked to him. They looked at that mug of his and they figured, "You can trust this guy."

He had, in common with all great reporters, enormous energy, enthusiasm and curiosity. He'd get on kicks and drive you crazy with them.

I remember when he discovered double-knits. You would have

thought he invented them. You couldn't go near him without getting a commercial and being encouraged to scrunch up his pant leg in your fist.

Then there was the time he learned a new way to hang trousers so that they wouldn't wrinkle. That whole week he walked around the office with a hanger, demonstrating.

It was all part of his reporter's instinct, that child-like delight he took in telling you something you hadn't known before, to deliver the news.

I talked to him for the last time less than two weeks before his death. He was ill and failing fast but he called me in Washington. He wanted to tell me something.

An editor in Des Moines had killed a column of mine and I hadn't heard about it yet. Gammack got wind of it and called to get my reaction. His voice was weak, but there was almost a lilt in it.

He felt no malicious joy at a colleague suffering a professional loss—there was no envy in the man—but his pleasure at being the first one to tell me the news was undisguised.

He was born a reporter, he died a reporter. Few of us will live so rich and satisfying a life.

This week there was a reunion of veteran war correspondents